'This sprightly and gracious, yet robust, work i: and scripturally based response to those who understood Paul's doctrine of justification. Al for those familiar with the debate between the various scholarly perspectives on Paul, it is in fact a straightforward and reasonably succinct exposition of Tom's interpretation that incorporates a defence of his approach to Paul in general and his exegesis of specific passages in Galatians and Romans in particular. This is definitely one of the most exciting and significant books that I have read this year. Like all of the author's work, I found it hard to set down once I had started to read it. Strongly commended!'

I. Howard Marshall, Honorary Research Professor of
New Testament Exegesis, University of Aberdeen

'N. T. Wright provides yet again another fresh and exciting exposition of the Apostle Paul. Here Wright shows how Paul proclaimed justification by faith as part of the Bible's theodramatic story of salvation, a story that stretches from Creation to Abraham to Israel and all the way through to Jesus the Messiah. Wright responds to many criticisms including those of John Piper and, regardless of whether one gravitates towards Wright's or Piper's unpacking of Paul, you cannot help but enjoy the sparks that fly when these two great modern Pastor-Scholars cross swords over the Apostle. Moreover, Wright artfully brings readers into the narrative world of Paul and he sets before us a stirring portrait of the Apostle to the Gentiles and his gospel.'

Michael F. Bird, Lecturer in New Testament Highland Theological College

'Like Paul himself writing to the Galatians, Bishop Tom expounds and defends in this book his interpretation of the apostle's teaching on justification with passion and power. At the same time, he seeks to move beyond divisive categories so that Paul can speak from within his own context and thereby to us in ours. The result is an extraordinary synthesis that should be read by the sympathetic, the suspicious and everyone else.'

Michael J. Gorman, The Ecumenical Institute of Theology
St Mary's Seminary & University Baltimore, Maryland

'For some time now, I have watched in puzzlement as some critics, imagining themselves as defenders of Paul's gospel, have derided Tom Wright as a dangerous betrayer of the Christian faith. In fact, Paul's gospel of God's reconciling, world-transforming grace has no more ardent and eloquent exponent in our time than Tom Wright. If his detractors read this book carefully, they will find themselves engaged in close exegesis of Paul's letters, and they will be challenged to join Wright in grappling with the deepest logic of Paul's message. Beyond slogans and caricatures of "Lutheran readings" and "the New Perspective", the task we all face is to interpret these difficult, theologically generative letters afresh for our time. Wright's sweeping, incisive sketch of Paul's thought, set forward in this book, will help us all in that task.'

Richard B. Hays, George Washington Ivey Professor of
New Testament, The Divinity School, Duke University

'I find it quite stunning that a book dealing with the subject of justification could be this compelling a read – along the way you find yourself getting caught up in the momentum and energy of the book, which pulls you into the momentum and energy of THE BOOK – which is, of course, Tom's point . . .'

Rob Bell, founding pastor of Mars Hill Bible Church

'John Piper, it turns out, has done us all a wonderful favour. In writing the critique that invited this response, he has given Bishop Wright the opportunity to clearly, directly, passionately and concisely summarize many of the key themes of his still-in-process yet already historic scholarly and pastoral project. Wright shows – convincingly – how the comprehensive view of Paul, Romans, justification, Jesus, and the Christian life and mission that he has helped articulate embraces "both the truths the Reformers were eager to set forth and also the truths which, in their eagerness, they sidelined". Eavesdropping on this conversation will help readers who are new to Wright to get into the main themes of his work and the important discussion of which it is a part. And it will give Wright's critics a clearer sense than ever of what they are rejecting when they cling to their cherished old wineskins of conventional thought.'

Brian McLaren, pastor (crcc.org) and author (anewkindofchristian.com)

'This is a sharply polemical book, and N. T. Wright occasionally rises to Pauline heights of exasperation at his opponents. At bottom, though, it is about Pauline basics – about Abraham and Israel, eschatology and covenant, courtroom and Christology. With debates about perspectives old and new swirling around him like a cyclone, Wright does what he always does – he leads us carefully through the text. Some will doubtless remain sceptical about the Copernican revolution Wright proposes, but we are all indebted to him for reminding us once again of the breadth of the gospel of God and the majesty of the God of the gospel.'

Peter Leithart, author of Solomon among the Postmoderns

'Frank theological table talk is sometimes a necessary endeavor. Tom Wright's *Justification* is his substantive reply to critical work by many, including John Piper, on the New Perspective. Wright correctly reminds us that this approach should be better called New or Fresh Perspectives. The goal is to open up the text connecting what it originally said in the first century, not change it. This book sets up a meaningful and significant conversation between the camps in this debate through its direct interaction with the critique. It should be read and reflected on, just as work on the other side should be. So I recommend this book and say, pull up a chair to the table and pay careful attention to the conversation. In the dialogue, all of us will learn more about what Paul and Scripture say about justification (and a few other things as well).'

Darrell Bock, Research Professor of New Testament Studies
Dallas Theological Seminary

JUSTIFICATION: GOD'S PLAN AND PAUL'S VISION

TOM WRIGHT
Bishop of Durham

First published in Great Britain in 2009

Society for Promoting Christian Knowledge
36 Causton Street
London SW1P 4ST

British Library Cataloguing-in-Publication Data
A catalogue record for this book is available from the British Library

ISBN 978–0–281–06090–0

1 3 5 7 9 10 8 6 4 2

Typeset by Graphicraft Ltd, Hong Kong
Printed in Great Britain by Ashford Colour Press

Produced on paper from sustainable forests

Contents

Preface

When I heard about John Piper's book, *The Future of Justification: A Response to N. T. Wright*, I was torn between two reflections. On the one hand, as they say, the actor doesn't mind whether he's playing the hero or the villain as long as it's his name on the board outside the theatre. On the other hand, there is a danger that if people typecast you as the villain the image may stick and you won't get any other parts. So, despite my initial reluctance to get drawn into the details of debate when I am really far too busy with other things, I eventually decided that an initial response was called for.

I say 'initial response', because I do not suppose that this book is in any way complete. Piper is one of an increasing number who, supposing the great Reformation tradition of reading and preaching Paul to be under attack, has leapt to its defence, and every passing week brings a further batch of worried and anxious ripostes to the 'new perspective on Paul' and to myself as one of its exponents. I cannot begin to enter into debate with all of this, and indeed there are many important writers with whom I simply cannot engage here in any detail. I hope, as I say in the first chapter, to sketch something which is more like an outflanking exercise than a direct challenge on all the possible fronts. The latter exercise would result in hand-to-hand fighting, not only on every line in Paul, but also on what everyone else has said about every line in Paul. There is a place for that sort of book, but this is a different sort.

But what's it all about? One cheerful English reviewer, from a part of the church that has not usually worried over-much about the details of 'the doctrine of justification', spoke in terms of text-trading and theological arm-wrestling, implying that this was a curious indoor sport for those who might like that sort of thing but not enormously relevant to wider concerns facing the church. It will come as no surprise that I do not share that view. Justification is hugely important. The debates which have gone on around the doctrine in a variety of contexts are actually the focal points of several other issues we all face.

What is so contentious about it, then? This is of course what the book is all about. But it may help if I set out very briefly where some at least of the main pressure points lie.

In part, to begin with, the question is about *the nature and scope of salvation*. Many Christians in the Western world, for many centuries now, have seen 'salvation' as meaning 'going to heaven when you die'. I and others have argued that that is inadequate. In the Bible, salvation is not God's rescue of people *from* the world but the rescue of the world itself. The whole creation is to be liberated from its slavery to decay (Romans 8.21). I have written about this at length elsewhere, notably in *Surprised by Hope* (London and San Francisco: SPCK and HarperOne, 2007/8). Many in the Reformed tradition represented by John Piper would agree with this point. But I do not think they have yet allowed it to affect the way they think about the questions that follow.

Second, the question is about the *means* of salvation, how it is accomplished. Here John Piper, and the tradition he represents, have said that salvation is accomplished by the sovereign grace of God, operating through the death of Jesus Christ in our place and on our behalf, and appropriated through faith alone. Absolutely. I agree a hundred per cent. There is not one syllable of that summary that I would complain about. But there is something missing – or rather, some*one* missing. Where is the holy spirit? In some of the great Reformed theologians, not least John Calvin himself, the work of the spirit is every bit as important as the work of the son. But you can't simply add the spirit on at the end of the equation and hope it will still have the same shape. Part of my plea in this book is for the spirit's work to be taken seriously in relation both to Christian faith itself and to the way in which that faith is 'active through love' (Galatians 5.6). And the way that spirit-driven active faith is at work, through love and all that flows from it, explains how God's final rescue of his people from death itself has been accomplished (Romans 8.1–11).

Third, the question is about *the meaning of justification*, what the term and its cognates actually refer to. Some Christians have used terms like 'justification' and 'salvation' as though they were almost interchangeable, but this is clearly untrue to scripture itself. 'Justification' is the act of God by which people are 'declared to be in the right' before him: so say the great Reformation theologians,

John Piper included. Yes, indeed. Of course. But what does that declaration involve? How does it come about? Piper insists that 'justification' means the 'imputation' of the 'righteousness' – the perfect obedience of Jesus Christ – to the sinner, clothing him or her with that status from the first moment of faith to the final arrival in heaven (Piper, 9). I understand the force of that proposal, and the sense of assurance which it gives. What's more, I agree that this sense of assurance is indeed offered by the doctrine of justification as Paul expounds it. But as I argue in this book, Paul's way of doing it is not Piper's. Paul's doctrine of justification is the place where four themes meet, which Piper, and others like him, have managed to ignore or sideline.

First, Paul's doctrine of justification is about *the work of Jesus the Messiah of Israel.* You cannot understand what Paul says about Jesus, and about the significance of his death for our justification and salvation, unless you see Jesus as the one in whom 'all the promises of God find their Yes' (2 Corinthians 1.20). For many writers, of whom Piper is not untypical, the long story of Israel seems to function merely as a backdrop, a source of proof-texts and types, rather than as itself the story of God's saving purposes. Piper and others like him have accused me of downplaying the significance of the saving, indeed substitutionary, death of Jesus within Paul's doctrine of justification. I hope this book will put such suggestions to rest – while reminding my critics of how that part of Paul's theology actually works.

Second, Paul's doctrine of justification is therefore about what we may call *the covenant* – the covenant God made with Abraham, the covenant whose purpose was from the beginning the saving call of a worldwide family through whom God's saving purposes for the world were to be realized. For Piper, and many like him, the very idea of a 'covenant' of this kind remains strangely foreign and alien. He and others have accused me of inventing the idea of Israel's story as an ongoing narrative in which the 'exile' in Babylon was 'extended' by hundreds of years so that Jews in Paul's day were still waiting for the 'end of exile', the true fulfilment of the covenant promises. Despite the strong covenantal theology of John Calvin himself, and his positive reading of the story of Israel as fulfilled in Jesus Christ, many who claim Calvinist or 'Reformed' heritage today resist applying it in the way that, as I argue in this book, Paul himself does, in line with the solid biblical foundations for the 'continuing exile' theme.

Third, Paul's doctrine of justification is focused on the divine *lawcourt*. God, as judge, 'finds in favour of', and hence acquits from their sin, those who believe in Jesus Christ. The word 'justify' has this lawcourt as its metaphorical home base. For John Piper and others who share his perspective, the lawcourt imagery is read differently, with attention shifting rather to the supposed moral achievement of Jesus in gaining, through his perfect obedience, a 'righteousness' which can then be passed across to his faithful people. Piper and others have accused me of superimposing this 'lawcourt' framework on Paul; I argue that it is Paul himself who insists on it.

Fourth, Paul's doctrine of justification is bound up with *eschatology*, that is, his vision of God's future for the whole world and for his people. Right through Paul's writings, but once more especially in Romans, he envisages two moments, the *final* justification when God puts the whole world right and raises his people from the dead, and the *present* justification in which that moment is anticipated. For John Piper and the school of thought he represents, present justification appears to take the full weight. Piper and others have then accused me of encouraging people to think of their own moral effort as contributing to their final justification, and hence of compromising the gospel itself. I insist that I am simply trying to do justice to what Paul actually says, and that when we factor in the Spirit to the whole picture we see that the charge is groundless.

All these debates rest on one foundation: the text of Paul's letters. Piper claims to be faithful to scripture; so, of course, do I. Some critics of the so-called 'new perspective' write as if they are the ones who know 'what the Bible says' while others of us play fast and loose with it. Well, they appeal to exegesis, and to exegesis we shall go, particularly in the second half of the present book. Though the treatment of key passages is necessarily brief, it is a lot fuller – and deals with the whole texts, not simply a few verses snatched from them – than those offered by most of my critics.

These advance summaries of much more complex arguments must serve to alert the reader, not indeed to the full sweep of what can be said on either side, but to the general areas of agreement and disagreement.

I regret very much that pressure of other duties, and the urgency of the publisher's deadlines, have meant that I have not been able to share initial drafts of this book either with the various friends who had offered to help, or with John Piper himself (as he so graciously did with me). However, though I hope to have presented things in a new light and with fresh clarity, I do not suppose I am actually saying very much that I have not already said elsewhere, in the various works listed in the bibliography. No doubt kind people would have made comments that would have improved the book, but the mistakes and unclarities are as usual, and this time unavoidably, all my own. I am still hoping before too long to complete the fourth volume (which deals with Paul) in my series *Christian Origins and the Question of God*. That, I trust, will help to clarify things further.

I am delighted to dedicate this book to my old friend and sparring-partner, Jimmy Dunn. The fact that he will disagree with some of it is neither here nor there. I am enormously grateful for his friendship and fellowship in the work of the gospel here in the north-east of England and in Durham in particular. I must also express my gratitude to the many friends and colleagues who have encouraged me to write, however briefly, in response to John Piper, and to those who share my heavy load in Durham, and in the Church of England, for encouraging me to see the ministry of expounding scripture in person and in print as a vital part of that vocation.

N. T. Wright
Auckland Castle

Abbreviations

Climax N. T. Wright, *The Climax of the Covenant*. Edinburgh: T&T Clark, 1991

JVG N. T. Wright, *Jesus and the Victory of God*. London: SPCK, 1996

NTPG N. T. Wright, *The New Testament and the People of God*. London: SPCK, 1992

Piper John Piper, *The Future of Justification: A Response to N. T. Wright*. Wheaton, IL: Crossway Books, 2007

Part 1

INTRODUCTION

1

What's all this about, and why does it matter?

Imagine a friend coming to stay who, through some accident of education, had never been told that the earth goes round the sun. As part of a happy evening's conversation, you take it upon yourself to explain how the planetary system works. Yes, from where we stand it does of course seem that the sun circles around us. But this is merely the effect of our perspective. All that we now know of astronomy confirms that the earth on which we live, in company with a few other similar planets, is in fact revolving around the sun. You get out books, charts and diagrams, and even rearrange objects on the coffee-table to make the point. Your friend alternates between incredulity, fascination, momentary alarm, and puzzlement. Eventually you smile, have another drink, and head for bed.

Very early in the morning, while it is still dark, there is a tap at the bedroom door. He is up and dressed and invites you to come for an early walk. He takes you up the hill to a point where the whole countryside is spread out before you, and, as the sky begins to lighten, you can just see, far off to the east, the glistening ocean. He returns to the subject of the previous night. So many wise people of old have spoken of the earth as the solid-fixed point on which we stand. Didn't one of the Psalms say something about the sun celebrating as it goes round and round, like a strong giant running a race? Yes, of course modern scientists are always coming up with fancy theories. They may have their place, but equally they may just be fads. Wouldn't we do better to stick with the tried and tested wisdom of the ages?

As he warms to his theme, so at last, out of the sea, there emerges the huge, dazzling, shining ball. You stand in silence, watching its majestic rise, filling the countryside with golden light. As its lower edge clears the ocean, you wait with a sense of frustrated inevitability for the punch-line. Here it comes.

'Now, you see,' – a gentle hand on the arm, he doesn't want to make this too harsh – 'we have the evidence of our own eyes. It really *does* go round the earth. All those wonderful theories and clever new ideas – they may have a lot to teach us, but ultimately they take us away from the truth. Better to stay with tried and tested truth, with the ground firm beneath our feet. Aren't you happy we came on this walk?'

Now I can well imagine that, as with the Pharisees listening to Jesus' Parable of the Wicked Tenants, there may be some readers who will at once be angry, realizing that I have told this story against them. And it may be a dangerous move to start a book by alienating still further those with whom, it appears, I am engaged in dialogue. But I use this story for one reason in particular: to make it clear that, at the present moment in the debate about St Paul and the meaning of 'justification', *this is how it appears*, to me at least. We are not in dialogue. I have been writing about St Paul now, on and off, for thirty-five years. I have prayed, preached and lectured my way through his letters. I have written popular-level commentaries on all of them, a full-length commentary on his most important one, and several other books and articles, at various levels, on particular Pauline topics. And the problem is not that people disagree with me. That is what one expects and wants. Let's have the discussion! The point of discourse is to learn with and from one another. I used to tell my students that a least 20 per cent of what I was telling them was wrong, but I didn't know which 20 per cent it was: I make many mistakes in life, in relationships and in work, and I don't expect to be free of them in my thinking. But whereas in much of life one's mistakes are often fairly obvious – the shortcut path that ended in a bed of nettles, the experimental recipe that gave us all queasy stomachs, the golf shot that landed in the lake – in the life of the mind things are often not so straightforward. We need other minds on the job, to challenge us, to come back at us, to engage with our arguments and analyses. That is how the world goes round.

Well, some might reply, is that not what's happening? What are you grumbling about? Here are all these writers, taking you on. Might they not have spotted the 20 per cent you were talking about? Shouldn't you be glad to be corrected?

Well, yes. But my problem is that that's not how things are working out. I have thought about writing this book for some time, but have finally been prodded into doing it because one of my critics – John Piper, of Bethlehem Baptist Church in Minneapolis, Minnesota – has gone one better than the rest and devoted an entire book to explaining why I'm wrong about Paul, and why we should stick with the tried and trusted theology of the Reformers and their successors. (Or at least some of them; actually, the Reformers disagreed among themselves, and so do their successors.[1]) And the problem is not that he, like many others, is disagreeing with me. The problem is that he hasn't really listened to what I'm saying. He has watched with growing alarm as I moved the pieces around the coffee-table. It has given him a sleepless night. And now he has led me up the hill to show me the glorious sight of another sunrise. *Yes*, I want to say. *I know about the sunrise. I know it looks to us as if the sun goes round the earth. I'm not denying that. But why couldn't you hear what I was trying to tell you?*

The answer may well be, of course, 'Because you didn't explain it properly.' Or, perhaps, 'Because what you were saying was so muddled and confused that it's better to stick with a straightforward, plain account which makes sense.' And, on the chance that one of these is true, I am writing this book to try, once more, to explain what I have been talking about – which is to explain what I think St Paul was talking about. But there is a more worrying possible answer. My friend – and most of the people with whom I shall here be in debate are people I would like to count as friends – has simply not allowed the main things I have been trying to say to get anywhere near his conscious mind. He has picked off bits of my analysis and argument, worried away at them, shaken his head, and gone back to the all-powerful story he already knew. (As I was drafting this, the new issue of *Christian Century* landed on my desk, with an article by a teacher to whom a student said, 'I loved what I was learning, but I couldn't make it stay in my head. It was too different from what I had already learned, so my brain just kept switching back to default.'[2]) And, partly because I am more than a little weary with this happening again and again, on websites, in questions after lectures, in journalistic interviews, and increasingly in academic and quasi- or pseudo-academic articles and books, I am determined to have one more go at setting things out.

Actually, this book is not my intended 'final account' of the matter. There remains the large task, towards which I have been working for most of my life, of the book on Paul which is now planned as the fourth volume of my series about Christian origins.[3] But I do not want to spend two hundred pages of that book in detailed discussions with Piper and other similar writers. There are many other issues to be dealt with, in quite different directions, and to concentrate in the larger book on the fierce little battles that are raging in the circles I must now address would pull that project out of shape.

There are two other reasons why I have begun with the story of the friend who thinks the sun goes round the earth. The first is that, within the allegorical meaning of the story, the arguments I have been mounting – the diagrams, the pictures, the objects on the coffee-table – stand for fresh readings of scripture. *They are not the superimposition upon scripture of theories culled from elsewhere.* But the response, which puts itself about as 'the evidence of our eyes', 'the most obvious meaning', and so on, is deeply conditioned by, and at critical points appeals to, tradition. Yes, human tradition – albeit from some extremely fine, devout and learned human beings. Ever since I first read Luther and Calvin, particularly the latter, I determined that whether or not I agreed with them in everything they said, their stated and practised method would be mine, too: to soak myself in the Bible, in the Hebrew and Aramaic Old Testament and the Greek New Testament, to get it into my bloodstream by every means possible, in the prayer and hope that I would be able to teach scripture afresh to the church and the world. The greatest honour we can pay the Reformers is not to treat them as infallible – they would be horrified at that – but to do as they did. There is a considerable irony, at the level of method, when John Piper suggests that, according to me, the church has been 'on the wrong foot for fifteen hundred years'. It isn't so much that I don't actually claim that. It is that that is exactly what people said to his heroes, to Luther, Calvin and the rest. Luther and Calvin answered from scripture; the Council of Trent responded by insisting on tradition.[4]

The second reason I have begun with the parable of the friend, the earth and the sun is deeper again. It is serious for theological and pastoral reasons, and is near the heart of what is at stake in this debate and many others. The theological equivalent of supposing that the earth goes round the sun is the belief that the whole of Christian truth *is all about me and my salvation*. I have read dozens of books and articles in the last few weeks on the topic of justification. Again and again the writers, from a variety of backgrounds, have assumed, taken it for granted, that the central question of all is, 'What must I do to be saved?' or (Luther's way of putting it), 'How can I find a gracious God?' or, 'How can I enter a right relationship with God?'

Now do not misunderstand me. Hold the angry or fearful reaction. Salvation is hugely important. Of course it is! Knowing God for oneself, as opposed to merely knowing or thinking *about* him, is at the heart of Christian living. Discovering that God is gracious, rather than a distant bureaucrat or a dangerous tyrant, is the good news that constantly surprises and refreshes us. *But we are not the centre of the universe.* God is not circling around us. We are circling around him. It may look, from our point of view, as though 'me and my salvation' are the be-all and end-all of Christianity. Sadly, many people – many devout Christians! – have preached that way and lived that way. This problem is not peculiar to the churches of the Reformation. It goes back to the high Middle Ages in the Western church, and infects and affects Catholic and Protestant, liberal and conservative, high and low church alike. But a full reading of scripture itself tells a different story.

God made humans for a purpose: not simply for themselves, not simply so that they could be in relationship with him, but so that *through* them, as his image-bearers, he could bring his wise, glad, fruitful order to the world. And the closing scenes of scripture, in the book of Revelation, are not about human beings going off to heaven to be in a close and intimate relationship with God, but about heaven coming to earth. The intimate relationship with God which is indeed promised and celebrated in that great scene of the New Jerusalem issues at once in an outflowing, a further healing creativity, the river of the water of life flowing out from the city, and the tree of life springing up, with leaves that are for the healing of the nations.

What is at stake in the present debate is not simply the fine-tuning of theories about what precisely happens in 'justification'. That quickly turns, as one reviewer of Piper's book noted somewhat tartly, into a kind of evangelical arm-wrestling, a text-trading contest in which verses from Paul, Greek roots, arcane references to sources both ancient and modern, and sometimes (alas) unkind words fly around the room. Many people will look on with distaste, like neighbours overhearing an unpleasant family row. Yes, there will be some text-trading in this book. That is inevitable, given the subject-matter, and the central importance of scripture itself. But the real point is, I believe, that the salvation of human beings, though of course extremely important for those human beings, is part of a larger purpose. God is rescuing us from the shipwreck of the world, not so that we can sit back and put our feet up in his company, but so that we can be part of his plan to remake the world. *We* are in orbit around *God and his purposes*, not the other way around. If the Reformation tradition had treated the gospels as equally important to the epistles, this mistake might never have happened. But it has, and we must deal with it. The earth, and we with it, go round the sun of God and his cosmic purposes.

Ironically, perhaps, this statement can be heard as the radical application of justification by faith itself. 'Nothing in my hand I bring,' sings the poet, 'simply to thy cross I cling.' Of course: we look away from ourselves to Jesus Christ and him crucified, to the God whose gracious love and mercy sent him to die for us. But the sigh of relief which is the characteristic Christian reaction to learning about justification by faith ('You mean I don't have to *do* anything? God loves me and accepts me as I am, just because Jesus died for me?') ought to give birth at once to a deeper realization down exactly the same line: 'You mean it isn't all about ME after all? I'm not the centre of the universe? It's all about God and his purposes?' The problem is that, throughout the history of the Western church, even where the first point has been enthusiastically embraced – sometimes particularly where that has happened – the second has been ignored. And with that sometimes wilful ignorance there has crept back into theology, even into good, no-nonsense, copper-bottomed Reformation theology, the snake's whisper that actually it *is* all about us, that 'my relationship with God' and 'my salvation' is the still point at the centre of the universe. I am the hero in this play. Even Jesus comes on stage to help me out of the mess I'm in. And, way back behind all talk of 'new perspectives', 'old perspectives', 'fresh perspectives' and any other perspectives you care to name, what I am contending for, and the reason I am writing this book, is not just to clarify a few technical details, or justify myself – the crowning irony in a book on this topic! – against my critics. ('It's a very small matter', wrote Paul himself, 'that I should be judged by you or by any human court; I don't even judge myself . . . it is the Lord who judges me.'[5]) The reason I am writing this book is because the present battles are symptoms of some much larger issues that face the church at the start of the twenty-first century, and because the danger signs, particularly the failure to read scripture for all its worth, and the geocentric theology and piety I've mentioned, are all around us. I am not, in other words, simply appealing to my critics to allow my peculiar interpretations of St Paul some house room, or at least permission to inhabit a kennel in the back yard where my barks and yaps may not be such a nuisance. I am suggesting that the theology of St Paul, the whole theology of St Paul rather than the truncated and self-centred readings which have become endemic in Western thought, the towering and majestic theology of St Paul which, when you even glimpse it, dazzles you like the morning sun rising over the sea, is urgently needed as the church faces the tasks of mission in tomorrow's dangerous world, and is not well served by the inward-looking soteriologies that tangle themselves up in a web of detached texts and secondary theories . . .

It is, after all, an interesting question as to why certain doctrinal and exegetical questions suddenly explode at particular points. I sat down to lunch last November with a man I had not met until that day. We were in company, in a very nice restaurant. As we took our places, he turned to me and said energetically, 'How do you translate *genōmetha* in 2 Corinthians 5.21?' I stared around the table. Everyone was waiting for my answer. I'll get to that later in the book, but my point here is to ask: What is going on in our culture, our times, our churches, our world, that suddenly makes us itch at this point, itch so badly that we have to scratch like mad even in public? Answering that question would take several other books, but the answer cannot *simply* be 'because the gospel is at stake', or 'because souls need to be saved'. We live in a highly complex world, and the sudden volcanic eruption of angry, baffled concern at the so-called 'new perspective on Paul' can be located interestingly in a socio-cultural, and even political, milieu where an entire way of life, a whole way of understanding the Christian faith and trying to live it out, a whole way of being human, is suddenly perceived to be at risk. It is cognate (for instance) with a large and difficult problem in Western Christianity, the problem characterized by the implicit clash between those who get their faith from the four gospels, topped up with a few bits of Paul, and those who base it on Paul, topped up with a few illustrations from the gospels. These issues in turn need to be mapped onto broader questions within parts of the Western church, as is done (for instance) by Roger Olson in a recent book, where he distinguishes 'conservatives' (people like Don Carson of Trinity Evangelical Divinity School) from 'post-conservatives' (people like me).[6] It's always intriguing to discover that you belong to a group you didn't know existed. That particular cultural divide is a fairly solidly American one, and, as they say over there, I don't think I have a dog in that fight. Behind Olson's divide there are, of course, much larger cultural and social tectonic plates shifting this way and that. We should not imagine that we can discuss the exegesis of 2 Corinthians 5.21, or Romans or Galatians, in a vacuum. Everything is interconnected, and when people feel the floor shaking and the furniture wobbling, they get scared.

Test this out. Go to the blogsites, if you dare. It really is high time we developed a Christian ethic of blogging. Bad temper is bad temper even in the apparent privacy of your own hard drive, and harsh and unjust words, when released into the wild, rampage around and do real damage. And as for the practice of saying mean and untrue things while hiding behind a pseudonym – well, if I get a letter like that it goes straight in the bin. But the cyberspace equivalents of road-rage don't happen by accident. People who type vicious, angry, slanderous and inaccurate accusations do so because they feel their worldview to be under attack. Yes, I have a pastoral concern for such people. (And, for that matter, a pastoral concern for anyone who spends more than a few minutes a day taking part in blogsite discussions, especially when they all use code-names: was it for this that the creator God made human beings?) But sometimes worldviews have to be shaken. They may become idolatrous and self-serving. And I fear that that has happened, and continues to happen, even in well-regulated, shiny Christian contexts – including, of course, my own. John Piper writes, he tells us, as a pastor. So do I.

In fact, he writes as one who, when it all comes down to it, shares my own concern. When his book came out, he sent me a copy, and in it he wrote kindly, in his own hand: 'For Tom, with love and admiration and concern and the desire and prayer that Jesus Christ, the Lord of the universe, who holds our lives in his hands, will bring us to one mind for the sake of the fullness of his glory and for the good of this groaning world.' That is my desire and prayer as well. The earth goes round the sun. Jesus is the hero of the play, and we are the bit-part players, the Fifth Servant and Seventh Footman who come on for a moment, say one word, and disappear again, proud to have shared his stage and, for a moment, been a tiny part of his action. It is because I sense that picture in John Piper's work, and because, unlike some of my critics (including some of those whose words are quoted on the back cover of his book!), he has been scrupulously fair, courteous and generous in all our exchanges, that I write, not with a heavy heart ('Oh, what's the use? He'll never get it. Let him think the sun goes round the earth if it makes him happy!') but with the hope that maybe, just maybe, if we take some time, get out some more books and perhaps telescopes, the penny will drop, the 'aha' moment will happen, the new worldview will click into place, and all will become clear. And, critics please note, I do not expect to remain unchanged through that process. I am not defending a fortress called 'The new perspective' against all comers. I hope not just to make things clearer than I have done before, but to see things clearer than I have done before as a result of having had to articulate it all once more. Perhaps if I succeed in seeing things more clearly I may succeed in saying them more clearly as well.

At this point, in fact, questions about the 'new perspective' and its various rivals become less important. There are times when I wish that the phrase had never been invented; indeed, perhaps for Freudian reasons, I had quite forgotten that I had invented it myself (though even then it was borrowed from Krister Stendahl) until J. D. G. Dunn, who is normally credited with it, graciously pointed out that I had used it in my 1978 Tyndale Lecture, in which, as I well remember, he was sitting in the front row.[7] My relationship with Jimmy Dunn, sometimes stormy, sometimes puzzling, now happy (he astonished and humbled me by dedicating his recent big book, *The New Perspective on Paul*, to me, and my returning of the compliment herewith is a small thank-offering for a long and properly tangled collegial friendship), should inform onlookers of the most important thing about the new perspective, namely that there is no such thing as *The* new perspective (despite the title of his recent book!). There is only a disparate family of perspectives, some with more, some with less family likeness, and with fierce squabbles and sibling rivalries going on inside. There is no united front (like Schumann's famous 'League of David against the Philistines', fighting against Rossini on the one hand and Wagner on the other) pushing back the recalcitrant Westminster-Confession hordes with the ox-horns of liberal biblical scholarship. It doesn't work like that.

Indeed, anyone giving close attention to the work of Ed Sanders, Jimmy Dunn and myself (for some reason we are often mentioned as the chief culprits:[8] why not Richard Hays? Why not Douglas Campbell, or Terry Donaldson, or Bruce Longenecker?[9]) will see that we have at least as much disagreement between ourselves as we do with those outside this (very small, and hardly charmed) circle. Jimmy Dunn and I have disagreed for the last thirty years on Paul's Christology, on the meaning of Romans 7, on *pistis Christou*; more recently, and perhaps importantly, on the question of Israel's continuing exile. Ed Sanders has had no particular reason to disagree with me – I am not aware that he has taken an enormous interest in anything I've written – but my gratitude for the stimulus of his work has been cheerfully matched by my major disagreements with him on point after point not only of detail but of method, structure and meaning. I well remember one Oxford term when I was lecturing on Romans at 11 a.m. on Mondays, Wednesdays and Fridays, and Ed Sanders was lecturing on Paul's Theology on the same days at 10 a.m. Students would come straight from his lecture to mine, and on more than one occasion I said something which provoked a ripple of laughter: I had exactly but unintentionally contradicted what Sanders had said in the previous hour.

All of which, anecdotal but perhaps significant, is to say: critics of the 'new perspective' who began by being afraid of Sanders should not assume that Dunn and I are flying under the same flag. In fact, as another old friend, Francis Watson, is now making clear, it is time to move beyond the 'new perspective', to develop quite different ways of reading Paul which will do more justice to him historically, exegetically, theologically and (it is hoped) pastorally and evangelistically.[10] This may involve retrieving some elements of the so-called 'old perspective', but Piper and others like him should not cheer too soon. The stray lambs are not returning to the Reformation fold – except in the sense that, for me at least, they remain absolutely committed to the Reformers' method of questioning all traditions in the light of scripture. It is time to move on. Actually, I had hoped to have indicated this in the title of my last book on Paul, though the American publisher muted this somewhat (the English title was *Paul: Fresh Perspectives*, which when translated into American came out as *Paul in Fresh Perspective*). Anyway, what follows is an attempt, not to defend something monolithic called 'the new perspective', certainly not to rescue some of the stranger things that Ed Sanders has said, but to launch one more time into Paul, his letters and his theology, in implicit and sometimes explicit debate with some at least of those who have expressed their very considerable alarm when I have tried to do this before.

Some at least. There are now quite a lot of people writing about all these issues. Michael Bird's recent mostly helpful book has an 18-page bibliography, mainly of English and American works (there are a lot more: the Germans, to look no further, are not inactive), and the 'Paul Page' website now updates this bibliography.[11] Even if I were able to devote all my time to the ever-increasing flood of literature, let alone to the wider studies on first-century Judaism, paganism and Christianity which would set it all in its proper context, and the new commentaries on particular books, it would be difficult to keep up. I have, as we say, a 'day job' which is quite demanding, and which includes, but goes a long way beyond, my responsibilities to expound and defend the teaching of the Bible. (The fact that I am finishing work on this book during the 2008 Lambeth Conference speaks for itself.) It is clearly impossible for me to engage explicitly, in the way one might like, with more than a fraction of the relevant recent writing. However, I think we can make a virtue out of this necessity. Many of the books and articles in question have got to the point, in engagement with secondary literature, that up to half of each page is taken up with small-print footnotes. I have written a fair number of footnotes in my time, and they have their own potential for elegance and even humour. (When my parents proof-read my doctoral thesis, they nicknamed it 'The Oxford Book of Footnotes'; when they did the same for my brother Stephen, some years later, his was called 'The Durham Book of Footnotes'.) But for most readers, even most scholarly readers, such a way of writing can become turgid and scholastic, with the text and the main questions buried under a heap of dusty rubble. I recall the late and much-missed Ben Meyer speaking of those who ask for the bread of insight and are given instead the stone of research. One might extend this: instead of the fish of the gospel, one is presented with the scorpion of scholarly infighting. In trying to avoid this danger, I am well aware of the opposite one: key points made in debate may go unanswered. That can't be helped. I shall try to address what seem to me the central issues, and the curious details where they are relevant, in the main text.

To use a dangerous metaphor: there are two ways of winning a battle. You can do your best to kill as many enemies as you can until few if any are left to oppose you. Or you can simply outflank your opponents so that they realize their position is unsustainable. Much recent literature has been trying the first method. This book is aiming for the second. I know there will be plenty of footsoldiers out there who will continue to hide in the jungle, believing their side is still winning. But I hope that the next generation, without pre-existing reputations to lose and positions to maintain, will get the message.

II

Another image comes to mind. Sometimes, faced with a jigsaw puzzle, one is tempted to make it apparently easier by ignoring half the pieces. Put them back into the box! I can't cope with that many! The result is of course that the puzzle is harder, not easier. However, one can imagine someone, having made this initial disastrous move, trying to remedy the situation by brute force, joining together pieces that don't quite fit in order to create some sort of picture anyway. (I am reminded of the old joke about the former officers of the Stasi, the East German secret police. In order to find out what jobs they might be suited for in the new Germany, they were required to take an intelligence test. They were given a wooden frame with several holes of different shapes, and a set of wooden blocks shaped to fit the holes. When the test was complete, all the blocks were slotted into the frames; but it turned out that, while some of the ex-Stasi officers were indeed quite intelligent, most of them were simply very, very strong.)

The application of this jigsaw image should be obvious. In preparing to write this book, I read quickly through not only the key texts I wanted to deal with, but the articles on 'justification' in the theological and biblical dictionaries that came to hand. Again and again, even where the authors appeared to be paying close attention to the biblical texts, several of the key elements in Paul's doctrine were simply missing: Abraham and the promises God made to him, incorporation into Christ, resurrection and new creation, the coming together of Jews and Gentiles, eschatology in the sense of God's purpose-driven plan through history, and, not least, the holy spirit and the formation of Christian character. Where were they? Reading texts like Romans and Galatians, it is hard to imagine how one could write three sentences about justification without bringing in most of those elements, but those articles managed it. (I should cite an honourable exception. The great conservative scholar J. I. Packer, in his article in the *New Bible Dictionary*, includes virtually all of the above, so that even though I question some aspects of his synthesis he offers a much more fully rounded picture than most of his rivals.[12])

Nor is it only themes that go missing. You can tell a lot about a book on Paul by seeing which passages don't appear in the index. John Piper, astonishingly, has no discussion of Romans 2.25–29 or 10.6–9, absolutely crucial passages in Paul and certainly in my exposition of him. Nor does he deal at any point with what is central for me, the question of Paul's understanding of God's promise to

Abraham in Genesis 15. His only reference to the latter passage is to say that Paul 'picks up the language of imputing' from Genesis; at this point, Piper is exactly on all fours with Ed Sanders, regarding Paul's use of Genesis as merely an incidental convenience, without reference to the wider context, let alone the place of Genesis 15 within one of Paul's greatest controlling stories. Even Jimmy Dunn, discussing whether Paul is a 'covenant theologian', manages not even to address the question of why Paul chooses Genesis 15, not just for a prooftext but for the underlying theme of two of his most crucial chapters.[13]

A further example is provided by the characteristically engaging, substantial and scholarly review of the subject by Stephen Westerholm.[14] Despite the wonderful acclaim from leading scholars printed on the back of the book, Westerholm has managed to leave two-thirds of the jigsaw pieces in the box. One would not know, after over four hundred pages, that justification, for Paul, was closely intertwined with the notion of 'being in Christ' – even though the stand-off between 'juristic' and 'participationist' categories has dominated major discussion of Paul's theology for a hundred years, with the work of Sanders as simply another high point (following Schweitzer and many others) in the elevation of 'participation' to primary position. Westerholm has screened out an entire theme, despite the fact that many, not least in the Reformed as opposed to the Lutheran tradition, have suggested that it is in fact the appropriate context for understanding justification itself. Perhaps this is cognate with the fact that Westerholm, one of the greatest anti-new-perspective champions in current writing, does not seem to notice the existence, let alone the importance, of 'the imputed righteousness of Christ' which, for Piper and others, is *the* central issue; and with the fact that he places C. E. B. Cranfield within his account of 'Lutheran' scholarship, despite acknowledging that Cranfield belongs emphatically in the 'Reformed' camp – and has spent much of his scholarly career trying to prise the reading of Paul out of the hands of a perceived antinomian Lutheranism. Far too many pieces of the jigsaw are swept off the table by this kind of treatment.

Two bits of the jigsaw in particular, neither of them particularly characteristic of either 'old perspective' or 'new', seem to me to be forced on our attention by Paul himself. Actually, they go together quite closely. First, there is Paul's rich and subtle use of the Old Testament. Here I follow, and then go beyond, the seminal work of Richard Hays.[15] When Paul quotes scripture, he regularly intends to refer, not simply to the actual words quoted, but to the whole passage. Again and again, when you look up the chapter from which the quotation is taken, a flood of light streams back onto Paul's actual argument. Among many favourite examples, I mention 2 Corinthians 4.13. 'We have the same spirit of faith,' declares Paul, 'in accordance with scripture, "I believed, and so I spoke"; so we believe, and so we speak.' What does the quotation of Psalm 116.10[16] add to his argument? Surely believing-and-so-speaking is rather obvious? Isn't that what one normally does? Yes, but look at the whole Psalm – the one we know as 116 in the Hebrew and English, divided into two in the Septuagint. It is a prayer of one who is suffering terribly, but who trusts in God and is delivered. In other words, it is exactly the prayer of someone in the situation of Paul in 2 Corinthians 4. Paul has the whole Psalm in mind, and wants his readers to catch the 'echoes' of it as well. This principle of interpretation is now widely established as at least one way among others in understanding Paul's use of scripture. It is not peculiar to, or indeed particularly characteristic of, the 'new perspective' – though it is characteristic of various strands in second-Temple Judaism, the study of which is of course important, if controversial, as one element in the 'new perspective'.

Second, and as far as I am concerned absolutely central for Paul, there is the apostle's understanding of the story of Israel, and of the whole world, as a single continuous narrative which, having reached its climax in Jesus the Messiah, was now developing in the fresh ways which God the creator, the Lord of history, had always intended. This, too, is a characteristic second-Temple Jewish idea, though again it has not at all been prominent in the 'new perspective'.

This is so important for everything that follows in the present book that I need to spell it out a bit more. Highlighting Paul's reading of 'the story of Israel' isn't a matter simply of 'narrative theology' in the reductive sense that, while some people like to do theology in abstract propositions, others prefer, as a matter of cultural taste, to think in story-mode. It is an attempt to understand how Paul's references to Adam and Abraham, to Moses and the prophets, to Deuteronomy and Isaiah and even the Psalms, mean what they mean because he has in his head and heart, as a great many second-Temple Jews did, a grand story of creation and covenant, of God and his world and his people, *which had been moving forwards in a single narrative and which was continuing to do so.* This time the howls of protest come not so much from the anti-new-perspective brigade – so far as I can see, they have mostly not even noticed the point, try as I may to get it across – but from the older writers like Ernst Käsemann, whose debate with Krister Stendahl on this and related matters formed the subject of my Tyndale Lecture in 1978, to which I referred above, and from Käsemann's successors such as J. Louis Martyn. As burnt children, declared Käsemann with a reference back to the Nazi 'salvation-history' of the 1930s ('God has raised up the German nation to carry forward his purposes, and all we have to do is get on board'), we are unwilling to put our hands into the fire again. Point taken; but Stendahl was on to something, even though he did not, in my view, explore it fully in its Pauline dimensions.[17] Paul does indeed think of history as a continuous line, and of God's purpose in history sweeping forwards unbroken from Abraham to Jesus and on, through himself and his work, into the mission of the church. But within this continuous line there is an almighty crash, like the great chord in the 'Surprise' symphony which wakes everyone up with a start even though it belongs exactly within the harmony and rhythm of the movement: an apocalyptic moment *within* the covenant story, the moment – to change the musical image – when the soloist bursts into the music with a torrent of violent chords, which yet reveal themselves on reflection as the point towards which the orchestral introduction had been heading all along. Paul's view of the cataclysmic irruption of God into the history of Israel and the world in and through the death and resurrection of Jesus the Messiah was that this heart-stopping, show-stopping, chart-topping moment was, despite initial appearances, and certainly despite Paul's own earlier expectations and initial understanding, the very thing for which the entire history of Israel from Abraham onwards, the entire history of Israel under Torah from Moses onwards, and indeed the entire history of humanity from Adam onwards, had been waiting. It is central to Paul, but almost entirely ignored in perspectives old, new and otherwise, that *God had a single plan all along through which he intended to rescue the world and the human race, and that this single plan was centred upon the call of Israel, a call which Paul saw coming to fruition in Israel's representative, the Messiah.* Read Paul like this, and you can keep all the jigsaw pieces on the table. Ignore this great narrative, and you will either have to sweep half of them out of sight or try the Stasi trick.

Where all this is ignored – as it routinely is, both in the new perspective and the old, as well as in the nine hundred and ninety-nine righteous readers of Paul who are unaware that they need any 'perspective' at all – we are back to the question of the jigsaw. Take away the single story, and Romans 9—11 becomes a detached musing on predestination, or 'the future of Israel' as a different topic from the rest of the letter. Take away the single story, and the thrust of Paul's climactic statements in Galatians 3 is not only blunted, it is ignored. In 3.29, after heaping up almost all his great theological themes into a single pile – law, faith, children of God, 'in Christ', baptism, 'putting on Christ', 'neither Jew nor Greek', 'all one in Christ' – the conclusion is not 'you are therefore children of God' or 'you are therefore saved by grace through faith', but *'you are therefore Abraham's seed'.* Why does that matter to Paul, and at that point? Most 'new perspective' writers have no answer for that. Virtually no 'old perspective' ones even see that there is a question to be asked. But until we have found the answer we have not been reading Paul, but only a fictitious character of our own invention, cobbled together from such Pauline jigsaw-pieces as we already know and like, forced together with the power of self-assured dogma and stuck in place with the glue of piety and pastoral concern.

Later dogma and piety will themselves, of course, set up a whole new train of thought. A further musical illustration. Hold down the loud pedal on a piano, and strike a low A. If the piano is in tune, you will soon hear the next A vibrating in sympathy. Then the E above that. Then the next A. Then C sharp. Then another E. Things then get a little confused – the next note in the true harmonic sequence ought to be a slightly flat G natural – but this is enough for my present point. All those notes – several As, reinforcing the basic one, with Es and at least one C sharp – are actually *part of* the original note. Few humans can hear them without the aid of a piano or near equivalent, but they are there. But supposing someone, alert perhaps to one of the Es, were to strike that instead ('Listen! This is the note we've been hearing!'). It would indeed belong with the original A. But now, having itself been struck, it would set up *a different set of resonances* to the earlier ones: another E, then a B, a further E, then G sharp, another B, and so on.

This is what has happened, I suggest, in the uses to which Paul has been put in the centuries following the Reformation. Let us grant for the moment that Luther and Calvin (for all their major differences – another point often glossed over in the hasty and sometimes angry anti-new-perspective movement) really did hear a true overtone from what Paul was saying – say, the E which forms the fifth of the chord based on the pedal A. What has then happened? Things have not stood still within Protestantism. All kinds of movements have come and gone. The eighteenth-century Continental Enlightenment was, in some respects, a thoroughly Protestant movement, getting rid of authoritarian religion and asking demystifying, rational, historical questions. The Romantic movement, in reaction against dry Enlightenment rationalism, carried a further strain of Protestant sentiment, this time insisting that what mattered was the inward feeling, not the outward action. Different kinds of pietism have sprung up, flourished, mutated and left their legacy within all of this. Finally (this, of course, cuts several long stories exceedingly short) there has been existentialism, looking to authentic human experience as both the key to, and the yardstick for, genuine faith. There is no such thing as a pure return to the Reformers. They themselves have been heard and re-heard repeatedly in echo chambers that they would not have recognized. And their own readings of Paul have been passed on through those echo chambers to the point where the voice of the apostle has become all but unrecognizable. All the notes on the piano are jangling away merrily, and any attempt to discern which pedal note was struck first appears hopeless.

Unless, of course, we return to history. History was where Paul looked to see the roots of the story whose climax he believed was Jesus Christ. History is where we have to go if, as we say, we want to listen to scripture itself rather than either the venerable traditions of later church leaders or the less venerable footnotes of more recent scholars. For too long we have read scripture with nineteenth-century eyes and sixteenth-century questions. It's time to get back to reading with first-century eyes and twenty-first-century questions.

2

Rules of engagement

Anyone trying to write about Paul, or (for that matter) about anyone who wrote many books on interrelated topics, is faced with a choice. Either you work through the existing texts and deal with the topics as they come up – in which case you will either repeat your discussions of particular topics or gather them together in one place. Or you will select the topics you think important, and work through them, dealing with the relevant texts as they appear – in which case you will either repeat your remarks about the individual books or, again, have to gather them together in one place. You either have commentary plus system, or system plus commentary.

This purely structural dilemma, which you would meet whether you were discussing anyone from, say, Aristotle to Jane Austen, carries a theological edge when the books we are dealing with form part of Holy Writ. Of course, historical scholarship on the New Testament is open to all, whether Jewish or Christian, atheist or agnostic. But the present debate about Paul and justification is taking place between people most of whom declare their allegiance to scripture in general, and perhaps to Paul in particular, as the place where and the means by which the living God has spoken, and still speaks, with life-changing authority. This ought to mean, but does not always mean, that exegesis – close attention to the actual flow of the text, to the questions that it raises in itself and the answers it gives in and of itself – should remain the beginning and the end of the process. Systematize all you want in between; we all do it, there is nothing wrong with it and much to be said for it, particularly when it involves careful comparing of different treatments of similar topics in different contexts. But start with exegesis, and remind yourself that the end in view is not a tidy system, sitting in hard covers on a shelf where one may look up 'correct answers', but the sermon, or the shared pastoral reading, or the scriptural word to a Synod or other formal church gathering, or indeed the life of witness to the love of God, through all of which the church is built up and energized for mission, the Christian is challenged, transformed and nurtured in the faith, and the unbeliever is confronted with the shocking but joyful news that the crucified and risen Jesus is the Lord of the world. That is letting scripture be scripture.

Scripture, in other words, does not exist to give authoritative answers to questions other than those it addresses – not even to the questions which emerged from especially turbulent years such as the sixteenth and seventeenth centuries. That is not to say that one cannot deduce from scripture appropriate answers to such later questions; only that you have to be careful and recognize that that is indeed what you are doing. One older writer, in a volume much quoted in present discussion, declares that Paul used Old Testament terminology (specifically, the phrase 'the righteousness of God') 'not simply because false teachers sought to use the Old Testament against him, but because the Old Testament provides the revelation from which the salvation in Christ must be understood'.[1] There is the problem in a coffee cup. We know, it seems, ahead of time, that 'the salvation in Christ' is the topic to be discussed; Paul for some reason uses Old Testament language to address it; well, this wasn't just for polemical reasons, but because scripture gave him authoritative revelation. It never occurs to Clowney, apparently, that Paul might have wanted to discuss God's righteousness, as many other first-century Jews did, in and for its own sake. And it never occurs to him that the structure of the letter to the Romans, and many indications within that, declare that this is precisely what he was doing. Romans is, after all, primarily about God. Along, perhaps, with Genesis and Isaiah, it is the most obviously heliocentric section of the whole Bible. We go round the sun, not the other way about.

If we are to give primary attention to scripture itself, it is vital to pay attention to the actual flow of the letters, to their context (to the extent that we can discern it), and to the specific arguments that are being mounted at any one time. We must ask, with each succeeding letter, each major section, each sub-section, each paragraph, each sentence and each word: What is Paul basically talking about? What is he saying about that? What relation (if any) does that discussion have to the questions we may want to ask? If those latter questions jangle so loudly in our own heads, we may presume that he is addressing them when he may not be, or may be only as part of a larger discussion which is important to him but not (to our own disadvantage!) to us.

An illustration. After the death of Diana, Princess of Wales, in the late summer of 1997, many in England were in a state of shock which reached a climax with her dramatic funeral the following Saturday. Millions of people all over the country seemed unable to think of anything else all week. The day after the funeral, preachers were faced with a choice. Since everyone is thinking about Diana, do you preach about her, discerning if you can some message, however oblique, in the day's readings, and trying to help people deal both with genuine grief and with (as some cynics suggested) media-generated mass hysteria? Or do you do your best to change the subject and move people on (as we say) by simply preaching, with or without the lectionary, about something else entirely?

I chose the former route. I remember it well. Indeed, my then colleagues insisted that, as the team leader, it was my responsibility to gather up the mood of the moment and address it with a fresh word from God. But I know of a church where the preacher made the other decision, and preached an entire sermon about Mary the mother of Jesus. One of the worshippers there told me afterwards that she had come upon a young woman after the service, in tears as much of puzzlement as of grief. 'I didn't understand what he was saying,' she said. 'Can you help me get the point?' She had assumed, throughout the sermon, that the preacher was *in fact* speaking about Princess Diana, however obliquely; and she was determinedly trying to decode, from his totally different discourse, a message that might help her in her grief.

The history of the reading of Paul is littered with similar mistakes – not always quite so obvious, but mistakes none the less: texts pressed into service to address questions foreign to the apostle, entire passages skimmed over in the hunt for the key word or phrase which fits the preconceived idea. And the problem is not purely one of the misuse of texts, a minor hermeneutical peccadillo for which a scripture professor would give you a bad mark or low grade. If you read your own question into the text, and try to get an answer from it, when the text itself is talking about something else, you run the risk, not only of hearing only the echo of your own voice rather than the word of God, but also of missing the key point that the text was actually eager to tell you, and which you have brushed aside in your relentless quest for your own meaning. Thus, for instance, the attempt to read a text like 1 Corinthians 1.30 ('[God] is the source of your life in Christ Jesus, who became for us wisdom from God, and righteousness and sanctification and redemption') in terms of an 'ordo salutis', the order of events in the progress towards salvation, is not only unlikely to make much sense in itself, but is highly likely to miss the point that Paul is making, which is the way in which the status of the believer in Christ overturns all the social pride and convention of the surrounding culture. And that is a fairly mild example. It is as though a music critic, studying the overture to Mozart's opera *The Magic Flute*, were to write an article about the development of the modern trombone, used there to such wonderful effect, as though the reason Mozart wrote what he did were simply to showcase the instrument rather than to introduce the entire opera.

In particular, it is vital (within any Christian theology; and, indeed, within good hermeneutical practice on any corpus of texts) to allow one writing to illuminate another. Most biblical preachers would agree. (From time to time scholars insist, naturally and rightly, on making sure we have heard the distinctive message of each letter, to check that we are not simply flattening things out; but, even if we conclude that there is tension, or perhaps development, between two letters, we still ought to do our best to hear them symphonically.) But this means, not least, that we must listen not only to Romans and Galatians, but also to the two Corinthian and the two Thessalonian letters, and also to Philippians; and, not least, to Ephesians and Colossians.

Here we encounter an interesting irony. In much Protestant scholarship of the last hundred or more years, Ephesians has regularly been deemed post-Pauline, and Colossians has frequently joined it in that 'deutero-Pauline' category. Like my teacher George Caird, and more other leading scholars than one might imagine from some of the mainstream literature, I have long regarded that judgment with suspicion, and the more I have read the other letters the more Ephesians and Colossians seem to me very thoroughly and completely Pauline. The problem is, of course, that within the liberal Protestantism that dominated New Testament scholarship for so many years Ephesians and Colossians were seen as dangerous to the point of unacceptability, not least because of their 'high' view of the church. There are, to be sure, questions of literary style. But with the Pauline corpus as small as it is – tiny by comparison, say, with the surviving works of Plato or Philo – it is very difficult to be sure that we can set up appropriate stylistic criteria to judge authenticity. But the point is this. At least in America (things are different in Germany), the 'conservative' Pauline readers who have opposed the 'new perspective' are pretty much in favour of Pauline authorship of these letters, for reasons (presumably) to do with their view of scripture. Yet the same implicit critique of Ephesians and Colossians holds sway over their reading as well. Romans and Galatians give us the framework for what Paul really wanted to say; the other letters fill in the details here and there.

Suppose we conduct a thought experiment. Suppose we come to Ephesians first, with Colossians close behind, and decide that we will read Romans, Galatians and the rest in the light of them instead of the other way round. What we will find, straight off, is nothing short of a (very Jewish) cosmic soteriology. God's plan is 'to sum up all things in Christ, things in heaven and things on earth' (Ephesians 1.10; compare Colossians 1.15–20). And we will find, as the means to that plan, God's rescue both of Jews and Gentiles (Ephesians 1.11–12; 1.13–14) in and through the redemption provided in Christ and by the spirit, so that the Jew-plus-Gentile church, equally rescued by grace through faith (2.1–10), and now coming together in a single family (2.11–22), will be Christ's body for the world (1.15–23), the sign to the principalities and powers of the 'many-splendoured wisdom of God' (3.10). Supposing that had been the vision that gripped the imagination of the Reformers in the sixteenth century. Supposing they had had, engraved on their hearts, that close and intimate combination of (a) saving grace accomplishing redemption in the once-for-all death of the Messiah and putting it into operation through faith, without works and (b) the proleptic unity of all humankind in Christ as the sign of God's coming reign over the whole world. And supposing they had then, and only then, gone back to Romans and Galatians . . . The entire history of the Western church, and with it the world, might have been different. No split between Romans 3.28 and 3.29. No marginalization of Romans 9—11. No scrunching of the subtle and important arguments about Jew-plus-Gentile unity in Galatians 3 onto the Procrustean bed of an abstract antithesis between 'faith' and 'works'. No insisting, in either letter, that 'the law' was just a 'system' that applied to everyone, and that 'works of the law' were the moral requirements that encouraged people to earn their own salvation by moral effort. In short, the 'new perspective' might have begun then and there. Or perhaps we should say, the 'new perspective' *did* begin – when Ephesians was written. No wonder Lutheran scholars have been so suspicious of it. But why should that apply to conservative readers for whom it is every bit as much Holy Writ as Romans or Galatians?

In particular, what scripture actually says must be brought into creative dialogue with tradition. This is standard fare in beginner-level doctrine courses, and 'conservative' churches within the Protestant tradition have always insisted that they are 'biblical', whereas other churches down the road are in thrall to human traditions of this or that kind. But here is the problem, which I hinted at in the opening chapter. Again and again, when faced with both the 'new perspective' and some of the other features of more recent Pauline scholarship, 'conservative' churches have reached, not for scripture, but for tradition, as with Piper's complaint that I am sweeping away fifteen hundred years of the church's understanding.[2] Of course, Piper himself wants to sweep away most of the same fifteen hundred years, especially anything from mediaeval Catholicism, and to rely instead on the narrow strand which comes through Calvin and the Westminster Confession. But whichever way you look at it, the objection is odd.

What is needed – admittedly a large and bulky requirement – is what Tony Thiselton has recently and massively described as 'A Hermeneutics of Doctrine'.[3] We need to understand 'doctrines', their statement, development, confutation, restatement, and so on, within the multiple social, cultural, political and of course ecclesial and theological settings of their time. Thus, for instance, it is well known – and very germane to this book – that Anselm of Canterbury, who gave a massive impetus to Western thought on the person and work of Jesus, the meaning of his death, and the notion of justification itself, was working within a highly 'judicial' context. He drew on Latin concepts of law and 'right' and applying them to the biblical sources in a way which, as we can now see, was bound to distort both the essentially Hebraic thought-forms in which the biblical material was rooted and the first-century Greek thought-forms within which the New Testament was designed to resonate. This is not a major objection to Anselm, certainly not a knock-down argument. All theologians and exegetes are involved in the same kind of hermeneutical circle. But, in coming to grips with the particular formulations that have been adopted down the centuries, we must always ask: Why did they emphasize *that* point in *that* way? What were they anxious to safeguard, what were they eager to avoid, and why? What were they afraid of losing? What aspect of the church's mission were they keen to take forward, and why? And, in particular: Which scriptures did they appeal to, and which ones did they seem to ignore? Which bits of the jigsaw did they accidentally-on-purpose knock onto the floor? In the passages they highlighted, did they introduce distortions? Were they paying attention to what the writers were actually talking about, and if not what difference did that make?

After all, the great Confessions of the sixteenth and seventeenth centuries were hardly the product of leisured academics, saying their prayers and thinking through issues in an abstract way, without a care in the world. Those were turbulent, dangerous and violent times, and the Westminster Confession on the one hand, the 39 Articles of my own church on the other, and many more besides, emerged from the titanic struggle to preach the gospel, to order the church, and to let both have their proper impact on the political and social world of the day, while avoiding the all too obvious mistakes of large parts of mediaeval Catholicism (equally obvious, it should be said, to many Roman Catholics then and now). When people in that situation are eager to make their point, they are likely to overstate it, just as we are today. Wise later readers will honour them, but not canonize them, by thinking through their statements afresh in the light of scripture itself.

As an example: it is fascinating to see two essentially Reformed thinkers both insisting, against John Piper and others, that the 'imputed righteousness' of Christ (or of God – we shall explore this confusion below) is on the one hand a legitimate thing to talk about from a systematic theological standpoint, but is on the other hand not actually found stated as such anywhere in Paul. Michael Bird is a younger scholar who might be discounted, when he insists on this, by the Reformed 'old guard'. But listen to this: 'the phrase [the imputation of Christ's righteousness] is not in Paul but its meaning is.' That is J. I. Packer, cautiously making the distinction between what Paul said and did not say and what Reformed theology, rightly in his view, can say in summarizing him.[4] The question presses, however: if 'imputed righteousness' is so utterly central, so nerve-janglingly vital, so standing-and-falling-church important as John Piper makes out, isn't it strange that Paul never actually came straight out and said it?[5] Yes, I shall look at the relevant passages in due course. But I note, for the moment, that when our tradition presses us to regard as central something which is seldom if ever actually said by Paul himself we are entitled, to put it no more strongly, to raise an eyebrow and ask questions. And, yes, that applies to me as well.

II

In our effort to understand scripture itself – a never-ending quest, of course, but one to which each generation of Christians is called afresh – we are bound to read the New Testament in its own first-century context. That is a highly complex task, which keeps several highly intelligent people in full employment all their lives, but the attempt must be made. This applies at every level – to thought-forms, rhetorical conventions, social context, implicit narratives, and so on – but it applies particularly to words, not least to technical terms. To take an example which is controversial, but not in our present context: in 1 Thessalonians 5.3, Paul says 'When they say "peace and security", then sudden destruction will come upon them.' Now, of course, it is easy to read this text against the background of a placid German society on, say, 30 October 1517; or a placid American scene on 10 September 2001. But it helps to understand Paul if we know – as we certainly do – that phrases such as 'peace and security' were part of the stock in trade of Roman imperial propaganda at the time.

And that is simply a start. The more we know about first-century Judaism, about the Greco-Roman world of the day, about archaeology, the Dead Sea Scrolls, and so on, the more, in principle, we can be on firm ground in anchoring exegesis that might otherwise remain speculative, and at the mercy of massively anachronistic eisegesis, into the solid historical context where – if we believe in inspired scripture in the first place – that inspiration occurred. This is the point where, at last, I must engage in a certain amount of close-quarters debate with John Piper. The title of his opening chapter offers a warning to his readers: 'Not all Biblical-Theological Methods and Categories are Illuminating'. Well, that is hard to disagree with. But as the chapter progresses it is clear that what he means is: 'Please do not be seduced, by N. T. Wright or anyone else, into imagining that you need to read the New Testament within its first-century Jewish context'. And at that point – foundational for his whole argument, and mine – I must protest.

Piper knows, of course, that it is part of the task of exegesis to understand what words meant at the time. But he claims that first-century ideas can be used 'to distort and silence what the New Testament writers intended to say'. This can happen, he says, in three ways. First, the interpreter may misunderstand the first-century idea. Yes, of course. But Piper's back-up to this is extraordinary. 'In general', he writes, 'this literature has been less studied than the Bible and does not come with a contextual awareness matching what most scholars bring to the Bible.'[6] This is very strange. Of course literature like the Dead Sea Scrolls, being only recently discovered, has not been so extensively discussed, and its context remains highly controversial. But to say that we *already* have 'contextual awareness' of the Bible while screening out the literature or culture of the time can only mean that we are going to rely on the 'contextual awareness' of earlier days – of, say, Whiston's *Josephus*, or Alfred Edersheim's *Life and Times of Jesus the Messiah*, both of which had an honoured place on the shelves of many clergy and theologians over the last century, but which are massively outdated by the discoveries and research of the last century.[7] It is simply not the case, as Piper asserts, that to pay proper heed to first-century texts means to bring an assured interpretation of extra-biblical texts to illumine a less sure reading of a biblical text. The true historian tests everything and takes nothing for granted. Yes, scholarly fashions change, and what looks assured today may well not look so sure tomorrow. But the works that Piper cites to reassure his readers that they need not worry about these silly new readings of first-century texts – especially the first volume in the set called *Justification and Variegated Nomism* – will not bear the weight he wants to put on them. To the extent that the essays there are fully scholarly, they do not make the case their principal editor claims they do; to the extent that they appear to do so, they are themselves subject to question as being, to put it mildly, *parti pris*.[8] Saying this does not, of course, settle the question. We shall return to it in due course. It is just to say that all investigation of words and terms must be located within their historical context.

In particular, Piper seems to me to lean far too heavily in a dangerous direction in a key footnote,[9] warding off – so it seems – the possibility of reading Paul in ways other than his own, before they even appear over the horizon. Responding to my claim (which had seemed to me uncontroversial) that, to understand a word, 'we must begin with the wider world [the writer] lived in, the world we meet in our lexicons, concordances, and other studies of how words were used in that world, and must then be alive to the possibility of a writer building in particular nuances and emphases of his or her own', Piper says that this obscures two facts: first, that the author's use of the word 'is *the* most crucial evidence concerning its meaning', and second that 'all other uses of the word are themselves other instances that are as vulnerable to misunderstanding as is the biblical use'. We have no access to 'how words were used in that world', he claims, 'other than particular uses like the one right there in the Bible'. This seems to me dramatically to overstate the case. Yes, of course, every use in every source must be subject to question. But when we meet a word or term which is used in a consistent way across a range of literature of a particular period, and when we then meet the same word or term in an author we are studying, the natural presumption is that the word or term means there what it meant elsewhere. Until, that is, the context rebels, producing a sense so odd that we are forced to say, 'Wait a minute, something seems to be wrong; is there another meaning for this word we were taking for granted?' And as for Piper's insistence – with which, in the last analysis, I of course agree – that 'the final court of appeal is the context of an author's own argument' (61), I respond: Yes, absolutely: and that means taking Romans 3.21—4.25 seriously *as a whole argument*, and discovering the meaning of its key terms within that. It means taking Romans 9.30—10.13 seriously *as a whole argument*, and discovering within that why Paul makes the use of Deuteronomy 30 that he does, and how that helps us, precisely from within his own argument, to discover the meaning of his key terms. It means, as well and behind those two, taking Romans 2.17—3.8

seriously *as part of a single train of thought* and discovering the meaning of its key terms within that. And I note, sadly, that in this book at least Piper never deals with any of those great arguments, but contents himself with picking piecemeal at verses here and there. Almost anything can be proved that way.

This is by no means an abstract or theoretical point about lexicography. It relates directly to the phrase 'the righteousness of God', as we shall see, and indeed to many other Pauline words, phrases and entire trains of thought. After all, what is the alternative? Sadly, it is plain in Piper's own work. If we do not bring first-century categories of thought, controlling narratives, and so on, to the text, we do not come with a blank mind, a *tabula rasa*. We come with the questions and issues we have learned from elsewhere. This is a perennial problem for all of us, but unless we are to declare, here and now, that God has no more light to break out of his holy word – that everything in scripture has already been discovered by our elders and betters and that all we have to do is read them to find out what scripture says – then further research, precisely at a historical level, is what is needed. I know John Calvin would have wholeheartedly agreed with this. It is (in other words) no argument to say that a particular paradigm 'does not fit well with the ordinary reading of many texts and leaves many ordinary folk not with the rewarding "ah-ha" experience of illumination, but with a paralysing sense of perplexity'.[10] I could respond, of course, by saying that I know many 'ordinary folk' who are flat bored with the 'ordinary reading' of many Pauline texts, and who, not from a love of novelty (of which Piper also accuses me;[11] if only he knew!) but from a genuine hunger for spiritual and theological depth, grab on for dear life to the perspectives I have tried to offer. Piper would no doubt say that such folk are sadly deluded. But the point is this: there is no neutral, 'ordinary reading'. What seems 'ordinary' to one person will seem extraordinary to others. There are readings which have grown up in various traditions, and all need testing historically and exegetically as well as theologically. And, as I have argued before and hope to show here once more, many of the supposedly 'ordinary readings' within the Western Protestant traditions have simply not paid attention to what Paul actually wrote.

In fact, where first-century meanings are held at bay, concepts and debating points from completely other centuries come in to take their place. Hence all the discussion of the 'formal cause' of justification as against the 'material cause', the debates about what is to count as the 'ground' or 'means' of justification, and so on. Where do we find these in Paul, or indeed in first-century Judaism? Answer: we don't, but some traditions have employed such language to try to help them to get Paul to answer the questions they wanted to ask (and that they either assumed or hoped he was himself asking). In particular, the sixteenth and seventeenth century supplied so many new ideas and categories from the concepts and controlling stories current at the time that, while they remain a wonderful example and encouragement in many things, they must not be taken as the final court of appeal. (The same could be said, once more, of Anselm and the categories of his day.) It is worrying to find Piper encouraging readers to go back, not to the first century, but to 'the Christian renewal movements of sixteenth-century Europe'.[12] To describe that period as offering the 'historic roots' of evangelicalism is profoundly disturbing. Proper evangelicals are rooted in scripture, and above all in the Jesus Christ to whom scripture witnesses, and nowhere else.

The rules of engagement for any debate about Paul must be, therefore: exegesis first and foremost, with all historical tools in full play, not to dominate or to squeeze the text out of the shape into which it naturally forms itself, but to support and illuminate a text-sensitive, argument-sensitive, nuance-sensitive reading. One of the first insights I came to in the early stages of my doctoral work on Romans, wrestling with the commentaries of the 1950s and 1960s as well as with the great traditions (which I respected then and respect still) of Luther and Calvin, was that, when you hear yourself saying, 'What Paul was really trying to say was . . .' and then coming up with a sentence which only tangentially corresponds to what Paul actually wrote, it is time to think again. When, however, you work to and fro, this way and that, probing a key technical term here, exploring a larger controlling narrative there, enquiring why Paul used *this* particular connecting word between these two sentences, or *that* particular scriptural quotation at this point in the argument, and eventually you arrive at the position of saying, 'Stand *here*; look at things in *this* light; keep in mind *this* great biblical theme, and then you will see that Paul has said exactly what he meant, neither more nor less' – then you know that you are in business. Even if – perhaps especially if! – it turns out that he is not talking about what we thought he should have been, or that he is not saying exactly what our tradition, or our favourite sermon, had expected him to say about it.

In this context, I must register one strong protest against one particular translation. When the New International Version was published in 1980, I was one of those who hailed it with delight. I believed its own claim about itself, that it was determined to translate exactly what was there, and inject no extra paraphrasing or interpretative glosses. This contrasted so strongly with the then popular New English Bible, and promised such an advance over the then rather dated Revised Standard Version, that I recommended it to students and members of the congregation I was then serving. Disillusionment set in over the next two years, as I lectured verse by verse through several of Paul's letters, not least Galatians and Romans. Again and again, with the Greek text in front of me and the NIV beside it, I discovered that the translators had had another principle, considerably higher than the stated one: to make sure that Paul should say what the broadly Protestant and evangelical tradition said he said. I do not know what version of scripture they use at Dr Piper's church. But I do know that if a church only, or mainly, relies on the NIV it will, quite simply, never understand what Paul was talking about.

This is a large claim, and I have made it good, line by line, in relation to Romans in my big commentary, which prints the NIV and the NRSV and then comments on the Greek in relation to both of them. Yes, the NRSV sometimes lets you down, too, but nowhere near as frequently or as badly as the NIV. And, yes, the NIV has now been replaced with newer adaptations in which some at least of the worst features have, I think, been at least modified. But there are many who, having made the switch to the NIV, are now stuck with reading Romans 3.21–26 like this: 'But now a righteousness from God, apart from law, has been made known . . . this righteousness from God comes through faith in Jesus Christ to all who believe. . . . [God] did this to demonstrate his justice . . . he did it to demonstrate his justice at the present time, so as to be just and the one who justifies those who have faith in Jesus.' In other words, 'the righteousness of God' in 3.21 is only allowed to mean 'the righteous status which comes to people from God', whereas the equivalent term in 3.25 and 3.26 clearly refers to God's own righteousness – which is presumably why the NIV has translated it as 'justice', to avoid having the reader realize the deception. In the following paragraph, a similar tell-tale translation flaw occurs, to which again we shall return. In 3.29, Paul introduces the question, 'Is God the God of Jews only?' with the single-letter word *ē*, normally translated 'or'; '*Or* is God the God of Jews only?' – in other words, if the statement of 3.28 were to be challenged, it would look as though God were the God of Jews only. But the NIV, standing firmly in the tradition that sees no organic connection between justification by faith on the one hand and the inclusion of Gentiles within God's people on the other, resists this clear implication by omitting the word altogether. Two straws in a clear and strong wind. And those blown along by this wind may well come to forget that they are reading a visibly and demonstrably flawed translation, and imagine that this is what Paul really said . . .

Whereas, of course, a reading of Paul more wide awake to the world in which he lived and thought would have seen the connections and meanings at once. But to go further with this we need another chapter.

3

First-century Judaism:
covenant, law and lawcourt

I

I distinctly remember when the shock first hit. I was reading through the complete works of Josephus, partly because that was what a young graduate student was supposed to do, and partly because I was due to teach an undergraduate who wanted to study second-Temple Judaism. Josephus is such a rattling good read, albeit sad and gory at times, that it is easy to get carried along by the flow and forget where you are. And then, rather like reading an account of something that happened in the summer of 1964 and suddenly thinking 'that's when I canoed up the Caledonian Canal', it dawned on me. I was reading Josephus' account of the build-up to the Roman/Jewish war of AD 66–70, particularly the part describing events in Jerusalem and Galilee in the mid-50s. Josephus was writing about revolutionary parties, would-be leaders, prophetic movements, incompetent Roman governors, and urgent little groups reading scripture to try to make sense of it all. And, as I remember suddenly thinking, *this was when St Paul came back to Jerusalem for his final visit, having just written Romans.*

Then and there I realized that most Jews of the time were not sitting around discussing how to go to heaven, and swapping views on the finer points of synergism and sanctification. There were of course plenty of Jews who did discuss things like the interrelationship between divine and human agency, and indeed the question of who would inherit 'the age to come', the great time of salvation, but for the most part they were not engaged in the debates on which our own traditions have concentrated. They were hoping and longing for Israel's God to act, to do what he had promised, to turn history the right way up once again as he had done in the days of David and Solomon a thousand years before. Nor were they

37

obsessed with 'going to heaven when they died'. Some believed in resurrection: they would die, but God would raise them on the last day. Others did not. Others again believed in a future disembodied immortality. But all this was not, to put it mildly, the main or central topic of their conversations, their poems, their legal discourses, their late-night meetings. The rabbis (meaning, in a broad sense, the Pharisees, of whom Paul had been one, and their successors over the next few hundred years) do not for the most part say, when discussing their particular interpretations of the ancestral law, 'this is what you need to do to make sure you go to heaven', or 'to make sure you will be raised from the dead'. The worry about the afterlife, and the precise qualifications for it, which have so characterized Western Christianity, especially (it seems) since the Black Death, and which have shaped and formed Western readings (both Catholic and Protestant) of the New Testament, do not loom so large in the literature of Paul's contemporaries.

All generalizations are misleading, including that one. There are exceptions to every rule, just as there were to the striking 'rule' that 'All Israel has a share in the world to come'.[1] There is absolutely no guarantee that the literature and the archaeological remains, including coins, that give us historical access to the world of first-century Judaism enable us to map anything like an exact picture of how people thought, what motivated them, which controlling stories they understood themselves to be part of. What has come down to us is often representative only of a literate and cultured elite. But, in addition, Judaism was richly varied, right across the period from the last two or three centuries BC to the second century AD, so much so that many have understandably wanted to speak of 'Judaisms', plural. There are many different theologies, many different expressions, many different ways of standing within, or on the edge of, or in tension with, the great ancestral traditions of Israel. There is what has, perhaps unhappily, been called 'Variegated Nomism', a rich panoply of ways of understanding Israel's law and trying to obey it. Not only is it too simple to say, as some versions of the new perspective have said, that all first-century Jews believed in grace; they meant many different things by 'grace', and responded to those meanings in a rich variety of ways. Yes. All this I grant.

And yet. There is a swell, a surge, an incipient flood tide, which sweeps through between the sand dunes of history and soaks into acre after acre of the evidence, whether it be the cynical politician Josephus or the wild sectarians scribbling the scrolls, whether it be the agonized visionary who wrote the book we call 4 Ezra or the wonderfully detailed lawyers' minds we see revealed in the early rabbinic traditions. The tide which was carrying all Israel along in the time of Jesus and Paul was the tide of hope, hope that Israel's God would act once more and this time do it properly, that the promises made to Abraham and his family would at last come true, that the visions of the prophets who foretold a coming restoration would find their ultimate fulfilment. What we in the Western world have come to see as the 'individual' hope, and indeed the individual life of faith, piety or virtue, found their place within that. So I and many others have argued, up and down and at length. I do not know how to make the case more clearly than I have already done.[2]

In particular – I sigh as I write this, because I know it remains not only controversial but also straightforwardly incomprehensible to many – many first-century Jews were hoping that this deliverance, this promise-fulfilling divine action, would happen *at that time.* That is what Josephus says, and we have ample evidence from several quite disparate sources to back it up. Many Jews, throughout this period, were *calculating* when the great deliverance would happen, and they were doing so on the basis of the prophecy to which, it seems, Josephus was referring: the ninth chapter of the book of Daniel.[3]

Daniel 9 is mostly a prayer. Daniel (scholars normally assume that the book was written, or at least edited, in the second century BC, but 'Daniel' here is the character in the book, a high official at the royal court of the Chaldeans four centuries earlier) is studying the writings of Israel's prophets to see how long the awful exile of God's people would last. He reads in Jeremiah that it will be seventy years.[4] He is not the only one to read that prophecy: the authors of 2 Chronicles, and of Ezra (supposing them to be different) knew it, and so did the prophet Zechariah.[5] But Daniel is the only one to receive a startling reinterpretation of Jeremiah's promise.

Daniel 9.3–19 contains one of the most moving of all biblical prayers: a lament for all the devastation that has happened to Judah and Jerusalem, a deep, radical confession of the sin and guilt of the people that had so richly deserved such punishment, and a humble prayer that the promised seventy-year mercy would not now be delayed further. His prayer is answered with a heavenly visit and a reinterpretation of the promise. The angel Gabriel is sent to tell him that the prophecy is not for seventy years, but for *seventy weeks of years*: 'Seventy weeks are decreed for your people and your holy city: to finish the transgression, to put an end to sin, and to atone for iniquity, to bring in everlasting righteousness, to seal both vision and prophet, and to anoint a most holy one.'[6] The prophecy continues with detailed descriptions of the rebuilding of Jerusalem, the cutting off of 'an anointed one', the setting up of 'an abomination that desolates', and an ultimate destruction.[7] Of these things, as the letter to the Hebrews says, we cannot now speak in detail.

The point is this. Daniel was (again according to Josephus) popular in the first century, not as what we would call 'devotional reading' (though no doubt devout Jews shared in the prayer of chapter 9, as well one might), but as what we would call a political tract. 'Seventy weeks of years' translates as $7 \times 70 = 490$: *when would they be up?* When would this prophecy of prophecies be fulfilled? When would the great Redemption finally happen? When would this extended term of 'exile' finally be over? How could one tell?

Well, it would depend on when the period actually started. Granted the fairly rudimentary chronology available to first-century Jews reckoning up their own history, there were plenty of options available. From the detailed studies scholars have made, it appears that some were inclined to place the end of the 490-year period around what we now call the turn of the eras. That position was adopted by some at least of the authors of the scrolls, which offers a plausible reason why some Essenes thought the house of Herod might provide the coming Messiah. Others did their calculations quite differently, and came up with the middle of the first century AD, or even some time in the second. And of course those are exactly the times when great revolts took place. Josephus understood: 'what more than all else incited them to the war [he is referring to the war of AD 66–70] was an ambiguous oracle, found in their sacred scriptures, to the effect that at that time one from their country would become ruler of the world'.[8] The Bible said it; they believed it; that settled it – and off they went to fight God's battles.

What on earth has all this to do with Pauline theology? Three things in particular.

First, *many first-century Jews thought of themselves as living in a continuing narrative stretching from earliest times, through ancient prophecies, and on towards a climactic moment of deliverance which might come at any moment.* Once again, we cannot say 'all first-century Jews thought like this', any more than you can say 'all Americans like hamburgers'. But plenty do, and plenty did. They were not, in other words, understanding themselves as living in a narrative which said, 'all humans are sinful and will go to hell; maybe God will be gracious and let us go to heaven instead and dwell with him; how will that come about? Let's look at our scriptures for advance clues.' No: scripture was seen, in its many-sided and multifarious characteristics and modes, as at least this: a large-scale controlling narrative *whose ending had not yet arrived.* Scripture was not simply a source-book for doctrine or ethics, a manual of piety. It was all that, of course, but it was more. *It offered the earlier acts in the drama that was still taking place.* I find it curious that, though I have tried in many different places to emphasize this as the context for understanding Paul, and though critics like John Piper have clearly read those books, they pass over this theme in silence. It is (to coin a phrase) just as if I'd never said it.

The second thing, equally important and this time frequently noted and attacked, is this: *this continuing narrative was currently seen, on the basis of Daniel 9, as a long passage through a state of continuing 'exile'.* I put 'exile' in inverted commas because I know perfectly well – and if I didn't a host of well-meaning but incomprehending critics have been eager to point it out – that of course the geographical 'exile' ended, in a sense, when the captives returned from Babylon. They came back, rebuilt Jerusalem and the Temple, and started up life once more. Some, as we saw, hailed this as the fulfilment of Jeremiah's seventy years. But it wasn't just that the glorious promises had not all been fulfilled (the wonderful visions of Isaiah 40—55, the fabulous new Temple promised by Ezekiel, and above all YHWH himself returning to Zion). It was, more darkly, that Israel was 'enslaved' to foreign overlords and their pagan culture and customs. 'Here we are,' says Ezra, 'slaves to this day – slaves in the land that you gave to our ancestors'; 'from the days of our ancestors *to this day* we have been deep in guilt, and for our iniquities we ... have been handed over to the kings of the lands ... and to utter shame, *as is now the case* ... for we are slaves; yet our God has not forsaken us.'[9] Similar statements can be found in a variety of literature of the time, from Qumran to Tobit, from the book of Baruch to Second Maccabees, and on into rabbinic literature.[10] A study of the book of Malachi would make the same point: Israel has returned to the land, but things are far from satisfactory, the great prophecies have not yet been fulfilled, and in particular YHWH himself has not yet returned to the Temple – though, warns the prophet, he soon will. The exile (the real exile, as opposed to the merely geographical exile in Babylon) is still continuing. And this exile is, in turn, to be understood, relatively straightforwardly, as the result of the 'covenantal curse' articulated so strikingly in Deuteronomy 27—29. Scripture said that YHWH would bring the curse on his people if they disobeyed, and that the curse would end in exile under foreign overlords; that is a good description (thought many first-century Jews) of where we still are; therefore we are still under the curse, still in exile.

Attempts to controvert this, which have often taken the form, 'But they *were* back in the land, so they can't have been in exile', or 'but 1 Peter thinks of the churches as a community of exiles, so the gospel can't have been about the return from exile', show merely that the fundamental point has not even been grasped: *many first-century Jews thought of the period they were living in as the continuation of a great scriptural narrative, and of the moment they themselves were in as late on within the 'continuing exile' of Daniel 9.*[11] I appreciate that for so many people in late Western modernity the idea of people 'living within a controlling narrative' seems foreign (though we all do it cheerfully: every time people say 'in this day and age' they are appealing to an assumed idea of modernity, or progress, or enlightenment); that for many Christians within the Protestant traditions the idea of continuing history as having importance in itself, and of expecting deliverance within history, is not on the radar screen, perhaps for implicit religious reasons; and that for many, perhaps most, contemporary Western readers of the New Testament (John Piper's 'ordinary folk', perhaps), the effort required to think into a worldview where people were thinking to themselves, *When is God going to do what he's promised?* is all too much, and they shake their heads and settle back into the comfort of a non-historical soteriology the long and the short of which is 'my relationship with God' rather than 'what God is going to do to sort out his world and his people'. Or, alternatively, the question, 'When will God do what he's promised?' splurges back onto the theological scene in the form of lurid speculations about the Rapture: drive eschatology out of the front door, and it will break in through the back window. And with all of these strategies we thereby put ourselves in the position of musicians who, finding the score of a Beethoven symphony, reckon that because the only instruments they themselves possess are guitars and mouth-organs, that must be what Beethoven had in mind. Or, if you like, that because the only music they know is a collection of songs none of which last longer than four minutes, that must be what Beethoven actually intended.

One of the rhetorically pleasing features of my insistence on this 'return from exile' motif is that it puts a lot of clear water between me and Ed Sanders, who does not reckon with the idea, and particularly Jimmy Dunn, who has never been able to see what I am talking about. So the 'new perspective' falls apart at this point! Good: let us proceed into the uncharted territory beyond, and particularly to the third point that emerges from Daniel 9. This is where we come at last within earshot of Paul. And we do not need to turn the volume up very loud for the echoes to resonate:

Ah, Lord, great and awesome God, keeping covenant and steadfast love with those who love you and keep your commandments, we have sinned and done wrong, acted wickedly and rebelled, turning aside from your commandments and ordinances. We have not listened to your servants the prophets ... To you, Lord, belongs righteousness (LXX: *soi, kyrie, hē dikaiosynē*, translating *leka adonai hatsedaqah*) but to us belongs open shame ...

To the Lord our God belong mercy and forgiveness, for we have rebelled against him ... All Israel has transgressed your law and turned aside, refusing to obey your voice. So the curse and the oath written in the law of Moses, the servant of God, have been poured out upon us, because we have sinned against you. He has confirmed his words, which he spoke against us and against our rulers, by bringing upon us a calamity so great ... Just as it is written in the law of Moses, all this calamity has come upon us. We did not entreat the favour of the Lord our God, turning from our iniquities and reflecting on his fidelity (LXX: *dikaiosynē*; Theodotion: *alētheia*, translating *emeth*). So the Lord kept watch over this calamity until he brought it upon us. Indeed, the Lord our God is right (*dikaios kyrios ho theos hēmōn*, translating *tsadiq* YHWH *eloheynu*) in all that he has done; for we have disobeyed his voice.

And now, O Lord our God, who brought your people out of the land of Egypt with a mighty hand and made your name renowned even to this day – we have sinned, we have done wickedly. O Lord, because of your righteousness (*kata tēn dikaiosynēn sou*, LXX; *en pasē hē eleēmosynē sou*, Theod., translating *cecol tsidqotheka*), let your anger and wrath turn away from your city . . .

We do not present our supplication before you on the ground of our righteousnesses (*epi tais dikaiosynais hēmōn*, translating *'al tsidqothenu*), but on the ground of your great mercies. O Lord, hear; O Lord, forgive; O Lord, listen and act and do not delay! For your own sake, O my God, because your city and your people bear your name! (Daniel 9.4–19)

You are in the right, and we are in the wrong. That is the basic meaning of verse 7: in the implicit lawsuit between God and Israel, God is in the right. All this is the language of the *covenant* (v. 4); more specifically, of the covenant in Deuteronomy 27—30, referred to here in verses 11–14: Moses warned of a curse that would come, a curse that would involve exile and horrible judgment on Israel. God is *righteous*, not just (in other words) as though in a lawsuit, but in terms of the covenant. These were the terms and conditions; Israel broke them; and the exile – the specific covenantal curse – has come upon the people. So what is now to happen? The very same attribute of God because of which God was right to punish Israel with the curse of exile – i.e. his 'righteousness' – can now be appealed to for covenantal restoration the other side of punishment. The God of the exodus – and an exodus, of course, is what people enslaved in a foreign land need, as all the 'exilic' prophets knew – has acted in the past to fulfil his covenantal promises, as indeed he did in the first exodus.[12] So now, 'in accordance with all your righteousnesses', in other words, 'your righteous acts', the prophet beseeches God to have mercy on Israel and Jerusalem. In case there is any doubt, 'righteous acts' here clearly does not mean 'virtuous acts'. It means 'acts in fulfilment of God's covenant promises'. God has acted before to fulfil the covenant. He must now do so again. 'Covenant' and 'lawcourt' belong together.[13]

The single narrative; the single narrative now going through an extended period of 'exile'; the exile, and its hoped-for reversal, as the fulfilment of God's righteousness. And all of this, not in some dubious or difficult-to-interpret out-of-the-way second-Temple text, such as John Piper is so anxious about, but right there in the Old Testament canon, in a book, and a chapter, which according to the Synoptic tradition was dear to the heart of Jesus himself.

From here it would be easy to say, 'Well, now we know what "God's righteousness" means; let us go now in haste to Romans and see this great sight, how the letter makes sense if we read it with Daniel 9 in mind.' Alas, there is a roadblock in the way before we can even begin to approach that task. Are we quite sure we know, even from this apparently clear passage, what 'the righteousness of God' really means?

II

John Piper is quite sure. He has written about this subject again and again. I actually reviewed his first book when it came out, and remarked then, as he has done now,[14] that he and I had been working on similar topics and reading the same scholars, albeit coming to different conclusions (not *very* different, by the way, but with obviously significant divergencies). Then and subsequently he has expounded a view of 'the righteousness of God' which, he claims, goes deeper than 'covenant faithfulness', deeper also than the 'lawcourt' implications. God's righteousness, he claims, is God's concern for God's own glory. He expounds this view, briefly and in summary, on pp. 62–71, referring to his much fuller treatments elsewhere.

There is no time to explore these fuller discussions. We would need to examine literally dozens of Old Testament passages, as well as the key ones in Paul, to which we shall return. I simply content myself with five observations which place worrying question-marks beside Piper's proposal. In each case this is not simply a matter of showing why I think Piper is wrong (not massively wrong, just out of alignment and lacking in precision). It is, more importantly, a matter of introducing key points, from within Paul's Jewish world and within his own writings, which are foundational for where we need to go.

First, there is a huge mass of scholarly literature on the meaning of 'God's righteousness', and Piper simply ignores it. I am not aware of any other scholar, old perspective, new perspective, Catholic, Reformed, Evangelical, anyone, who thinks that *tsedaqah elohim* in Hebrew or *dikaiosynē theou* in Greek actually means 'God's concern for God's own glory'. Rather, the widespread view is that *tsedaqah/dikaiosynē* in general (i.e. the Hebrew meaning, still reflected in biblical Greek as opposed to classical Greek where *dikaiosynē* means 'justice') refer to 'conformity with a norm', and when this is further contextualized as *God's* 'righteousness' the strong probability is that this refers to God's fidelity to the norms he himself has set up, in other words, the covenant. Thus J. I. Packer: 'the reason why these texts (Isaiah and the Psalms) call God's vindication of his oppressed people His "righteousness" is that it is an act of faithfulness to His covenant promise to them'.[15] Of course, when God acts in faithfulness to his own promises, this results in his name, his honour and his reputation, being magnified or glorified. Nobody would deny that. But nowhere is it clear that 'God's righteousness' actually *denotes* that glorification. Piper's attempt to show that there must be a 'righteousness' *behind* God's 'covenant faithfulness' is simply unconvincing. It begins to look as though Piper has simply not understood what covenant faithfulness means, and its enormous significance throughout scripture. As many representatives of both old and new perspectives have said, following Ernst Käsemann who, though in some ways a classic Lutheran and therefore naturally an 'old perspective' person, was too good an exegete not to notice many of the phenomena which then turned into the 'new perspective', God's *dikaiosynē* is, not least, his faithfulness to, and his powerful commitment to rescue, creation itself. It always has in view God's utter commitment to put things right. But, as we shall see presently, in scripture, in second-Temple Jewish literature, and in Paul himself, not least in Paul's reading of scripture, *God's way of putting the world right is precisely through his covenant with Israel*. This is the theme that will emerge clearly in the exegesis in due course. *God's single plan to put the world to rights is his plan to do so through Israel.*

(A grammatical note at this point. It is often said that this reading of *dikaiosynē theou* makes the genitive 'subjective'. This is so only to the extent that the noun, *dikaiosynē*, is a noun-referring-to-an-action: 'righteousness' as 'acts of righteousness'. To the extent that *dikaiosynē* refers to an aspect of God's character, albeit one which clearly implies that God will act in certain ways, the genitive *theou* would not be subjective, but possessive. The two shade into one another but are still clearly distinguishable. If we speak of 'Paul's dictation of the letter', the word 'Paul's' is subjective, designating the *subject* of the action. If we speak of 'Paul's wisdom', the word 'Paul's' is possessive, designating the *owner* or *possessor* of the wisdom in question.)

At least, however, Piper does not go in the far more frequent wrong direction, that of deducing, from the fact that 'righteousness' in the Bible is a 'relational' term, that it refers to the 'relationship' between God and humans, making 'justification' mean 'the estab-lishment of a relationship between me and God'. The word 'rela-tionship' in contemporary English is in any case far too slippery to be of any use at this point. The 'relationality' of 'righteousness' does not have to do with 'getting to know someone personally', as 'relationship' implies to most people today, but rather with 'how they are related to one another' (which might be true, say, of cousins who had never met and were even unaware of one another's existence), 'how they stand in relation to one another' (which might be true of parties in a lawsuit who did not know one another at all), or to what is 'the status of their relationship'. And, once this is clear, it moves the language back where most people today place it: in a mixture, yet to be explored, of covenant and lawcourt.

Second, it is not at all clear how Piper's idiosyncratic definition of 'God's righteousness' works out within the scheme of imputation that lies at the heart of his own reading. If 'God's righteousness' is 'God's concern for God's own glory', what does it mean to sug-gest that this is imputed to the believer? It could only mean '*the believer's* concern for God's own glory'. But concern for someone else's glory is not the same as concern for one's own. Here we meet, not for the last time, the confusion that arises inevitably when we try to think of the judge transferring, by imputation or any other way, his own attributes to the defendant. And, in any case, though it is true that Paul does see Abraham, for instance, as 'giving God glory' (Romans 4.24), there is nothing to say that this is what was meant by his having 'righteousness' imputed to him. Indeed, Paul says in 4.22 that this 'giving glory to God', along with faith, and trust in God's promise, and full conviction of God's power, was the *reason why* God 'reckoned it to him as righteousness'. The two can then hardly be the same thing, though since Piper does not discuss Romans 4.20–22 in this book I cannot be sure.

In any case, Paul's repeated quotation of Genesis 15 throughout chapter 4 indicates strongly what is going on. That chapter was where God established his covenant with Abraham. To be sure, this was for God's own glory. But Abraham's 'righteousness' is his right standing within that covenant, and God's 'righteousness' is his unswerving commitment to be faithful to that covenant – including the promise (4.13) that Abraham would inherit the world. Here we have it: *God's single plan, through Abraham and his family, to bless the whole world*. That is what I have meant by the word 'covenant' when I have used it as a shorthand in writing about Paul. My justification for using it is not that every time the idea is present Paul uses the word *diathēkē*, the normal Greek for *berith*, 'covenant', because obviously he doesn't. My justification is that this massive, many-sided and multiply explanatory narrative is rooted, by Paul himself, in classic 'covenantal' passages such as Genesis 15, Deuteronomy 27—30, and Daniel 9.

Third, Piper's failure to grapple with the larger context of Romans 3 and 4 – specifically, the great argument that runs from 3.21 to 4.25 as a whole on the one hand, and the smaller train of thought in 3.1–8 on the other, picking up 2.17–29 – means that his attempts to distance 'God's righteousness' from the notion of covenant faithfulness (pp. 67–70) fail to convince. For this I refer to my larger commentary.[16] Again, it seems that Piper has read it, but he never engages with the basic proposal I make, which is that – fully in line with Daniel 9 and the multitude of Isaiah and Psalms passages that talk in the same way – 'God's righteousness' here is his faithfulness to the covenant, *specifically to the covenant with Abraham made in Genesis 15*, and that it is because of this covenant that God deals with sins through the faithful, obedient death of Jesus the Messiah (3.24–26). As we saw in Daniel, 'God's righteousness' includes his duty to punish sin in line with the covenant provisions in Deuteronomy 27—29. This link cannot be waved away, as Piper tries to do, in a footnote.[17] Further, Piper's discussion of 3.1–8 never even attempts to come to terms with what the paragraph is *about*, because Piper has held at arm's length – or perhaps has never even glimpsed, despite the various things he has read which make it clear enough – that *the point of the covenant always was that God would bless the whole world through Abraham's family*. The point of Romans 3.1–8 is not a general discussion about God's attributes and human failure. Likewise, the 'unfaithfulness' of the Israelites is not their lack of 'belief'. The point is that God has promised to bless the world through Israel, and Israel has been faithless *to that commission*. That is why, against Piper,[18] we can indeed understand 'covenant faithfulness' as a translation of *dikaiosynē theou* in Romans 3.5. As in Daniel 9, it is because of God's faithfulness to the covenant that he must punish his faithless covenant people, and as a result their covenant failure ('unrighteousness') thus shows up his covenant faithfulness all the more. All this (not merely a general condemnation of all humanity, though to be sure that is there as well) is what sets up the peculiar dramatic tension of 3.19–20, and what then drives the single, united train of thought in 3.21—4.25. God has made a plan to save the world; Israel is the linchpin of this plan; but Israel has been unfaithful. What is now required, if the world's sin is to be dealt with and a worldwide family created for Abraham, is a faithful Israelite. That is what God has now provided. To all this we shall return.

Fourth, Piper's attempt to downplay the importance of the lawcourt metaphor within the whole discussion is deeply unconvincing.[19] (He says the same about me, too, at this point; how can we move beyond this mutual incomprehension?) The language of 'righteousness' in the Old Testament regularly refers to lawcourt, or quasi-lawcourt situations: Judah declares that Tamar is 'righteous rather than me', not meaning 'she is more virtuous than I am', but rather that the implicit lawcourt in which they are squared off against one another has clearly, without actual need for a judge, found in her favour and against him.[20] Similarly, Saul says to David, 'You are righteous rather than me', again not meaning that David is virtuous and he is not (that is true, but it is not the point Saul is making), but rather that, in the implicit lawcourt situation, David is 'in the right' and Saul is 'in the wrong'.[21] But the status of 'righteousness' possessed by Tamar in the first example, and David in the second – and the status of 'righteousness' which any acquitted defendant, or vindicated plaintiff, would have in the Hebrew law-court once the court had found in their favour – is simply not the same thing as the 'righteousness' of the judge who tries the case. I have argued this before and am still puzzled that it should be so difficult to understand.[22]

Try the exchange either way. Let us imagine a fictitious scenario in ancient Israel. Azariah and Bildad go to law before Gamaliel, acting as judge. Azariah accuses Bildad of stealing a sheep. Gamaliel hears the case and finds in favour of Bildad: the court declares that the accusation is unfounded and that Bildad is innocent. That 'finding in favour', that declaration, is 'justification'; its result is that Bildad is now 'righteous', that is, 'in the right'. This does not mean, primarily, that Bildad is virtuous, certainly not that he has a special concern for the glory of the judge. It is quite possible that Gamaliel has mistried the case, that morally and actually Bildad is guilty, and that his only concern is for his own saving of his skin. But he is 'righteous' in terms of the court's decision. He is, in other words, the vindicated defendant.

But that status, though it is *received from* the judge, was not the judge's own status. Gamaliel was not a vindicated defendant, and even if he had been at some time in the past that would not have been the point. When the judge in the lawcourt justifies someone, he does not give that person his own particular 'righteousness'. He *creates* the status the vindicated defendant now possesses, by an act of *declaration*, a 'speech-act' in our contemporary jargon.

Conversely, Gamaliel hears the case according to the rules laid down for judges: no bribes, no favouritism, uphold the law, punish the wrongdoer, vindicate the person in the right, make sure widows and orphans get their proper due. If he does all this, he is 'righteous' in the way that a judge is supposed to be 'righteous'. When he finds in favour of Bildad, however, Bildad is 'righteous', but not at all in that way. He has not done any of those things, nor did he need to. Nor is the verdict 'righteous' a way of saying that he has, really, even though it doesn't look like it. Once again: 'righteous' and its cognates, in their biblical setting, are in this sense 'relational' terms, indicating how things stand with particular people *in relation to the court*. (Not, we note, in their 'relationship' to the judge, as though the possibility that Bildad and Gamaliel might go off arm in arm for a drink were the point of it all; in fact, if they did so, eyebrows might be raised.) This works completely, satisfyingly, and thoroughly across the entire range of Pauline exegesis and theology. Conversely, it makes no sense to suggest, with Piper,[23] that for both defendant and judge 'righteousness' means 'an unwavering allegiance to treasure and uphold the glory of God', and that 'in this lawcourt it is indeed conceivable for the Judge's righteousness to be shared by the defendant'. Anticipating his later argument for the imputation of God's/Christ's righteousness (why else would he want to make this strange argument?), Piper suggests that 'it may be that when the defendant lacks moral righteousness' (where did *moral* righteousness come from all of a sudden?), 'the Judge, who is also Creator and Redeemer, may find a way to make his righteousness count for the defendant, since it is exactly the righteousness he needs – namely, an unwavering and flawless and acted-out allegiance to the glory of the Judge'. This, to be frank, looks suspiciously like a *deus ex machina* kind of theological exegesis: 'I know this is impossible and illogical, but because God is God he can do it!' The trouble is that this, as we shall see, is not how the language actually works. The result Piper is really after – or rather, its proper Pauline equivalent – can be obtained without recourse to such tortuous argumentation.[24]

Fifth, there is a sense in which what Piper claims about 'God's righteousness' could be seen as going in exactly the wrong direction. He sees it as God's concern for God's own glory, which implies that God's primary concern returns, as it were, to himself. There is always of course a sense in which that is true. But the great story of scripture, from creation and covenant right on through to the New Jerusalem, is constantly about God's overflowing, generous, creative love – God's concern, if you like, for the flourishing and well-being *of everything else*. Of course, this too will redound to God's glory because God, as the creator, is glorified when creation is flourishing and able to praise him gladly and freely. And of course there are plenty of passages where God does what he does precisely not because anybody deserves it but simply 'for the sake of his own name'. But 'God's righteousness' is regularly invoked in scripture, not when God is acting thus, but when his concern is going out to those in need, particularly to his covenant people.

The *tsedaqah elohim*, the *dikaiosynē theou*, is an outward-looking characteristic of God, linked of course to the concern for God's own glory but essentially going, as it were, in the opposite direction, that of God's creative, healing, restorative love. God's concern for God's glory is precisely rescued from the appearance of divine narcissism because God, not least God as Trinity, is always giving out, pouring out, lavishing generous love on undeserving people, undeserving Israel, and an undeserving world. That is the sort of God he is, and 'God's righteousness' is a way of saying, Yes, and God will be true to that character. Indeed, it is because God will be true to that outward-facing generous, creative love that he must also curse those ways of life, particularly those ways of life within his covenant people, which embody and express the opposite. It isn't that God basically wants to condemn and then finds a way to rescue some from that disaster. It is that God longs to bless, to bless lavishly, and so to rescue and bless those in danger of tragedy – and therefore *must* curse everything that thwarts and destroys the blessing of his world and his people.

When we think more broadly about 'righteousness' in the Bible, it is of course true, as we saw in Daniel 9, that several things are so closely correlated that it is not easy at first sight to see what each of them means. This is a well-known problem in relation to 'righteousness' and 'salvation', as frequently in Isaiah 40—55. The two sit side by side so often that people have often been tempted to say that 'righteousness' there *means* 'salvation'. But that is misleading. Words cannot simply be telescoped into one another like that. Even when two different words *de*note the same thing, they will often *con*note different things. As has been shown so many times that it seems otiose to labour the point, God's righteousness is that quality or attribute *because of which* he saves his people. His 'acts of righteousness' are thus the acts he performs as outworkings or demonstrations of his covenant faithfulness. But, even at that point, 'righteousness' does not mean the same as 'salvation'. Even when the words *denote* the same thing – the mighty deeds by which God rescues his people – the word 'righteousness' *connotes* the notion of God's covenant faithfulness because of which he does such things, and the word 'salvation' *connotes* the fact that his people were in trouble and needed rescuing. All this needs to be borne in mind carefully as we proceed.

III

Where, then, does the law – the Jewish Law, the Torah – come into all of this? Here the ways divide among the heirs of the Reformation. For Martin Luther, Moses was regularly cast as the bad guy, the one who gave the wicked law that did nothing but condemn. For John Calvin, the Mosaic law was given as the way of life for a people already redeemed. 'It was to a delivered people that God addressed the words of his covenant at Sinai.'[25] And that, stated crisply by an old-fashioned Calvinist in a book of impeccable Old Perspective provenance, edited by Don Carson himself, is the long and the short of what Ed Sanders was arguing about Torah-keeping within Judaism. That is 'covenantal nomism': now that you're in the covenant, here is the law to keep.

Of course, it is a bit more complicated than that. But I have often reflected that if it had been the Reformed view of Paul and the law, rather than the Lutheran one, that had dominated biblical scholarship through the two hundred years since the Enlightenment, not only would the 'new perspective' not have been necessary (or not in the same form), but the polarized debates that have run for the last hundred years, between 'participationist' and 'juristic' forms of soteriology, would not have been necessary either. Many a good 'old perspective' Calvinist has declared that the best way to understand justification is within the context of 'being in Christ': the two need not be played off against one another, and indeed they hardly can be without tearing apart some of Paul's most tightly argued passages (e.g. Galatians 3.22–29 or Philippians 3.7–11). It was the relentless insistence on the wickedness of Judaism, the folly of arrogant self-righteous lawkeeping on the one hand and the gloom of depressing lawkeeping on the other, the sense of Judaism as 'the wrong kind of religion', and so on – all of which slurs, though frequent in many would-be Christian traditions, were always far more endemic in Lutheranism than in Calvinism – that represented the problem to which Sanders, following Moore, Davies, Schoeps, Stendahl and others, was offering a fresh solution.[26] God gave Israel the Torah as the way of life for the people with whom he had already entered into covenant, and whom he had now rescued from slavery. The Torah was itself the covenant charter, setting Israel apart from all the other nations: Which other country, Israel was to ask itself, has laws like these?[27] All the 'obedience' that the law then required would fall under the rubric of 'response to God's saving grace', even when this was not explicitly mentioned.

Actually, in writing those sentences I find it hard to tell whether I am summarizing Calvin or Sanders. In Calvin and his followers – think of Karl Barth, think of Charles Cranfield – the great emphasis is on the single plan of God, the fact that God has not changed his mind. There are plenty of theologians who have suggested that God initially gave people a law to see if they could save themselves that way, and then, finding that they could not, decided on a Plan B, namely incarnation and crucifixion and 'justification by faith'. But that is what Calvinism has always rejected, partly because it is a pretty hopeless view of God and partly because it makes little or no sense exegetically. And, within this kind of Calvinism, the point of the Law – think of the endless debates over the meaning of *telos* in Romans 10.4 – is not that God has brought it to an end, has put a stop to all that nonsense, but that he has brought it to its glad and proper goal. If we have to choose between Luther and Calvin, we must in my judgment choose Calvin every time, for both theological and exegetical reasons. I suspect that John Piper would heartily agree – though he, like other anti-new-perspective writers, may not enjoy having the large fissures in the Old Perspective so relentlessly exposed.

It is at this point, ironically, that suddenly all Piper's warnings about the danger of trying to read second-Temple Judaism as the context for Paul rebound on those who are trying to prop up the 'old perspective'. Sanders has offered a massive but, to many, deeply unconvincing reading of the 'pattern of religion' in second-Temple Judaism: unconvincing because it is too uniform, unconvincing also because it is insufficiently theological (in Sanders' defence, he was offering a study in religion, not theology, but it may of course be questioned whether one can ultimately separate the two). With the sole exception of 4 Ezra (actually, I would have thought it was quite a good fit, but that is a question for another time),[28] Sanders claimed that Judaism in Paul's day, not least Rabbinic Judaism, put a priority on keeping Torah not in order to earn membership in God's people but in order to express and maintain it. Judaism, he concludes, was therefore not a religion of 'legalistic works-righteousness' such as generations of scholars, preachers and 'ordinary folk' (Piper's term!) have imagined.

The shock of this conclusion, and the apparent undermining of much that the Lutheran tradition at least had held dear, eventually brought forth a massive response in the form of a multi-author project, *Justification and Variegated Nomism*, whose first volume is subtitled 'The Complexities of Second Temple Judaism'.[29] The essays in large part support Sanders' overall case more than (we may suppose) the editors had hoped when they commissioned them, and even Don Carson in his conclusion (now generally recognized to be somewhat tendentious) has to admit that Sanders has a point even if he has overplayed it. The main problem then emerges: if second-Temple Judaism, having in theory at least accepted that one was a Jew by God's choice, by election and covenant, then reckoned that one had to perform the works of the law in order to remain a member, to inherit the ultimate blessings of membership, how was that further law-keeping to be understood theologically? What account might one give of it? And this, unfortunately, takes us into deep waters not only of Pauline theology but of a much longer and more complex tradition, namely the question, to which we shall return, of the interplay of divine and human agency at the point of obedience.

But that is where the irony comes, at least from Piper's point of view. If, as we saw above, he is so unsure of whether we can trust our reading of post-biblical second-Temple sources, how does he know from these sources that second-Temple Judaism was after all a legalistic, works-righteousness sort of religion? He engages with me on the whole question of 4QMMT, the one document in second-Temple Judaism where the phrase 'works of the law' is to be found, and then, more broadly, on the question of whether second-Temple Judaism was as 'legalistic' as has been thought, or as free from that blight as Sanders had argued.[30] And the irony is of course that Piper is himself dependent, for his judgment, on such knowledge of second-Temple sources as we are able to have. How does he know they were accurate? Ought he not to be looking back to the Old Testament itself and asking himself whether, with some aspects of Luther's thought, he supposes that the Hebrew scriptures themselves teach the sort of 'legalism' that he supposes Paul demolishes, and if so what account he gives of this phenomenon (is Paul contradicting scripture?), or whether, with Calvin, he sees the scriptural commands to lawkeeping and godliness as divinely given and intended, and not retracted? According to the Sermon on the Mount, Jesus said that he had not come to abolish the law but to fulfil it. A Calvinist will find that much easier to grasp than a Lutheran – though it would be interesting to hear an 'old perspective' expositor explain how Jesus' brisk commands in that great Sermon are to be obeyed by his followers without any sense of moral effort, synergism, and so on.

The problem comes, it seems, not so much at the stage of 'getting in'. Most scholars of whatever persuasion are agreed that for most Jews, or at least any who thought about it, the answer was that one was a Jew because of God's gift of membership by birth and by the ancestral covenants sealed in Exodus and Sinai. Even those who believed that covenant membership was being redrawn, so that they had now to opt in (as in Qumran), also developed some kind of predestinarian theology to cover that as well, corresponding at that level to the strong statements in Deuteronomy about God's uncaused choice of Israel. The problem then relocates itself, into the area that remains controversial and which we shall pursue further below. If initial membership is by grace, but final judgment is according to works – and the New Testament, at first glance, including the Pauline corpus, does seem quite clear at this point – then what account of those 'works' can we give? Is this not, at last, the moment when Jewish 'legalism' is exposed?

There is no room in the present volume to discuss the second-Temple texts in question, and in any case it is not necessary, since I do not disagree with those scholars, and there are now many, who insist that at this level 'works' were demanded within many Jewish frameworks of thought, and that there was a variety of accounts given as to how to understand these theologically. Rather – and building further on my previous work on MMT[31] – I conclude this chapter by restating what I take to be massively demonstrated about the place of the Torah within that scheme of covenantal thought which Paul knew and took for granted as the basis of his ongoing dialogue with the Judaism he had himself formerly embraced.

First, the key question facing Judaism as a whole was not about individual salvation, but about God's purposes for Israel and the world. If God was going to be faithful to the covenant, what form would this take, when would it happen, and who would be the beneficiaries when it happened? The 'present age' would give way to the 'age to come', but who would inherit that 'age to come'? It was assumed, by the Pharisees at least, that the righteous dead would be raised to new life in that coming 'age'; who of those presently alive would be joining them? The answer, from source after source in the second-Temple period, confirming what we might have guessed from scripture itself, was this: Israel will be vindicated, will inherit the age to come – but it will be the Israel that has kept Torah, or that, through penitence and amendment of life (as in Daniel 9, looking back to Deuteronomy 30), has shown the heartfelt desire to follow God's ways and be loyal to his covenant. Torah, of course, included the sacrificial system through which Israelites could atone for their sins, so that one did not need or expect to be always perfect in all respects. The broad assumption was that Torah, in all its complexity, was the badge that Israel would wear, the sign that it really was God's people. 'All Israel will inherit the age to come', said the Rabbis, with the following clauses indicating that some would not, opting out by their own rank refusal to follow Torah.[32]

Torah thus functioned, implicitly at least, within not only a covenantal framework but also a broadly eschatological one. The 'age to come' would see Israel vindicated at last. But the way to tell, in the present, who would thus be vindicated in the future was to see who was keeping Torah (in some sense at least) in the present. The debates within Judaism at the time, which were often extremely fierce, tended then to turn on the question: What exactly does it mean to keep Torah in the present? These questions could be addressed in terms of a theological account of how much of this law-keeping was up to one's own initiative, and how much would be owed to God's grace and help. But they could also, and I think more characteristically, be addressed in terms of the actual regulations involved.

This is where MMT comes in. 'These are the specific works', says the writer, 'which will show in the present that you are the people who will be vindicated in the future.'[33] And this is set – though Piper does not comment on this, perhaps tellingly – within an exposition of the same passage in Deuteronomy 30 that Paul expounds in Romans 10, and for exactly the same reason. Deuteronomy 30 is the point where the Torah itself points to the renewal of the covenant, which Qumran believed God had put into effect in their community, and Paul believed had been put into effect through Jesus the Messiah. Where they were united was on the sense that there was indeed one divine purpose, from creation through Abraham and Moses to the monarchy and the prophets, and on into the long exile from which (both believed, in their different ways) God's people had now emerged. Where they diverged was on the questions (a) What events have precipitated the advance covenant renewal with us in the present? (b) Who will be vindicated when God finally completes what he has thereby begun? (c) What are the signs in the present which mark out those who will be vindicated in the future? and perhaps also, as we shall see, (d) What theological account can we give of how those present signs are accomplished, and hence of how one passes from present grace-given membership to future salvation? These are interesting and important questions, but before we can pursue them further, specifically by offering exegesis of the relevant Pauline texts, we must first pause and set out the rather important question: Are we sure we know what exactly we mean by 'justification' in the first place?

4

Justification: definitions and puzzles

I

What is the question to which the 'doctrine of justification' is the answer? What do the different views of justification say about that question and that answer? How do these concerns relate to Paul's central concerns in his letters? And how do those specific concerns of Paul relate to the rest of the New Testament, not least the gospels? Why is the doctrine of justification divisive, and in what sense is it to be seen, as Luther saw it, as the article by which a church stands or falls? To answer these questions properly would take, of course, entire books on their own, quite apart from my main task here; but we must at least acquire some sense of the terrain before we try to walk across it in terms of examining Paul's letters themselves.

I begin with some remarks of Alister McGrath, whose remarkable two-volume history of the doctrine is required reading for anyone who wants seriously to engage with it.[1] Having proposed that the heart of the Christian faith is found in 'the saving action of God towards mankind in Jesus Christ', stressing that this larger saving activity, rather than a specific doctrine of justification, is the centre of it all, he proceeds with some enormously important observations:

> The *concept of justification* and the *doctrine of justification* must be carefully distinguished. The *concept* of justification is one of many employed within the Old and New Testaments, particularly the Pauline corpus, to describe God's saving action towards his people. It cannot lay claim to exhaust, nor adequately characterise in itself, the richness of the biblical understanding of salvation in Christ.[2]

This is already highly significant. McGrath is creating hermeneutical space in which one might say: there are many equally biblical ways of talking about how God saves people through Jesus Christ, and justification is but one of them. This (for instance) enables us at once to note that the four gospels, where the term 'justification' is scarce, are not for that reason to be treated as merely ancillary to, or perhaps preparatory for, the message of Paul – as has sometimes happened, at least de facto, in the Western church. But there is more:

> The *doctrine* of justification has come to develop a meaning quite independent of its biblical origins, and concerns *the means by which man's relationship to God is established.* The church has chosen to subsume its discussion of the reconciliation of man to God under the aegis of justification, thereby giving the concept an emphasis quite absent from the New Testament. The 'doctrine of justification' has come to bear a meaning within dogmatic theology which is quite independent of its Pauline origins . . .[3]

I cannot overstress the importance of this statement, made by the scholar who, as much as any and more than almost all, has researched the entire history of the doctrine through many twists and turns unimagined by the ordinary devout Protestant. It is this statement, as much as any of my own, which justifies the claim, so threatening to writers like John Piper, that the church has indeed taken off at an oblique angle from what Paul had said, so that, yes, ever since the time of Augustine, the discussions about *what has been called* 'justification' have borne a tangled, but ultimately only tangential, relation to what Paul was talking about.

This raises all kinds of questions which press urgently upon us in current debate. If it is true that what the church has meant by 'justification' – simply by the *question* of justification, not even yet any particular *answer* to that question – is independent of, and goes beyond, what we find in Paul, then we must ask: Does this matter? Is the church free to use words and concepts in fresh ways which do not correspond to their biblical origins, while at least by implication claiming, through the biblical echoes that these words and concepts awaken, that they are thereby authorized by scripture itself? Most systematic theologians of my acquaintance would be quick to reply, Of course! The church can and must, under the guidance of the holy spirit, develop words, concepts, discourse of all sorts, out beyond the narrow confines of exegesis. That is what happened with Athanasius, holding out for the non-biblical term *homoousion* to express, against Arius, the radically biblical view of the divinity of Jesus Christ. We cannot reduce the task of theology to that of biblical commentary.

But notice what then happens. The word *homoousion* was not in scripture, but the word 'justification' was. As the church, within its own life and proclamation, uses a scriptural word or concept but denotes by that word or concept something more than, or even different from, what is meant by the word or concept in its scriptural origin, three effects are almost inevitable. First, it will then misread scripture at that point, imagining that when the Bible uses that word it is talking about the thing which the church normally talks about when it uses that word. And that may well not be the case. Second, such a reading will miss completely the thing that scripture *was* talking about at that point; it will fail to pay attention to the word of God. Third, it will imagine itself to have biblical warrant for its own ideas, when all it actually has are 'biblical' echoes of its own voice.

Things are of course more complicated than that. The many-sidedness of scripture, the grace and power of the holy spirit, and God's mercy in answering the preacher's prayers, regularly enable genuine understanding, real insight into the love and mercy and purposes of God, to leap across the barriers put up by our faulty and partial understandings. This is just as well, since otherwise, as systematic theologians often point out rather tartly, nobody would be able to do any theology until the great exegetical enterprise had signed off on its final footnote. We all live within the incomplete hermeneutical spiral, and should relish the challenges this presents rather than bemoan the limitations it places upon us.

But limitations there are. An example from another sphere will make the point. In Matthew 22.42, Jesus asks the Pharisees, 'What do you think of the Messiah? Whose son is he?' In its context, this is clearly a question about current opinion on the subject of 'the Messiah' – whoever he might be. 'What is the word on the street about the coming Messiah?' But the word 'Messiah', appearing in Greek as *Christos*, came quite early on to be treated as a proper name, the second name of Jesus himself, so that the King James translation, 'What think ye of Christ?', could float free from its original meaning, and present a very different question to a different audience: What is your opinion about *Jesus Christ* himself? Have you made your mind up about him? Not 'Tell me your views about the coming Messiah' (whom the reader believes to be Jesus), but 'Tell me your views about Jesus' (whom the questioner believes to be Messiah). Of course, the two questions are cognate. But they are not the same. In fact, the history of the word *Christ* itself offers all kinds of illustrations for our present matter, since it has regularly been taken as a 'divine' title, as though 'Jesus' were Jesus' 'human' name and 'Christ' his 'divine' name. The way the phrase 'the Christ' has been used to mean 'the incarnate one', or something similar, has meant that whole swathes of church life have been robbed of the very particular *Messianic* meaning of the word, with all its associations and resonances.

Nor is that merely something about which one can shrug one's shoulders and say, Well, they had lots of odd ideas in the first century, isn't it a good thing we've got out beyond those limitations. At this point the illustration moves from metaphor to metonymy: it is precisely the *Jewish, Messianic, covenantal, Abrahamic, history-of-Israel* overtones that later theology has screened out, both in its reading of 'Christ' and in its reading of 'justification'. Examples of this are legion. Out of all the dictionary articles I have read on 'justification' – and, though dictionaries are of course highly abbreviated, I know from my own experience in writing such articles that they can be a good index of what the author thinks really important – hardly any of them even mention Abraham and the whole covenantal story of Israel, though the three main expositions of justification (Romans 3.21—4.25 and 9.30—10.13, and Galatians 2.15—4.11) have those themes woven tightly into the fabric. A fascinating example is Alan Torrance's article in the *Oxford Companion to Christian Thought*, which provides an elegant and evocative account of that which 'justification' has become, with only a single glance – referring to the present writer! – at the Jewish and covenantal context of its biblical origins.[4] No: McGrath is right: despite the directions that 'the doctrine of justification' took from Augustine onwards, a serious reading of Paul in his own context shows that he is talking about something different. 'Paul's understanding of justification must be interpreted resolutely in terms of OT affirmations of God's faithfulness to the covenant, a faithfulness surprisingly but definitively confirmed through Christ's death and resurrection.'[5] As McGrath says elsewhere, 'if Pauline exegesis has achieved anything, it is to remind us of the need to interpret Pauline phrases within their proper context, rather than impose "self-evident" interpretations upon them'.[6] Back to John Piper's 'ordinary folk' again: what seems 'ordinary' or 'natural' as a reading of a particular biblical text may owe everything to habituation within a tradition (think of the mediaeval reading of 'repent' as 'do penance'!) and nothing to actual awareness of what Paul was talking about. The legend that makes the point most strikingly is the Calvinist commentator who headed the story of Salome's dance and the Baptist's beheading as 'the dangers of dancing'. That seemed natural enough at the time.

But does putting Paul's teaching in its actual, original context not risk making it marginal and therefore irrelevant? This is the nettle which must be grasped firmly, and which, once that is done, reveals itself to be the herb that heals all ills. Returning to McGrath's opening statement, we continue the sentence we broke off above:

> The 'doctrine of justification' has come to bear a meaning within dogmatic theology which is quite independent of its Pauline origins, so that even if it could be shown that it plays a minimal role in Pauline soteriology, or that its origins lie in an anti-Judaising polemic quite inappropriate to the theological circumstances of today, its significance would not be diminished as a result.[7]

Those familiar with the history of Pauline interpretation in the last hundred or so years will see at once what McGrath is getting at. Indeed, to put McGrath himself in his context, it may well be that his careful distinguishing of 'what Paul was actually talking about' from 'what the church has meant by justification' had this in mind all along: to free the developing doctrine from any attempt to pull it back into the black hole of 'mere Pauline polemic'. As is well known to Pauline scholars, though not always to dogmaticians, William Wrede and Albert Schweitzer argued a century ago that Paul's doctrine of justification was not central to his thought, but merely a bit of peripheral polemic.

Wrede, aware of the same phenomena which the 'new perspective' has highlighted, but without any glimmer of the larger theological context in which such phenomena could gain their true Pauline force, declared that 'justification by faith' was a mere polemical aside, designed to enable Gentiles to come into the church.[8] This in turn has generated counter-caricatures, not least that of Stephen Westerholm, who offers a witty but highly misleading rejoinder: the 'Lutheran' Paul is concerned with Christ's dying for our sins and the call to be reconciled to God, while the 'new perspective' Paul offers 'deliverance from a good deal of hassle', namely, the need to get circumcised.[9] Westerholm, revealingly, suggests that to relate justification to God's covenant faithfulness would be to 'reduce' it, which merely shows that he still has no idea what those of us who speak of 'covenant faithfulness' are thinking.[10] He does, however, retreat in the end from the false polarization: in his concluding short chapter he allows that for a full understanding of Paul one needs to note *both* that his teaching on justification is located within the debate about the inclusion of Gentiles *and* that it still has to do with the rescue of sinners from their sin and its consequences.[11] Well, precisely; but Westerholm, despite massive learning and ready wit, has not actually shown how Paul was able to sustain this combination of ideas within a thorough and coherent worldview.

Schweitzer, for his part, famously regarded 'justification' and the other 'forensic' language of Paul as a second-order way of thinking, a 'secondary crater' within the 'primary crater' which, for him, was 'being in Christ'.[12] Schweitzer's account of 'being in Christ', and of how lawcourt language related to it, lacked exegetical and theological staying power, but the basic insight has not gone away – and nor should Reformed theologians want it to, since it was John Calvin himself who insisted that one must understand justification with reference to the larger category of incorporation into Christ.[13] But the thrust of Wrede's and Schweitzer's point was lost on the continuing mainstream of Lutheran scholarship within the twentieth century. Even Käsemann, who in his retrieval of Jewish apocalyptic thought as the context for Paul's gospel owed more than a little to Schweitzer, retained justification as central – though bringing Wrede on board as well, with the observation that if justification is a polemical doctrine in Paul, this doesn't make it peripheral, but rather central, because Paul's theology *is* polemical, at its very core.

For Käsemann, himself nothing if not a polemical theologian, that seemed 'natural'.

This brings us back to McGrath's point by a different route. McGrath is saying, 'even if it could be shown that what Paul was doing was simply a polemical aside, that doesn't mean that later church doctrine about justification is all a mistake'. But this opens up an alternative set of possibilities: (a) Paul's doctrine did indeed have a polemical edge, but this didn't mean it was peripheral; (b) later theologies of justification, by abstracting the bits of Paul which they wanted and leaving behind the bits they didn't, have pulled Paul out of shape; (c) hardly surprisingly, then, they have not been able to agree on how precisely Paul's theology 'works' (back to the jigsaw with half the pieces still in the box); (d) a church that claims scriptural authority, not merely in the sense of finding a few texts upon which to hang its favourite ideas, but in the richer sense of soaking itself in the scriptures themselves to find fresh wisdom and energy for mission, holiness and unity, may now find itself called to do business afresh with the whole of what Paul was talking about, even if that means being precipitated into a constructively critical dialogue with the great tradition of 'the doctrine of justification'. For my part, that is exactly the challenge I have tried to respond to, and I have taken comfort from those many signs – not least, I should say, in John Calvin – that the best of exegetes were always pushing in this direction.

II

What, then, is 'justification' about? Most of the difficulties of the ongoing debate have arisen from the fact that the word, as McGrath points out, has regularly been made to do duty for *the entire picture of God's reconciling action towards the human race*, covering everything from God's free love and grace, through the sending of the son to die and rise again for sinners, through the preaching of the gospel, the work of the spirit, the arousal of faith in human hearts and minds, the development of Christian character and conduct, the assurance of ultimate salvation, and the safe passage through final judgment to that destination. To this I say: fine; if that's what you want to mean by 'justification', go ahead; but don't be surprised if, as Eliot put it,

Words strain,
Crack and sometimes break, under the burden,
Under the tension, slip, slide, perish,
Decay with imprecision, will not stay in place,
Will not stay still.

(Four Quartets, I.v)

And that, of course, is what has happened. Hence all the debate, the 'arm-wrestling', the 'text-trading', the endless footnotes, the massive scholastic tradition of mutual references, refutations, restatements, and so on. John Piper stresses that he writes 'as a pastor'; so do I – and I know that almost none of the thousands of souls for whom I am responsible have either the time or the inclination to wade through the logic-chopping of a thousand years and ten thousand monographs. There must be a way, as the sixteenth-century re-formers believed when faced with the similarly massive traditions of commentaries on Lombard's *Sentences* and similar works, to cut through all this, to get to the nub of the issue, to say what needs to be said, to shed clear light on the text of scripture itself instead of cutting that text into pieces and fitting those pieces – those that do not simply end up on the floor – into a different scheme of our own.

And there is such a way. It involves paying close attention – here it is again! – to what the words themselves actually meant, both in their Old Testament roots, their intertestamental uses (Jewish and Greco-Roman), and their specific contexts within Paul himself. And when we do that, we find that the *dikaios* root, though it is indeed *related closely to* the whole theme of human salvation by God's mercy and grace through Jesus Christ and the holy spirit, does not *denote* that entire sequence of thought – so that to force it to do that is necessarily to invent all kinds of extra bells and whistles of which Paul was innocent – but rather denotes *one specific aspect of* or *moment within* that sequence of thought. What has happened in the history of the 'doctrine of justification' is rather as though some-one, rightly convinced of the vital importance of the steering wheel for driving a car, were to refer to the car as 'the wheel', so that people who had never seen a car would be deceived into thinking that he was talking about the steering wheel itself as the entire ma-chine, and then were to imagine a gigantic steering wheel cunningly equipped with seats and a motor, but still really just a wheel . . .

Illustrations may deceive as well as illuminate, but let me drive this one a bit further down the road. What has then happened is that people who have seen actual cars – i.e. Paul's actual letters – have pointed out that they contain many other things alongside steering wheels. They have other wheels, the ones that run on the road! They have other things that the driver has to hold, press, push or fiddle with – gear levers, window handles, light-switches, and so on. Oh no, declare the 'steering wheel' purists. You can't say that! If you don't have a steering wheel you'll drive into the ditch! Everything *must* really be 'steering wheel'. And if you try to point out the genuine complexity of a car and how it works, they will quickly insist – and rightly, in a sense – that the steering wheel is organically connected to everything else, and that without it the whole point of the car is put in jeopardy. The 'steering wheel' purists are pastors, after all! They are anxious about drivers who might end up in the ditch!

So what is the 'steering wheel', and how does it relate to all the rest of the car? Let me put it as simply as I can, with the main supporting argument for all this being, 'Watch how, when you look at things like this, you discover that Paul has said exactly what he means, and that you can take his entire arguments, their full sweep of thought and their tiny details, and see how they fit together.' What I am offering, in other words, is a *hypothesis*: try this framework on Paul, and see whether it does not make sense of the data we have, getting it all in with appropriate simplicity, and shedding light on other areas also – in other words, doing the things that all hypotheses have to do if they are to work.[14]

'Justification', *diakiōsis*, though not a word Paul uses frequently, is the word he uses when he is summing up the other 'just' words which he does use more often. That is clear, for instance, in Romans 4.25. But before we can go any further we need – for the sake of anyone coming to all this for the first time, since those who regularly read books about this have met it countless times already – the obligatory note about the frustrating problem of the English and American languages. Or, perhaps I should say, about this particular frustrating problem of those languages.

English and American have two quite different root words, 'just' and 'righteous', where Greek and Hebrew have one each, *dikaios* and its cognates in Greek, *tsedaqah* and its cognates in Hebrew. The first

English/American root gives us (a) an adjective ('just'); (b) a verb ('justify'); (c) an abstract noun denoting an action ('justification'); (d) another abstract noun denoting a quality or virtue ('justice') and (e) some related double-word phrases ('just decrees', 'just requirements', and the like) which can be offered as translations of single words in Paul. The second root gives us (a) a different adjective ('righteous'); (b) an abstract noun ('righteousness'), denoting, variously, (i) a status, (ii) the behaviour appropriate to that status, and (iii) the moral quality supposed to underlie that behaviour; and (c) another abstract noun denoting 'that which is appropriate or correct' ('right', as in 'upholding the right'). The last of these can also function as an adjective, as in 'right behaviour', and a verb, as in 'to right the wrong', i.e. 'to put right' or, in English (but not normally, I discover, in American) 'to put to rights'. What the second root does not have is a verb corresponding to 'justify'. Sanders and one or two others have tried to revive the early English form 'to rightwise', but it has not caught on. (Sanders tried the same thing, for similar reasons, with using the word 'faith' as a verb, reflecting the fact that the Greek root *pistis* can go to 'faith' or to 'belief'. This, too, has not proved a success.[15])

This situation, frustrating and confusing to those without Greek and even to some who have it, is further complicated by the tendency for words, like bright three-year-olds, not to sit still where you told them to, but to wander around the room, start fiddling with things they weren't supposed to touch, form new friendships (especially when they bump into their Latin cousins, but that's another story), and generally enjoy themselves at the expense of the exegete who is trying to keep them under control. Some, as we saw, have tried to remedy all this by using old words like 'rightwise' for 'justify' and 'rightwising' for 'justification' (Sanders) or inventing horrible new ones based on the Greek ('dikaiosify' for 'justify' (Westerholm; he does have the grace to apologize)). Some Roman Catholic translators and commentators, being less anxious about the possible misleading implications of this, have replaced 'righteousness' with 'justice', but that does not quite relieve the problem across the board. And anyone who tries to echo *pistis* by speaking of 'justification by belief' had better have a good lawyer.

I propose no new words at this point. But I want to note, in addition to the point about the Latin cousins (*iustitia* carried its own meanings throughout the mediaeval period, massively conditioning the way Paul, and much besides, was understood, and setting up the questions which Luther and the others were answering in a very particular way), a point about the English/American word 'righteousness'. For many people in my world at least, this word has a strongly negative connotation: self-righteousness, a 'holier-than-thou' attitude, a cold, proud and disdainful view of oneself and the world. That is quite some way from the connotations of the Hebrew *tsedaqah*: that lovely word, especially as applied to God himself, is full of mercy and kindness, faithfulness and generosity. Yes, it also refers to the behaviour which is appropriate for God's people, and yes, it can from that point move towards the self-righteousness which, indeed, Paul names and shames. We shall come to that. But it is important to note connotations in order to ward off anachronisms.

In particular – something no English or American reader would ever guess from 'righteousness' itself – the Hebrew term and its cognates have particular functions in relation to the setting of the lawcourt. This is generally acknowledged, except where exegetes, watching their backs more than a little, are anxious to keep certain meanings out of the road in case they upset the theological applecart. And when Paul uses *dikaiosynē* and its cognates, though the context of Classical Greek would have suggested another, albeit overlapping, range of meanings, he regularly uses them with the Hebrew overtones in mind. What then does 'righteousness' mean within that lawcourt context? We have already begun to sketch the answer to this from another angle, and now return to it full on.

'Righteousness', within the lawcourt setting – and this is something that no good Lutheran or Reformed theologian ought ever to object to – denotes *the status that someone has when the court has found in their favour*. Notice, it does *not* denote, within that all-important lawcourt context, 'the moral character they are then assumed to have', or 'the moral behaviour they have demonstrated which has earned them the verdict'. As we saw in the previous chapter, anticipating this point, it is possible for the judge to make a mistake, and to 'justify' – that is, to find in favour of – a person who is of thoroughly bad character and who did in fact commit the crimes of which he or she had been charged. If that happens, it is still the case that the person concerned, once the verdict has been announced, is 'righteous', that is, 'acquitted', 'cleared', 'vindicated', 'justified'.

Note, too, that when the judge finds in favour of the plaintiff who had brought the charge, the plaintiff is then 'righteous', 'in the right', 'vindicated'. But since, in Romans 3, Paul's point is that the whole human race is in the dock, guilty before God, 'justification' will always then mean 'acquittal', the granting of the status of 'righteous' to those who *had* been on trial – and which will then also mean, since they were in fact guilty, 'forgiveness'. It is hugely important not to short-circuit all this in the interests of a quick-fix gospel or exegesis.

But if 'righteousness', within the lawcourt context, refers to the status of the vindicated person after the court has announced its verdict, we have undercut in a single stroke the age-old problem highlighted in Augustine's interpretation of 'justify' as '*make* righteous'. That always meant, for Augustine and his followers, that God, in justification, was actually *transforming the character* of the person, albeit in small, preliminary ways (by, for instance, implanting the beginnings of love and faith within them). The result was a subtle but crucial shifting of metaphors: the lawcourt scene is now replaced with a medical one, a kind of remedial spiritual surgery, involving a 'righteousness implant' which, like an artificial heart, begins to enable the patient to do things previously impossible.

But part of the point of Paul's own language, rightly stressed by those who have analysed the verb *dikaioō*, 'to justify', is that it does not denote *an action which transforms someone* so much as *a declaration which grants them a status*. It is the *status* of the person which is transformed by the action of 'justification', not the *character*. It is in this sense that 'justification' 'makes' someone 'righteous', just as the officiant at a wedding service might be said to 'make' the couple husband and wife – a change of status, accompanied (it is hoped) by a steady transformation of the heart, but a real change of status even if both parties are entering the union out of pure convenience.

But what is the effect of simply granting someone a status? Here we are back at once with the car and the steering wheel. The problems which immediately spring to the mind of panic-stricken theologians and pastors – If that's all it is, how will they become good

Christians?[16] If it's only a status, it must be a legal fiction! How can God make such a declaration anyway? – are all dealt with, in their proper time and place, once we realize that, however much the post-Augustinian tradition has used 'justification' to cover the whole range of 'becoming a Christian' from first to last, Paul has used it far, far more precisely and exactly. There are plenty of other bits to the car. Yes, the steering wheel remains important and vital, but we have an engine, a petrol tank, wheels on the road, seats and plenty besides. And if you try to turn the lights on by moving the steering wheel, or to fill the petrol tank through the steering shaft, your commendable attention to the steering wheel will have disastrous results. There is indeed a sense in which 'justification' really does *make* someone 'righteous' – it really does create the 'righteousness', the status-of-being-in-the-right, of which it speaks – but 'righteousness' in that lawcourt sense does not mean either 'morally good character' or 'performance of moral good deeds', but 'the status you have when the court has found in your favour'. And the urgent questions which this naturally raises, as to what on earth or in heaven is going on for God to make such a declaration, are all answered within the larger arguments which Paul is mounting, attention to which is vital if we are to understand the way *he* saw things rather than the ways in which little bits of his writings were fitted in to later constructions.

Notice where we have now got to. John Piper insists that God requires a moral righteousness of us, and that since we have none of our own God must reckon or impute such a moral righteousness from somewhere else – obviously within his scheme, from the 'righteousness' of Jesus Christ.[17] I can see how that works. But 'righteousness', within the very precise language of the courtroom which Paul is clearly evoking, most obviously in Romans 3, is not 'moral righteousness'. It is the status of the person whom the court has vindicated. And, yes, God has vindicated Jesus himself, by raising him from the dead, as is said explicitly in 1 Timothy 3.16 but indicated also in Romans 1.4. And, yes, that vindication is indeed the context within which the vindication of the believer is to be understood. On all this, more anon.

Now that that, I hope, is clear, it is time to move on to something altogether more demanding. What happens when we put all this into the context of that to which the Hebrew root *tsedaqah*

71

regularly referred, and that to which Paul's actual arguments regularly allude, namely God's covenant with Israel?

III

The other night I was a guest, and made a speech, at a dinner of church bell-ringers. The English art of campanology appears arcane to many people, who expect musical instruments to play tunes. Indeed, many church towers in America which have six, eight or even more bells are equipped, not with bell-ropes in the English style, so that there is one person to each bell and all together can be rung in sequence or in various orders, but with a mechanism that enables one person (or even a pre-set computer) to play tunes on them. This almost never happens in England – though I am glad to say that English-style change-ringing is now making inroads into America as well, and I was delighted to see several American enthusiasts at the dinner.

This is not the place (the reader may be glad to know) for describing English campanology, except to say that it involves 'ringing the changes' – the literal meaning of that phrase, unknown I suspect to many who use it metaphorically – on the eight (or however many) bells. There are literally hundreds of methods of working out how to make those changes, since the rules are that no bell can move more than one place in a row at a time and that no sequence must ever be repeated. For most people, walking by in the street or hearing cathedral bells from the other side of the city, it may appear simply as a confused noise. For those who know what it's about, it gives a deep and rich pleasure, the fresh expression of an ancient tradition.

The motto of my local association of bell-ringers reflects, somewhat self-deprecatingly, this sense that most people have no idea what it's all about: *Ars Incognita Contemnitur*, 'an unknown art is despised'. I ventured to suggest that the motto could be changed to something more upbeat: *Ars Audita Celebratur*, 'an art that is heard should be celebrated'. But my point here is quite simple: to many people, biblical covenant theology appears about as comprehensible as change-ringing is to the untutored person in the street. Indeed, 'despised' would not be too strong a word. 'Covenant romanticism', sniffs Mark Seifrid, making God's covenant with Israel 'the unexamined basis for resolving all questions about [Paul's] soteriology'.[18] That, of course, is just a smokescreen: the only 'lack of examination' on show here is not biblical covenant theology, which I and others have examined pretty thoroughly, but Seifrid's own persistent refusal to examine what is thereby actually being said.[19] Westerholm excuses his earlier failure to mention 'covenant' by saying, with gentler sarcasm than Seifrid, that it is because he has been narrowly preoccupied with the Pauline texts, 'which never link the vocabulary of "righteousness" with mention of "the" (or even *a*) covenant'.[20] And yet neither of them, nor the several other writers who take a similar tack, appear to be able to see that the key passages in Romans and Galatians are all drawing on, and claiming to fulfil, two central passages in the Pentateuch: Genesis 15, where God establishes his covenant with Abraham, and Deuteronomy 30, where Israel is offered the promise of covenant renewal after exile. Here, as elsewhere, Paul quotes one part of a chapter or passage and wants the whole to be in mind. But the unknown, unrecognized art is still despised. Can I, or anyone else, make it clearer than we have already tried to do? Will writers like Seifrid and Westerholm be able to hear what is being said, or will they once more walk me up the hill to view the sunrise?

Paul's view of God's purpose is that God, the creator, called Abraham so that through his family he, God, could rescue the world from its plight. That is the foundation. Call it 'God's single plan', if you like, to avoid the concordance-bound scruples of the doubters (not that the concordance gets in the way when they want to say something different themselves!) who complain that Paul doesn't much use the word 'covenant'. Call it 'the reason God called Abraham'. Call it 'the creator's purpose, through Israel, for the world'. Call it anything you like, but *recognize its existence* for Paul, for the world of thought he inhabited, and for any construction of his theology which wants to claim that it is faithful to his intention. For whenever you ignore it – which happens every time someone refers to Abraham in Romans 4 or Galatians 3 as an 'example' or 'illustration' – you are cutting off the branch on which Paul's argument is resting. To highlight this element, which Reformed theology ought to welcome in its historic stress on the single plan of God (as opposed to having God change his mind in mid-stream), is to insist on the wholeness of his train of thought.

Paul's understanding of God's accomplishment in the Messiah is that this single purpose, this plan-through-Israel-for-the-world, this reason-God-called-Abraham (you can see why I prefer the shorthand 'covenant'; this is going to be a very long book if I have to use multi-hyphenated phrases all the time) finally came to fruition with Jesus Christ. Here is the point which has so puzzled John Piper that he thinks a 'covenantal' reading would be a *belittling* of Paul's meaning. The single-plan-through-Israel-for-the-world was called into being by God as the means of addressing and solving the plight of the whole world. The 'covenant', in my shorthand, is not something other than God's determination to deal with evil once and for all and so put the whole creation (and humankind with it) right at last. When will it become clear to the geocentrists? *Dealing with sin, saving humans from it, giving them grace, forgiveness, justification, glorification – all this was the purpose of the single covenant from the beginning, now fulfilled in Jesus Christ.* Seifrid is right, and Käsemann was right, to stress that God's purpose in the Old Testament has the whole creation in view. That is precisely correct – though Seifrid is wrong to say that this covenant plan never had an Israel-dimension, just as Käsemann was wrong to say that Paul deliberately removed the Israel-dimension it had had until he took it on. *Of course* the plan of God had an Israel-dimension, and *of course* that remains central for Paul, as we shall see in relation to Romans 2—4 and 9—10. That, actually, is the only way fully and finally to understand Paul's Christology and the meaning of the cross itself, and with it – finally! – the truth of which 'imputed righteousness' is a half-parody . . . but that is to run too far ahead of myself . . .

'Covenant', in my usage at least, is a highly convenient and utterly appropriate shorthand to summarize four things and hold them in proper relation. These four are:

(a) the way in which Israelites in the Old Testament, and Jews in the second-Temple period, understood themselves as the people of the creator God, and – sometimes at least – thought of the purposes of this God as stretching beyond them and out into the wider world, into creation as a whole;

(b) the particular focus of this purpose, in scriptures that were foundational for Judaism as well as Paul, on the story of Abraham, not least God's establishment of his covenant with

him in Genesis 15 and, with circumcision, in Genesis 17, and
on the great covenantal promises and warnings in Deuteronomy
27–30;

(c) the sense in second-Temple Judaism that the single story of God
the creator with his (covenant) people Israel was continuing
to move forwards, battered but essentially unbroken, towards
whatever fulfilment, renewal, restoration or other great denouement God might eventually have in mind; and, not least,

(d) Paul's retrieval of this underlying story, and his dialectical
engagement with other contemporary Jewish versions of and
theories about it, and his rethinking (but not abandoning) of
it in the light of Jesus, the Jewish Messiah, the denouement-in-
person of the single-plan-through-Israel-for-the-world, the one
through whom at last the one God would fulfil the one plan to
accomplish the one purpose, to rid the world of sin and establish his new creation – and of the holy spirit, the operating
power of the single-saving-plan-through-Israel-for-the-world-
now-fulfilled-in-the-Messiah, Jesus.

(The reader may be thankful that this is in English. In German, that
entire last phrase might become a single word. As it is, I make no
apology for the length of the sentence thereby concluded. All these
things need to be held together – a task extremely easy in the first
century for someone like Paul, and apparently next to impossible
for those whose soteriology never had an Israel-dimension and who
don't want to start thinking about one now.)

Verbal statistics, and accidental occurrences of themes, are in any
case a dangerous guide in 'incidental' writings like Paul's. (In the
same way, we will only blow dust in our own eyes if we observe the
number of different 'covenants' in the Old Testament – with Noah,
with Phinehas, and so on – while ignoring the obviously covenantal
resonances of passages which are clearly central for Paul.[21] It is
often noted that, if we did not have 1 Corinthians 10 and 11, it
would be possible to claim that Paul knew nothing whatever about
the Lord's Supper or Eucharist, whereas that sudden discussion –
I recall a happy phrase of T. W. Manson's about 'the corner of
the argument being turned up at that point' – indicates that in
fact, within twenty-five years of Jesus' death, that celebratory meal
was a regular, central and vital part of the life of Paul's churches,

with its own already developed theology and praxis. This does not, of course, give us licence to claim that any and every incidental reference in Paul is in fact covert 'evidence' for a powerful and omnipresent theme. But when we look at the evidence for the single-plan-of-the-creator-through-Abraham-and-Israel-for-the-world, we discover tell-tale indications of how Paul might have spoken further.

For a start, there is the obvious reference, right in the middle of Galatians 3, when Paul talks explicitly about 'making a covenant', indicating that God did indeed make a covenant with Abraham and that the Torah cannot annul it (3.15–18). Is that enough of a clue? Let's look at the whole passage:[22]

> [15]My brothers and sisters, let me use a human illustration. When someone makes a covenanted will, nobody sets it aside or adds to it. [16]Well, the promises were made 'to Abraham and his family'. It doesn't say 'his families', as though referring to several, but indicates one: 'and to your family' – which means the Messiah. [17]This is what I mean. God made this covenanted will; the law, which came 430 years later, can't undermine it and make the promise null and void. [18]If the inheritance came through the law, it would no longer be by promise; but God gave it to Abraham by promise.

Verse 17 makes it impossible to say that the reference to the 'covenanted will' (my expanded translation of *diathēkē*, 'covenant') is purely 'an illustration from ordinary life'. The point of the remark about a 'human illustration' (v. 15) is not that Paul is introducing the idea of a 'will' (which happens to be denoted by the word *diathēkē*) into an argument where it was not already implicit, but that, since he is already thinking of *diathēkē* in terms of the covenant God made with Abraham in Genesis 15, he can extend that to the idea of a human 'will', which one cannot set aside or tamper with. The explanation in verse 17 makes this clear: *diathēkēn prokekyrōmenēn hypo tou theou*, 'this covenanted will having been made by God', is a summary of 'God made these promises to Abraham'. The contrast between promise and law is not merely that they function differently as abstract systems. The contrast is that 'the covenant' is what God made with Abraham, the agreement that through him God would bless the whole world, giving him a single worldwide family, while 'the law' is what God gave to Moses, for reasons that will become (more or less) apparent, but which cannot include abolishing or tampering with 'the covenant' God had already made with Abraham, which was the agreement, promised in Genesis 12 and established by solemn covenant in Genesis 15, the (here we go again) single-plan-through-Israel-for-the-world. Of course God made other 'covenants', plural, as Paul notes in Romans 9.4 – with Noah, with Moses, with David, and, at least in anticipation, with 'everyone who is thirsty' (Isaiah 55.1–3). Not to mention the promise of the 'new covenant' in Jeremiah 31, picked up and celebrated at length by . . . Paul, of course, in 2 Corinthians 3.[23]

But the obvious parallels between Galatians 3 and Romans 4 should indicate that, if Paul is referring to the promise of Genesis 15 in terms of 'covenant' in the former passage, there is no reason why he should not also be referring to it in the latter. And there is a particular reason to suppose, not only that he is doing so, but that he makes, in a characteristically subtle but powerful way, just that verbal link with the *dikaiosynē* language which Westerholm and others deny. In Romans 4.11, speaking of God's gift to Abraham of circumcision, Paul says that Abraham 'received the sign of circumcision as a seal *of the righteousness by faith* which he had in his uncircumcision'. But in the Genesis original, God says to Abraham that circumcision will be *a sign of the covenant* between them (17.11). Paul, quoting the passage about the establishment of the covenant, has replaced the word 'covenant' with the word 'righteousness'.

Why? Because he doesn't like 'covenant', wants to avoid it and its overtones, and decides to subvert it by substituting something totally different? Certainly not. The whole chapter (Romans 4) is a sustained exposition of the promises to Abraham, drawing on several chapters in Genesis but framing the whole thing particularly with Genesis 15, the chapter in which God made the covenant according to which (a) Abraham's seed would become as numerous as the stars of heaven, (b) his family would be exiles in a foreign land and eventually be brought out, and (c) his family would inherit the land of Canaan. What Paul has done in verse 11 is closely cognate with what he does two verses later, when (in line with some other second-Temple Jewish writings) he declares that the promises to Abraham and his family were that they should inherit (not 'the land', merely, but) 'the world' (4.13). This is exactly the point. Paul is not playing fast and loose with Genesis 15. He is reading it in its larger context, where, within the canonical shape of Genesis itself, it stands alongside chapters 12, 17 and 22, offering promises that, whereas the whole world had been cursed through Adam and Eve, through the human pride which led to Babel, the creator God would now bring blessing to that same whole world. That was the point of the covenant. And that was why, from the very start, the notions of dealing-with-sin-and-rescuing-people-from-it, on the one hand, and bringing-Jews-and-Gentiles-together-into-a-single-family, on the other, always were bound up together, as they always are in Paul. God's plan, God's single plan, always was to put the world to rights, to set it right, to undo Genesis 3 and Genesis 11, sin *and* the fracturing of human society which results from that sin and shows it up in its full colours (we might almost say: Genesis 3 needs the 'old perspective', and Genesis 11 needs the new!): to bring about new creation, through Abraham/Israel and, as the fulfilment of the Abraham/Israel-shaped plan, through the Messiah, Jesus.

This is why 'covenant', albeit clearly a shorthand, is an excellent way of understanding the full depth of Paul's soteriology. It is Paul's own shorthand, in Galatians 3; and, in Romans 4, he can say the same thing with the word 'righteousness'. We should not be surprised. As we saw in the previous chapter, careful exegesis of 'God's righteousness', both in the Old Testament and in second-Temple Judaism, indicates that, among the range of possible meanings, 'faithfulness to the covenant' is high on the list. Paul has announced in Romans 3.21 that God has been faithful to the covenant; Romans 4, so far from being an 'illustration' or 'example' of this (as though Abraham could be detached from his historical moorings and float around like a lost helium balloon wherever the winds of ahistorical hermeneutics might take him), is the full explanation of what Paul has in mind. The exegetical contortions, distortions, omissions and confusions which litter the field of anti-covenantal Pauline exegesis are the direct result of dismembering the sacred texts to which, piously, the exegetes still appeal.

How then does this 'covenantal' framework dovetail with the 'lawcourt' framework of meaning? Answer: by understanding the ways in which the Jewish people, from early on but especially in the second-Temple period, construed their own history in terms of

God's ongoing purpose, and saw, in particular, cosmic history in terms of a great Assize, a coming moment when God would set all things right – including vindicating his people. Here a passage like Daniel 7 comes naturally to mind, with the Ancient of Days taking his seat as judge, with the nations (in the form of the sequence of monsters) being judged and condemned, and with Israel (in the form of 'one like a son of man' and/or 'the people of the saints of the Most High') being vindicated, exalted after their suffering, like a defendant who has been on trial for a long time and is finally upheld. This scene – and the many other stories, poems, prophecies, expectations, flashes of insight and so forth which essentially say the same thing – is *covenantal*: the Creator God is acting at last in fulfilment of his ancient promises, as we saw when studying Daniel 9. It is also *forensic*, understanding the covenantal history within the lawcourt framework, not as an arbitrary metaphor chosen at random but precisely because the covenant was there as God's chosen means of putting things right. And it is also, of course, eschatological.

IV

The next dimension of the biblical, more especially the Pauline, doctrine of justification, belongs closely with the others – the lawcourt, the covenant. They cannot be understood without it, nor it without them, nor the exegesis of the key texts without all three. Eschatology completes a triangle.

Again, 'eschatology' is of course a shorthand. I am fond of telling the story of one early reader of *Jesus and the Victory of God*, who phoned me up to complain that he had looked up 'eschatology' in the dictionary several times and kept forgetting what it meant because it didn't seem to apply to what he was reading. Fair comment: the dictionary probably said 'death, judgment, heaven and hell', which is not how the word has been used within biblical studies for the last half-century at least.[24] By 'eschatology', to put it basically and clearly, I here at least mean this:

(a) that Paul, like so many (though no doubt not all) of his Jewish contemporaries, believed that the single purposes of the creator God were moving forwards with a definite goal in mind, the redemption of God's people and the ultimate rescue of the whole creation;

(b) that Paul, *unlike* his non-Christian Jewish contemporaries, believed that the definite goal God had in mind had *already* been launched in and through the Messiah, Jesus;

(c) that Paul, in parallel in some ways with Qumran and perhaps others, believed that this inauguration of the 'new age' had thus introduced a period of 'now-and-not-yet', so that the followers of Jesus were living *both* in the continuing 'old age' *and*, more decisively, in the already inaugurated new one.

Paul believed, in short, that what Israel had longed for God to do for it and for the world, God had done for Jesus, bringing him through death and into the life of the age to come. Eschatology: the new world had been inaugurated! Covenant: God's promises to Abraham had been fulfilled! Lawcourt: Jesus had been vindicated – and so all those who belonged to Jesus were vindicated as well! And these, for Paul, were not three, but one. Welcome to Paul's doctrine of justification, rooted in the single scriptural narrative as he read it, reaching out to the waiting world.

The eschatology, though, was as I said only partially realized. (That phrase doesn't quite catch the key point, since it implies that God's new world is, as it were, being introduced progressively, an inch at a time; whereas, for Paul, the events concerning Jesus the Messiah were nothing short of an apocalypse, the denouement of history, the bursting in of God's sovereign saving power to the world of corruption, sin and death.) There remains, of course, the final goal, the ultimate triumph, the moment when God will be 'all in all'. And so Paul's theology, as is often remarked, is held within this now-and-not-yet tension.

This introduces us at last to what appears the hardest point in the whole theology of justification, the whole discussion of the 'new perspective', the whole agony of conscience, pastoral concern, preachers' vocations, and so on. How does one describe the future, coming day of final judgment? How does one account for Paul's repeated statements about that judgment being in accordance with the 'works' that people have done? How does one describe, theologically, the interplay of grace and obedience among those who are already followers of Jesus?

Here, once again, we are back with the steering wheel and the car. There are many things which theologians and preachers find themselves compelled to say about these questions, but the sharp-edged question of 'justification' by itself will not necessarily help them to say it. This is the trouble with the great tradition, from Augustine onwards: not that it has not said many true and useful things, but that by using the word 'justification' *as though it described the entire process from grace to glory* it has given conscientious Pauline interpreters many sleepless nights trying to work out how what he actually says about justification can be made to cover this whole range without collapsing into nonsense or heresy or both. The answer is: get in the car, start the engine, take hold of the steering wheel firmly, but be thankful that it is part of a much larger machine through which, working together as a whole, the journey can be undertaken.

This is the point, too, of my earlier illustration about the jigsaw. In order to understand the *future* verdict which God, the righteous judge, will deliver on the last day, and how that future verdict is correctly anticipated in the *present* when someone confesses that Jesus is Lord and believes that God raised him from the dead (Romans 10.9), we need to understand one more level of the covenant: Christology. As John Calvin rightly saw – and as Paul himself said, in the first paragraph he ever wrote on the subject – we are 'justified in Christ' (Galatians 2.17).

V

The word 'Christology' covers several different topics (another case of systematicians, for perfectly good reasons, using shorthands to spare readers a multiplicity of hyphens). Each deserves a monograph, and will here receive a paragraph – enough, I hope, to set the scene for the exegesis which is following close behind.[25]

First, as to terms.

(a) Paul uses the word 'Jesus' to refer to Jesus himself, Jesus of Nazareth, the human being who lived in the Middle East, announced God's sovereign and saving rule, died on a cross, and rose again three days later.

(b) When he uses the word 'Christ' he denotes, of course, the same human being, but *connotes* the Jewish notion of 'Messiah'.

(c) When he uses the phrase 'son of God', he means *both* that Jesus is the Messiah, the son of David whom God had promised would be his (God's) own son (2 Samuel 7.14 and elsewhere), *and* that the human being Jesus is to be identified as one who was, all along, at one with 'the father', and has now been sent from him (Romans 8.3; Galatians 4.4).

(d) When he uses the word 'Lord', he means

   (i) that Jesus, precisely as the Messiah, is now exalted over all things;

   (ii) that Jesus has attained the position of sovereignty over creation marked out for human beings from the beginning, as in Genesis 1 and Psalm 8;

   (iii) that Jesus is therefore the reality of which all earthly emperors are mere parodies;

   (iv) and, strikingly, that he is to be understood in the role regularly marked out, in the Greek Old Testament, as *kyrios*, which renders the reverent Hebrew *adonai*, which stands of course for YHWH (e.g. 1 Corinthians 8.6; Romans 10.13).

This complex but utterly coherent usage, in which Paul is completely consistent throughout his writings, forms the platform for what is to come.

Second, the meaning of Messiahship. Paul uses *Christos*, designating Jesus as the Messiah, in the conscious belief that the Messiah is the one in whom two things in particular happen.

(a) 'The Messiah' is the one who draws Israel's long history to its appointed goal (Romans 9.5; 10.4). The single-plan-through-Israel-for-the-world was designed (so Paul believed, with many precedents in the Old Testament and second-Temple Judaism) to culminate in the Messiah, who would fight the victorious battle against the ultimate enemy, build the new Temple, and inaugurate a worldwide rule of justice, peace and prosperity. Paul, of course, saw all of these as being redefined, granted that the Messiah was Jesus (of all people!). But none of them is lost.

(b) 'The Messiah' is therefore the one – this is clearest in Paul, but there are significant antecedents – *in whom God's people are summed up*, so that what is true of him is true of them. To belong to the people over whom David, or David's son, was ruling was spoken of in the Old Testament as being 'in David' or 'in the son of Jesse' (2 Samuel 20.1; 1 Kings 12.16). Paul can therefore speak of Christians as 'entering into the Messiah' through baptism and faith, as being 'in him' as a result. He is the 'seed of Abraham', not simply as a single person but because he 'contains', as the goal of God's Israel-plan, the whole people of God in himself. The same point can be made by saying that Christians 'belong to the Messiah': 'if you are Messiah's, you are Abraham's family, heirs according to promise' (Galatians 3.29). This is the key that unlocks some of the most apparently stubborn and tricky bits of Paul, not least in Galatians 2—4.

Third, the accomplishment of the Messiah. Going back to (a) in the previous paragraph, the task of the Messiah, bringing to its appointed goal the single-plan-through-Israel-for-the-world, was to offer to God the 'obedience' which Israel should have offered but did not. It is striking that, in Romans 5.19, one of the most climactic ways in which Paul speaks of the accomplishment of Jesus the Messiah is in terms of his 'obedience'. This is picked up, famously, in Philippians 2.8: he was 'obedient all the way to death, even the death of the cross'. But if Romans 5.19 thus looks back to the obedient death of Jesus, as Paul has referred to it in 3.24–26, 4.25 and 5.6–11, he looks forward to exactly the same point with a closely correlated motif in chapter 3.

I shall say this more fully when we get to Romans in the exegetical section, but let me here summarize the point in advance. The problem with the single-plan-through-Israel-for-the-world was the 'through-Israel' bit: Israel had let the side down, had let God down, had not offered the 'obedience' which would have allowed the worldwide covenant plan to proceed. Israel, in short, had been *faithless to God's commission*. That is the point of the much-misunderstood, and actually in consequence much-ignored, but all-important, Romans 3.1–8. What is needed, following Romans 2.17–29 and 3.3, is *a faithful Israelite, through whom the single plan can proceed after all*. What Paul declares in 3.21–22 is that God has unveiled his own faithfulness to the single plan – through the faithfulness, which he will later refer to as 'obedience', of the Messiah. I shall have more to say on this when we reach the same point in our exegesis of

Romans, but I simply want here to note two things. (a) This is the true meaning of 'the faithfulness of the Messiah', *pistis Christou*, as opposed to the ideas which are sometimes rightly rejected as strange or unintelligible (e.g. that Paul is referring to Jesus himself being 'justified by faith'), and because of which exegetes frequently lapse back into the more familiar 'faith *in* the Messiah'. (b) This is the context, I believe, within which we can begin to make sense – biblical sense, Pauline sense – of the theme which some have expressed, misleadingly in my view, as 'the imputed righteousness of Christ'. To that we shall return.

Fourth, this faithful obedience of the Messiah, culminating in his death 'for sins, in accordance with the scriptures' as in one of Paul's summaries of the gospel (1 Corinthians 15.3), is regularly understood in terms of the Messiah, precisely because he *represents* his people, now appropriately *standing in for them*, taking upon himself the death which they deserved, so that they might not suffer it themselves. This is most clearly expressed, to my mind, in two passages: Romans 8.3, where Paul declares that God 'condemned sin in the flesh' (note, he does not say that God 'condemned Jesus', but that he 'condemned sin in the flesh' of Jesus); and 2 Corinthians 5.21a, where he says that God 'made him to be sin for us, who knew no sin'. There are of course many other passages in which Paul draws upon, and draws out, the stunning, majestic, grace-filled, love-expressing, life-giving message and meaning of the Messiah's cross.[26] But these are basic and clear. 'There is therefore now no condemnation for those who are in Christ Jesus, . . . for God . . . has condemned sin in the flesh [of his son].'[27] Sin was condemned *there*, in his flesh, so that it shall not now be condemned *here*, in us, in those who are 'in him'. Notice how the sterile old antithesis between 'representation' and 'substitution' is completely overcome. The Messiah is able to be the substitute *because* he is the representative. Once we grasp the essentially Jewish categories of thought with which Paul is working, many problems in a de-Judaized systematic theology are transcended.

Fifth, the resurrection of the Messiah is, for Paul, the beginning of the entire new creation. When God raised Jesus from the dead, that event was the divine declaration that he really had been his son all along (in the senses described above).[28] The resurrection was the 'vindication' of Jesus, his 'justification' after the apparent condemnation of the court that sent him to his death. But the resurrection is, for Paul, far more than an event which conveys truth concerning Jesus. It is the beginning of God's promised new age, which now awaits fulfilment when victory is won over all enemies, including death itself, so that God is all in all (1 Corinthians 15.28), when creation itself is set free from its slavery to corruption and decay, and comes to share the liberty of the glory of God's children (Romans 8.18–26). The death and resurrection of the Messiah are, for Paul, the turning-point of history – Israel's history, the world's history, even (if we can speak like this, not least in the light of the incarnation of Jesus) God's history. The gospel message, the proclamation of Jesus as the crucified and risen Lord, summons men, women and children – and, in a manner, the whole creation (see Colossians 1.23)! – to discover in Jesus, and in his messianic death for sins and new life to launch God's new creation, the fulfilment of the single-plan-through-Israel-for-the-world, the purpose through which, as a single act with a single meaning, sins are forgiven and people of every race are called into God's single family.

Sixth – it may feel like a different subject, but for Paul it belongs right here – the 'spirit of the son' (Galatians 4.6), the 'spirit of the Messiah' (Romans 8.9), is poured out upon the Messiah's people, so that they become in reality what they already are by God's declaration: God's people indeed, his 'children' (Romans 8.12–17; Galatians 4.4–7) within a context replete with overtones of Israel as 'God's son' at the exodus. The extremely close interconnection of Romans 8 and Galatians 4 with the discourse of justification in the earlier chapters of both letters warns us against attempting to construct a complete 'doctrine of justification' without reference to the spirit. Indeed, I and others have long insisted that the doctrine is Trinitarian in shape.[29] This is the point at which it is idle to complain that I, or others who take a similar position, are encouraging people to 'trust in anyone or anything other than the crucified and resurrected Savior'.[30] Is it wrong, or heretical, to declare that *as well as* and also *because of* our absolute faith in the crucified and resurrected Saviour, we *also* trust in the life-giving spirit who enables us to say 'Abba, father' (Romans 8.12–16) and 'Jesus is Lord' (1 Corinthians 12.3)? Of course not. For Paul, faith in Jesus Christ *includes* a trust in the spirit; not least, a sure trust that 'he who began a good work in you will bring it to completion at the day of the Messiah' (Philippians 1.6). In other words – though Paul does not mention the spirit here, this is certainly what is in mind – he can pray 'that your love may abound more and more, in knowledge and all discernment, so that you may be able to approve what is excellent, so that you may be pure and blameless at the day of the Messiah, filled with the fruits of righteousness which are through Jesus the Messiah to the glory and praise of God' (Philippians 1.9–11). Or, as he puts it later in the letter, 'God is at work in you, to will and to work for his good pleasure' (2.13). Shall we not trust in this God, in this spirit? Is that something other than a full and complete trust in Jesus the Messiah, the Saviour, the one sent by this God, the one through whom this God sends this spirit? How this works out, and what it means for a theological understanding of Christian life between present and final justification, we must explore through the exegesis.

Seventh, and finally, the point which has just been hinted at: for Paul, Jesus' Messiahship constitutes him as the judge on the last day.[31] Paul takes the Old Testament theme of 'the day of the Lord' and transforms it into 'the day of the Messiah' (Philippians 2.16, etc.).[32] Jesus is the king, the lord, the one at whose name every knee shall bow.[33] He is the one through whom, according to the gospel, God will judge the secrets of all hearts (the 'gospel', we note, is not simply 'here's how to be saved'; it is the good news that, through Jesus as Messiah, the creator God is putting the whole world right).[34] More specifically, 'we must all appear before the judgment seat of the Messiah'.[35] And at that judgment seat the verdict will be in accordance with one's 'works'. Here again we must return, via the exegesis, to understand how this final judgment will correspond to the one issued in the present on the basis of faith, and how the 'works' done by the Christian through the spirit (e.g. Romans 8.12–17) are properly to be understood.

This sevenfold story of Jesus as Messiah, woven deep into the structures of Paul's praying, thinking and working, forms the focus of the narrative in which he lived his life. This messianic story of Jesus, for him, was the eschatological climax of Israel's long history as the covenant people of the creator God, the narrative within which Christian identity was to be found, the reason for the favourable verdict in the lawcourt, and, above and beyond and around it all, the utter assurance of the overwhelming and all-powerful love of the creator God. This is the framework of thought which we now carry forward into the second part of this book, as we examine the actual passages, the actual arguments, the actual phrases in which Paul's famous theology of justification comes to primary expression.

Part 2

EXEGESIS

5

Galatians

I

In turning now to exegesis, I am once more under no illusions as to the enormity of the task. Great commentaries sit on my shelves, replete with collected and pondered learning and wisdom (and sometimes folly). Serious journals jostle for attention, with yet another interpretation of a key verse, a tricky passage, a vital theme. All scholars know this; some try to demonstrate their knowledge of the field with the massive annotation of which I spoke earlier. Having proved elsewhere that I can play that game to a reasonable standard, my regret at not being able to write this book in the same style is not at all that it may look naked and unadorned (that is a risk I have run before and will no doubt run again), but that some works which really would have helped my case will be ignored, and others which make good points diametrically opposed to my own could and should have been answered and will not be. This, too, cannot be helped. I have chosen a very limited selection of conversation partners for this short essay, and, with due apologies, I shall ask the others to be patient for another occasion. My method, too, is to be selective – one cannot write a full commentary on each of the letters within a book like this! – but to highlight two things: first, the larger arguments which Paul is advancing, and how, within them the framework of lawcourt, covenant, eschatology and Christology which I sketched in the previous chapter is worked out; second, the meaning of justification in particular. Other points must, with regret, be left to one side.

In launching in, I note what all exegetes know in their bones, that Paul never 'says it all' in any one place, that even when dealing with similar topics he comes at them from a slightly different angle, and that whatever else he is doing he is not attempting to write successive editions of a book hypothetically entitled 'What I basically think about God, Jesus and the gospel'. The letters are directed – as this book is directed, with all the imbalance that that entails – to particular situations, to particular attacks and questions which call forth particular kinds of rebuttal and response.

Someone in my position, in fact, is bound to have a certain fellow-feeling with Paul in Galatia. He is, after all, under attack from his own right wing. Knowing himself called to take the gospel of Jesus the Messiah to the pagan world, it must have been frustrating to find that those who shared with him the ancestral heritage which he now believed to have been fulfilled in Jesus had failed to grasp what he saw as central. Not, of course, that I wish to repeat the manifold hermeneutical dangers so evident in Luther's wonderful and deeply flawed commentary on Galatians, imagining that Paul is attacking exactly the same enemies as he is himself. But, since Galatians 1.8–9 is sometimes quoted against me (not, I hasten to add, by John Piper), and solemn anathemas are hurled at me for my teaching of 'another gospel', I thought it might help to redress the implicit hermeneutical balance a little.[1] Paul, after all, was standing for the cross and the scriptures against all human tradition, however venerable. He was insisting on the central importance of the breaking down of barriers between Jew and Gentile, to people who were eager to erect them. He, too, found himself frustrated that people to whom he thought he had explained things so clearly were still unable to get the point . . .

He was, in short, under attack from people whom scholars have come to call by a variety of names, but perhaps most straightforwardly (and following what Paul himself says in 1.7) 'agitators'. They are not, we note, 'Judaizers', despite often being called that; that word, properly, refers to Gentiles who are trying to become Jews – which is what the erstwhile pagan Galatians, having come to faith in Jesus the Messiah, were now being urged to do. The agitators, in other words, were trying to get the Galatians to 'Judaize'. Their reasons for doing so we may leave to one side, to be studied by those adept in the use of angled hermeneutical mirrors. Paul's answers lie before us on the page.

Or rather, they leap up at us off the page. As usual, Paul opens with a summary greeting which contains a strong hint of what is to come. 'Grace to you and peace from God our father and the Lord

Jesus the Messiah, who gave himself for our sins, to snatch us out of the present wicked age according to the will of God, our father, to whom be glory to the ages of ages, Amen.'² There we have it all: the single-plan-of-God; the eschatological framework (Jesus has broken through from the present age of sin and death into the new age, taking with him those whom he is rescuing from the latter and for the former); by implication the forensic context ('for our sins': something to do with his 'giving of himself' has, as in 1 Corinthians 15.3, had the effect of dealing with sin); and of course the central Christology, the achievement of Jesus as Messiah. And all to the praise and glory of God. All that follows will simply unpack this typically dense opening flourish.

We skip over the first chapter and a half, noting only that one of the key questions in the central sections of the letter is already raised in Paul's discussion of his early visits to Jerusalem: Titus was not compelled to be circumcised (2.3). Sadly, opinions differ as to whether he means 'Titus was circumcised, but this was undertaken freely, not under compulsion', or whether, as I am inclined to think more likely, 'Some people tried to compel Titus to be circumcised, but he and I successfully resisted.' Paul's comment on this, though, is telling: this event (whichever way it went) happened because of false members of the Christian family, who sneaked in alongside 'to spy out the freedom which we have in the Messiah, Jesus'. Freedom! There is that great word, beloved of reformers of every sort: but what did it mean for Paul? Clearly, here and throughout the letter, not least 'the freedom for Gentile Christians to stay as Gentile Christians, and not to have to become Jews in order to belong to the people of God'. But why, we want to ask, would a Jew of Paul's pedigree have come to think that belonging to the ethnic people of God, and living under its ancestral law, was a matter of slavery? Read on, says Paul, and find out.

The question of freedom and the law then dominates the vital and powerful paragraph 2.11–21. Paul intends this as the dramatic backdrop to the main argument he is then going to put directly to the Galatians, which begins in 3.1. What happened earlier at Antioch – and, equally important, the theological reflection which Paul now offers on what happened at Antioch – is designed, rhetorically, to open up the key issues and to do so with maximum theological, and also emotional, appeal.

Cephas (the Aramaic name for Peter) was in the wrong in Antioch. Prior to the arrival of people from James, Peter had been content to eat with Gentiles, presumably uncircumcised Gentile Christians. 'From James' meant 'from Jerusalem', where, as in Acts 21.20, the mood of most Christians was to be 'zealous for the Torah', as Paul himself had been (1.14). We need not be concerned here with the variety of beliefs held by different Jewish groups on the subject of table-fellowship with pagans. Enough to see that it was an issue which, in the overheated Middle-Eastern world of the first century, and in the excited world of early Christianity in particular, could and did arouse passions. So, when the 'men from James' arrived, Peter separated himself, and the other Jewish Christians did the same. So far, in this account, no question has been raised about whether the Gentiles concerned were true Christians. We must assume, in the light of what Paul says later (3.27), that they have been baptized. We certainly assume that they have believed in Jesus as the crucified and risen Lord. That is not at issue. What is at issue is the question: Is it right for Jewish Christians and Gentile Christians to eat together? Do they belong at the same table, or not? That is the question, in this, Paul's first and perhaps sharpest state-ment of 'justification by faith', to which he regards that doctrine as the answer.

Paul is clear as to the implication of Peter's withdrawal. Peter is saying, in effect, to the ex-pagan Christians, 'if you want to be part of the real family of God, you are going to have to become Jewish'. He is 'compelling them to Judaize' (2.14c) – the very thing which the 'agitators' are trying to do to the Galatians, which is of course why Paul is telling this story, and telling it this way. By way of chal-lenging Peter on this point, he says something very interesting about the person Peter has now become (2.14b): 'You are a Jew, but you are living like a pagan and not like a Jew.'

What can 'living like a pagan' mean here? That Peter has removed the marks of circumcision? Possible in theory, but exceedingly unlikely. That Peter is eating pork or other forbidden food? Possible, but still pretty unlikely. That Peter is disobeying the moral laws in Torah? Certainly not – Paul would have had other sharp words for that, as indicated in chapter 5. That Peter is no longer saying his prayers? Highly unlikely. Far and away the most likely solution is that in one of two ways Peter is no longer observing standard Jewish taboos. It is just possible that we should think in terms of a Christian refusal to keep the sabbath, or other Jewish special days (see 4.10). But the high probability – and few doubt this, but it was worth going round the other options just to make sure we are thinking in a first-century Jewish manner – is that Peter was by now well and truly used to eating with Gentile Christians, and to making no difference between himself and them. That, after all, is what Acts says Peter had learnt in the house of Cornelius.[3]

So something has happened to Peter – something so profound that he now has a new identity, which affects key behaviour patterns and taboos about that very central human activity, sitting down to a meal. And it is on that 'something', that change of identity, that transfer from one family to another, and the new position which membership in the new family creates, that Paul now concentrates, broadening what he has said to Peter (and hence, in the context of the letter, what he has said *about* Peter) to a more general statement (2.15–16) about all those who, though born Jewish, have become Christians.

'We are Jews by nature,' he writes, 'and not "Gentile sinners"' (2.15). That last phrase is a technical term: 'lesser breeds,' as it were, 'outside the law'. It represents, as do the boasts catalogued in Romans 2.17–20, what Paul knew to be a standard Jewish attitude, rooted of course in the scriptures themselves. He is talking about *ethnic identity*, and about the practices that go with that. And he is about to show that in the gospel this ethnic identity is dismantled, so that a new identity may be constructed, in which the things that separated Jew from Gentile (as in Ephesians 2.14–16, on which see below) no longer matter. This, and only this, is the context in which we can read the famous and dense verse 2.16 with some hope of success.

Despite the fact that 'we are Jews by nature [i.e. by birth], not Gentile sinners,' 'we nevertheless know', he says, '*that a person is not justified by works of the law*'. Here it is: the first statement of the Christian doctrine of justification by faith. Or rather, the first statement of its negative pole, that one cannot be justified by works of 'the law' – which, by the way, for Paul, *always* means 'the Jewish Law, the Torah'.

Now: another thought experiment. Let us suppose we only had a fragment of this letter, consisting of 2.11–16a, and stopping right here, 'not justified by works of the law'. What would we conclude about the meaning of 'justified'? We might well know, from extraneous verbal evidence, that 'justified' was a lawcourt term meaning 'given the status of being "in the right"'. But Paul is not in a lawcourt, he is at a dinner table. The context of his talking about 'not being justified by works of the law' is that he is confronted with the question of ethnic taboos about eating together across ethnic boundaries. The force of his statement is clear: 'yes, you are Jewish; but as a *Christian* Jew you ought not to be separating on ethnic lines'. Reading Paul strictly in his own context – as John Piper rightly insists we must always ultimately do – we are forced to conclude, at least in a preliminary way, that 'to be justified' here does not mean 'to be granted free forgiveness of your sins', 'to come into a right relation with God', or some other near-synonym of 'to be reckoned "in the right" before God', but rather, and very specifically, 'to be reckoned by God to be a true member of his family, and hence with the right to share table fellowship'. This does not clinch the argument for my reading of the whole doctrine. But the first signs are that, for Paul, 'justification', whatever else it included, always had in mind God's declaration of membership, and that this always referred specifically to the coming together of Jews and Gentiles in faithful membership of the Christian family.

What, then, are the 'works of the law', by which one cannot be 'justified' in this sense? Again, the context is pretty clear. They are the 'living like a Jew' of 2.14, the separation from 'Gentile sinners' of 2.15. They are not, in other words, the moral 'good works' which the Reformation tradition loves to hate. They are the things that divide Jew from Gentile: specifically, in the context of this passage (and we have no right to read Galatians 2.16 other than in the context of verses 11–15), the 'works of the law' which specify, however different Jewish groups might have put it at the time, that 'Jews do not eat with Gentiles'.[4] What one might gain by such 'works of the law' is not a treasury of moral merit, but the assured status of belonging to God's people, separated from the rest of humankind.

So what is the alternative? If we are 'not justified by works of the law', how *are* we 'justified'? Paul's answer opens up the now famous question of *pistis Iēsou Christou*, which can be translated either as 'the faithfulness of Jesus Christ' or as 'faith in Jesus Christ'.[5] For reasons I have given elsewhere, I have come to read the passage as follows: 'we know that a person is not justified by works of the law, but through the faithfulness of Jesus the Messiah; so we came to believe in the Messiah, Jesus, so that we might be justified by the faithfulness of the Messiah, and not by works of the law, because by works of the law no flesh shall be justified'. This fits together as follows.

'The faithfulness of the Messiah', in the sense described in the previous chapter – his faithfulness to the long, single purposes of God for Israel – is the instrument, the ultimate agency, by which 'justification' takes place. The Messiah's faithful death, in other words, redefines the people of God, which just happens to be exactly what Paul says more fully in verses 19–20 (always a good sign). And the way in which people appropriate that justification, that redefinition of God's people, is now 'by faith', by coming to believe in Jesus as Messiah. The achievement of Jesus as the crucified Messiah is the basis of this redefinition. The faith of the individual is what marks out those who now belong to him, to the Messiah-redefined family.

What is then added by the final clause of verse 16, which emphasizes once more what was said in the opening clause? 'By works of the law no flesh shall be justified': as in Romans 3.20, Paul quotes Psalm 143.2, though now writing 'flesh' (*sarx*) instead of 'no living thing', as in the Hebrew and Greek. He does not here explain things further, and we might be left to suppose that he is simply reinforcing the weight of the opening clause. 'Works of the law' cannot justify, because God has redefined his people through the faithfulness of the Messiah. But in Romans 3.20 Paul does explain the meaning of the quotation, by adding, 'for through the law comes the knowledge of sin'. As always when he writes quickly and densely, it is risky to fill in the gaps in his argument, but this point really does seem to be in his mind here as well.

There are, then, two interlocking reasons why 'works of the law cannot justify'. First, God has redefined his people through the faithfulness of the Messiah, and 'works of the law' would divide Jew from Gentile in a way that is now irrelevant. Second, 'works of the law' will never justify, because what the law does is to reveal sin. Nobody can keep it perfectly. The problem of Genesis 11 (the fracturing of humanity) is the full outworking of the problem of Genesis 3 (sin), and the promise to Abraham is the answer to both together.

Perspectives new and old sit comfortably side by side here, a pair of theological Siamese twins sharing a single heart.

It is impossible, without the rest of Romans and Galatians (and several bits of the other letters as well), to reconstruct the full implicit train of thought within which this makes the sense it does. But we may say cautiously, even at this stage, that Paul is working with the following idea (which will be filled out quite a bit in the next chapter of the letter). God's purpose in calling Abraham was to bless the whole world, to call out a people from Gentiles as well as Jews. This purpose has now been accomplished through the faithfulness of the Messiah, and all who believe in him constitute this fulfilled-family-of-Abraham. The law was given to keep ethnic Israel, so to speak, on track. But it could never be the means by which the ultimate promised family was demarcated, partly because it kept the two intended parts of the family separate, and partly because it merely served to demonstrate, by the fact that it was impossible to keep it perfectly, that Jews, like the rest of the human race, were sinful. The Messiah's death deals with (what seems to us as) this double problem.

Verses 17 and 18 raise and answer a question which must, like verse 16, be solidly anchored to the actual situation Paul is describing in verses 11–14.

'If, while seeking to be justified in the Messiah, we ourselves turn out to be "sinners", does that make the Messiah a servant of sin? Certainly not!' In other words (addressing Peter), 'Yes, we are seeking to find our identity as God's people "in the Messiah", trusting in his "faithfulness"; and yes, that means that in terms of the Torah as we know it we find ourselves standing alongside "Gentile sinners", as in verse 15. Technically, we are "sinners" like them.' This, I think, is preferable to the obvious alternative, which is to understand this as a reference to something like Luther's *simul iustus et peccator*: we are justified in Christ, but still sinners simply in the sense of committing actual sin.

But this does not mean – as some, perhaps those who had come from James, might have inferred – that the Messiah was simply stirring up 'sinful' behaviour, encouraging people to kick over the traces and live 'outside the law' along with . . . those Gentile idolaters! Certainly not! Rather, 'if I build up again the things which I tore down, I demonstrate myself to be a transgressor'. Paul has moved from 'we' to 'I' at this point, preparing for the intensely personal, and deliberately rhetorical, appeal of verses 19–21. What he is saying can be spelled out like this: 'If, having pulled down the wall of partition between myself and the Gentiles, having discovered that it is abolished through the Messiah, I then build it up again by separating myself from the Gentiles, all I accomplish is to erect a sign (the Torah itself!) which says "you have transgressed".' 'Transgression', we should note, is the actual breaking of the law, whereas 'sin' is any missing-of-the-mark, any failure to live as a genuine human being, whether or not the law is there to point it out.[6]

Paul is still, in other words, continuing to explore the theological dimensions of the situation Peter had put himself in. Either you stay in the Jew-plus-Gentile family of the Messiah, or you erect again the wall of Torah between them – but there will be a notice on your side of that wall, saying 'By the way, you have broken me' – both in general, because nobody keeps it perfectly, and in particular, because you have recently been living 'like a Gentile, not like a Jew' (v. 14).

This is the context within which we should understand the climactic and decisive statement of vv. 19–20, before the calm summary of verse 21. Paul begins with 'for': in other words, 19–20 explains further what he has just said. This is a statement about the radical change of identity which Paul has undergone – and not only Paul, but all those Jews who have come to be 'in Christ'. Here, as in Romans 7, the 'I' is a way of saying 'this is what happens to Jews', without saying it as though that were something which Paul could look at from the outside. 'I, through the Torah, died to the Torah, that I might live to God; I have been crucified with the Messiah, nevertheless I live, yet not I, but the Messiah lives within me; and the life I now live in the flesh I live in the faithfulness of the son of God, who loved me and gave himself for me.'

It should be obvious that this is not merely a statement of what we now call 'private religious experience'. That would scarcely contribute to the discussion ('that's all very well, Paul' they might say, 'but most of us have never had such an intense experience'). The point is that what happens to the Jew who believes in Jesus the Messiah is a dying and rising, a dying to the old identity defined by Torah (and thus separated from Gentiles) and a rising into the new identity defined by the Messiah himself, whose faithfulness unto death has brought his people out of the 'old age' and into the new. This event is an objective reality for all who believe in Jesus the Messiah and are baptized into him, whatever it 'feels like' at the time. To this statement Paul then adds the striking (and, even for him, rare) note that the Messiah's death on his behalf was an act of self-giving love, a love which put him in his debt, a love which embodied the very grace of God himself (verse 21), and which could not be refused (as to go back to a Torah-defined community would refuse it) without the grossest ingratitude. 'I do not nullify God's grace; for if righteousness (*dikaiosynē*) were through Torah, then the Messiah died in vain.'

The entire paragraph is a commentary on, a theological exploration of, the choices faced by Peter in Antioch, addressed through the device of the 'I' which explains, vividly and dramatically, what has happened not just to Paul, not just to Peter, but to all those Jews who believe in Jesus as Messiah. The Messiah's death and resurrection *reconstitutes the people of God*, in a way which means that they come out from under the rule of Torah and into the new world which God himself is making. Because the Messiah is the faithful Israelite who has carried God's single saving plan to its utmost conclusion, his death on their behalf ('he gave himself *for* me') carries them with him ('crucified *with* the Messiah').

And – the truly important conclusion from all of this – we discover what *dikaiosynē* really is. It denotes a *status*, not a moral quality. It means 'membership in God's true family'. Peter had supposed, for a moment at least, that this 'righteousness' was to be defined by Torah. That was why, suddenly feeling guilty when James's men arrived, he quickly 'rebuilt the wall of Torah' he had formerly torn down, separating himself from table-fellowship with Gentiles.

If, in other words (after all this careful walk through a complex paragraph), we are to adopt John Piper's strict criterion, and interpret the words Paul uses in the sense demanded by the passages in which we find them, then we are forced to conclude, at least in a preliminary fashion, as follows.

(a) 'Righteousness' denotes the status enjoyed by God's true family, now composed of both Jews and Gentiles who believe in Jesus the Messiah. The lawcourt metaphor behind the language of justification, and of the status 'righteous' which someone has when the court has found in their favour, has given way to the clear sense of 'membership in God's people'.

(b) 'Justification', as in the verbs of verses 16 and 17, two positive and two negative, denotes the verdict of God himself as to who really is a member of his people. The criterion on which the verdict is based is, for the negative verdict, sin: Israel under the Torah cannot be declared to be God's people, because the Torah merely points to sin. For the positive verdict, the criterion is the Messiah: the Messiah and his faithfulness unto death, the death to which he gave himself to 'deliver us from the present evil age' (1.4, echoed in the 'giving of himself' in 2.20), are the basis on which God makes the declaration 'Here are my people.'[7]

(c) The people over whom that verdict ('righteous', 'members of God's family') is issued are those who are 'in the Messiah' (v. 17), who have died and risen with him (vv. 19–20), who believe in him (vv. 16, 20).

Justification, in Paul's sense, cannot be played off against these other elements of his thought. They all belong together. It is, after all, one complete jigsaw, and all the pieces fit.

II

Galatians 3.1—4.11 forms, in essence, a single great argument, holding together within itself the tighter structure that runs from 3.6 to 3.29. The only way to understand the parts is to see them in relation to these larger wholes.

I choose to focus first on that slightly shorter section, 3.6–29. Here the parameters are clear. Paul is discussing the question, Who are the true children of Abraham? That is where he opens (3.6–7: 'Abraham believed God, and it was reckoned to him as righteousness; so you know that those who are "on the basis of faith" are the sons of Abraham'), and that is where he closes (3.29: 'and if you belong to the Messiah, you are Abraham's seed, heirs according to the promise').

Abraham, in other words, is not an 'example' of something else, an 'illustration' of a general point about different kinds of piety and their relative soteriological effectiveness. Paul is working, throughout this section, on the basis of the single-plan-of-God-through-Israel-for-the-world. This, and this alone, makes sense of the larger unit and the smaller details. Thus the short opening section continues simply by adding 'Gentiles' to the point already made: 'scripture foresaw that God would justify the Gentiles by faith, and so made that promise to Abraham; thus those of faith are blessed with faithful Abraham' (3.8–9). So far, so clear: God has begun the great single purpose, to bless the world through choosing Abraham, calling him, and making promises to him. Paul is aware, though many readers today may not be even after reading verses 15–17, that Genesis 15 (quoted in verse 6) is the chapter where God makes the covenant with Abraham, the covenant which envisages the exodus as one of its great fulfilments. This point will be highly relevant in the transition to chapter 4.

But what happens next? The markers, the concluding notes, in every section in this chapter are still all about Abraham and his family. Verse 9: those of faith are blessed with faithful Abraham. Verse 14: so that the blessing of Abraham might (after all!) come upon the Gentiles. Verse 18: the inheritance was given to Abraham by promise. Verse 22: no explicit mention of Abraham, but the same point: the promise belongs to believers. Then, finally, verse 29: if you are the Messiah's, you are Abraham's seed, heirs in accordance with the promise. The chapter is soaked in Abraham, and every section depends on the sense of a *historical sequence* in which Abraham comes first, the law comes next, and the Messiah – and/or 'faith' – comes to complete the sequence.

In particular, as the argument develops throughout the chapter, the main sub-theme is obviously the problem of the law. But the problem is not simply that the law condemns (though it does), shows up sin (though it does), or indeed encourages people into self-righteous 'legalism' (which Paul does not mention at all, in this chapter at least). The problem is that the Law *gets in the way of the promise to Abraham*, the single-plan-through-Israel-to-the-world, first by apparently choking the promise within the failure of Israel (verses 10–14), then by threatening to divide the promised single family into two (verses 15–18), then finally by locking everything up in the prison-house of sin. But at that point we become aware that this was, ultimately, a *positive* purpose. First, God always intended that the single-plan-through-Israel-for-the-world would be fulfilled, as announced to Abraham, on the basis of faith, and the Torah, by sealing off every other route, has made sure that this will indeed be the outcome. Just as the slavery in Egypt had appeared to place the promises in jeopardy, but was reversed in fulfilment precisely of those promises, so now with the effect of Torah. When deliverance comes, it will be seen to be by God's grace alone.[8] Second, sin itself *needed* to be dealt with, not merely ignored; Torah was right to draw attention to it.[9]

A word more – there could be a thousand words more, but this is not the place for them – about these three sections.[10] 3.10–14 has long been a favourite passage for those exploring the possibility that the origin of Paul's so-called 'law-free gospel' came in his recognition that God had vindicated the Jesus who had died under the law's curse (3.13, quoting Deuteronomy 21.23). That may or may not be the case – the question of the origin of Paul's thinking on particular subjects is not our concern at the moment – but I have to say that that line of thought does not have anything much to do with the actual argument of the passage. Michael Bird recounts his regular experience with his students, echoing mine over many years: when you ask people, 'Why did the Messiah become a curse for us?' the normal answer is something like, 'So that we might be freed from sin and share fellowship with God to all eternity.' Paul's is radically different: 'So that the blessing of Abraham might come upon the Gentiles, and so that we (presumably Jews who believe in Jesus) might receive the promise of the Spirit through faith'. That is where Paul at least thinks his argument is going. Once again, it is the context, not traditions brought in from outside, that really counts, and we must pay close attention.[11]

What then is the problem to which the curse-bearing death of the Messiah is the answer? The problem is that the law looked as if it would prevent the Abrahamic promises getting out to the nations, and thus prevent the single-plan-through-Israel-for-the-world coming to pass. This is exactly the point Paul summarizes in Romans 3.3: Israel, entrusted with the oracles of God, proved unfaithful to the commission (despite the boast of Romans 2.17–20). And, to make this point in a way again closely cognate to various parts of Romans, he draws on the great covenant passage in Deuteronomy 27—30, here particularly on the curses that come on those who do not obey the law. Like the author of 4QMMT and many others, Paul sees the entire history of Israel since Moses as the outworking of these great promises and warnings. In particular, he understands the long period since the geographical exile as the continuation of the period of the 'curse'. If Israel were to stay under that curse for ever – as appeared inevitable, granted that nobody in Israel did in fact abide by everything written in the Torah – then the promises would never be released into the wider world, and Israel itself could never be renewed. This plight is merely reinforced (verses 11–12) by the reiteration, in Habakkuk 2.4, of the Abrahamic motif of 'faith', and the counter-warning of Leviticus 18.5 that if you want to stay with the law then what matters is not merely possessing it, but doing it. But then comes the punch-line. The Messiah became a curse for us by hanging on the tree, coming himself to the place of the curse as indicated by Deuteronomy – and thereby making a way *through the curse and out the other side*, into the time of renewal when the Gentiles would at last come into Abraham's family, while Jews could have the possibility of covenant renewal, of receiving the promised spirit through faith (as in 3.2, 5). This reading of a dense and difficult passage is powerfully reinforced by a careful account of Romans 10.6–13, on which see the relevant discussion below.

The key to the next two sections is the notion of the single seed promised to Abraham. 'Seed' (*sperma* in Greek) can regularly mean 'family', and the point is that God promised Abraham one family, not two – but the Torah, left to itself, would divide that family into at least two, certainly into Jews and Gentiles and perhaps, on the same principle, into many families corresponding to many nations. This is where, as we saw earlier, Paul explicitly introduces the word 'covenant', making it clear in verse 17 that he is indeed thinking of God's covenant promise to Abraham (in other words, that the usage of *diathēkē* in verse 15 was not merely a piece of word-play by way of illustration), and of the historical sequence Abraham–Torah–Messiah/faith. The single 'seed' is the Messiah (verse 16): not, again, that Paul is playing word-games, imagining that the singular noun 'seed' must refer to a single individual (he knows perfectly well that that is not so, as verse 29 demonstrates), but that the Messiah is himself the one *in whom God's true people are summed up*. As in 2.15–21, which Paul has not forgotten even if some exegetes may have, the question at issue is whether Gentile Christians need to become Jewish, to get circumcised and keep those aspects of the law which mark them out from other Gentiles. The answer is: No, because in the Messiah you are already assured of full membership.

Chapter 3 verses 21–22 underscore the meaning we offered for the final clause of 2.16. By this stage in the argument Paul knew that it must have appeared that the law, which continually threatened to frustrate God's promises to Abraham, might in fact have been a terrible mistake. But this drives him deeper into the mystery of the overall single-plan-through-Israel-for-the-world. Yes, he says: there was nothing wrong with the law in itself, and had it been possible for a law to have been given which could have given life, *then righteousness would have been on the basis of the law* – the very thing which 2.21 had denied. Paul is here very close to Romans 7.7–12: the commandment was 'unto life', but it proved to be death. That passage helps us to understand what is in his mind here. The problem was not with the law, but with the people to whom the law had been given. This – to anticipate a later but vital point – is close to the heart of his theology, close to the reason why it often appears so complex and convoluted. There was always bound to be a problem with the single-plan-through-Israel-for-the-world, precisely at the 'through Israel' point, since Israel was made up entirely of human beings who, themselves sinful, were as much in need of redemption as the rest of humankind. Paul's conclusion here in 3.22 thus anticipates his sigh-of-relief moment at the end of the long argument of Romans 9—11 itself: scripture has concluded everything under sin, so that the promise, on the basis of the faithfulness of Jesus the Messiah, might be given to those who believe. God's single-plan-through-Israel-for-the-world has turned, as God always intended, into God's-single-plan-*through-the-faithful-Israelite*-for-the-world-*now-including-Israel-too*.

I hope it is already clear that God's dealing with sin as the root problem, and God's purpose to bring Jew and Gentile together in the single family 'in the Messiah', are so tightly intertwined throughout this passage so far that it would be futile to try to separate them. Here the normal caricatures of the 'new perspective' (which are sometimes of course richly deserved) simply break down. It is not *either* 'rescue from sin' *or* 'easy entry, without circumcision, into God's people'. Nor are these, as is sometimes suggested, merely to be thought of as 'vertical' and 'horizontal' dimensions, soteriology on the one hand and sociology on the other.[12] Part of the point is that soteriology itself, for Paul, is in that sense 'horizontal', having to do with the ongoing purposes of God within history, while sociology, for Paul, is 'vertical', because the single multi-ethnic family, constituted in the Messiah and indwelt by the spirit, is designed as God's powerful sign to the pagan world that Israel's God, Abraham's God, is its creator, lord and judge. In fact, what appear to Western eyes as two separate issues – salvation from sin on the one hand, a united people of God on the other – seem to have appeared to Paul as part and parcel of the same thing. That single same thing included God's dealing with humanity's idolatry, failure to reflect God's image, rebellion and sin, and not least fracturing into different nations and ethnic groups. As we shall see in the next chapter, they are all different ways of saying, ultimately, the same thing.

The final section of chapter 3 (verses 23–29) is like one of those symphonic finales where the composer seems to be trying to bring as many instruments into the action as possible, all playing different motifs but somehow combining into a glorious paean of praise. Certainly there are many more things going on in this passage than will emerge from a simplistic analysis in terms of the normal 'old perspective', and no doubt (!) from a simplistic analysis in terms of the new one, too. Is it possible to understand this rich and dense statement – which appears to be, from one point of view, a fuller restatement of 2.15–21, especially 2.19–21 – so that its main lines stand out and its details all fall into place?

The main line of thought should be clear, not least because it repeats, develops and sums up the main thrust of the whole chapter. All those who are 'of faith' are the children of Abraham; therefore God's people, Abraham's true family, are not defined by Torah. Think back to the situation in Antioch, and out into the situation in Galatia itself. Here are people coming from James to Antioch, to insist that Jewish believers should remain separated from uncircumcised Gentile believers, thereby putting pressure on those Gentile believers to get circumcised, to come within the fold of Torah. Here are people, similarly, coming (from James? Certainly from Jerusalem) to Galatia, to insist that Gentile converts there should get circumcised so that they may come, likewise, within the fold of Torah. Paul's answer is not that Torah is a bad thing, or that it wasn't after all given by God, or that its only purpose was to thunder warnings of judgment. Yes, Torah has had a seriously negative

106

purpose, as 3.10–22 has made clear. But the point is that Torah must be understood *within the strange single-plan-of-God-through-Israel-for-the-world*, the *covenantal and eschatological framework* (to say it out loud for once) within which the running metaphor of the 'lawcourt', always there by implication in the language of 'justification', is to be understood. This complex language is now itself transformed by two things: (a) the Messiah and his faithful, saving death, and (b) the faith/faithfulness which is now the single badge of his people, those who (like the 'I' of 2.19f.) have been crucified with him in baptism and raised with him into a new life, not merely personally but in terms of the corporate identity of God's people. And within this story, with these complexities, this historical story of Abraham–Torah–Messiah into which the Messiah's people are enfolded, the place of the law can finally be understood. I offer an expanded paraphrase to bring out the sense.

'Before faith came' – having spoken of 'faith' as he has done thus far, Paul can now use it as a synecdoche for the entire event of the Messiah, his faithful death, and the fact of a new community characterized by faith and faith alone rather than by ethnic markers – 'we', that is, the physical children of Abraham, 'were kept under guard by the Torah, shut up in prison against the day when this coming "faith" would be unveiled'. That last word, 'unveiled', translates *apokalyphthēnai*, from the root *apokalyptō*: this 'unveiling' is indeed an 'apocalypse', the parting of the heavens, the revelation of God's utterly shocking and surprising plan. But it was, none the less – and these verses make this abundantly clear – the surprise *which God had planned all along as part of his single-plan-through-Israel-for-the-world*. This was how it would work out! Torah had a purpose all right; it was indeed God's holy law; but its purpose was to keep Israel in check, to stop God's wayward people going totally off track, until the time when, through the Messiah, the long-term ultimate promises could be fulfilled. 'So, then, the Torah was our nanny, our babysitter, the slave hired to look after us while we were young and at risk, so that we might make it through to the coming of the Messiah, when God's people would be defined, justified, declared to be God's people indeed, on the basis of faith.' Paul is not saying, as traditional readings have had it, that 'the law was a hard taskmaster, driving us to despair of ever accomplishing its demands, so that we would be forced to flee to Christ and find an easier way, namely faith'. That is the large step back to an old caricature, well known but deeply inadequate, in which God has an initial plan about saving people (the law), but finds that nobody can make it that way, so devises an easier one (faith) instead.[13] That is not only bad theology, it is manifestly bad exegesis, not least of the present chapter in which the whole point is the single plan, the covenant promise to Abraham, and the strange but vital role of Torah within that.

But here now comes the point (v. 25): 'now that faith has come' (now, in other words, that God's new day has dawned, that the apocalypse has happened, that the Messiah's loving faithfulness to death (2.20) has delivered us from the present evil age (1.4) so that we are already living in the 'age to come' for which devout Jews had longed) – now that all this has happened, 'we are no longer under the rule of the babysitter'. In other words, Peter: you don't need to worry about those people who've come from James. They don't realize what time it is! They think it's still night-time, and you need the candles of Torah by which to see your way. They think you're still a young child who needs looking after, whereas you have grown up, you are now fully and completely a mature child of God. And you Galatians: the agitators who have been troubling you – they are wanting to drag you back into the night, to get you to light those candles, when the sun has risen and is pouring light all round the world. We are no longer under the rule of Torah: it belongs to the age of preparation, the strange pre-Messiah period when it seemed as though God's worldwide promises to Abraham were never going to be fulfilled.

All this is so (verse 26) 'because' (this is something of a climax at the moment, though in fact it is just the foundation for the larger, sustained, climax to the whole passage) 'you are all God's children (literally, 'sons'), through the faithfulness of the Messiah, Jesus'. God's children! One of the greatest Israel-titles of all, opening the list of privileges in Romans 9.4. Paul has glimpsed, in this paragraph, a theme which looked as though it was merely a metaphor – the young child under the rule of a babysitter – but which turns out to be a major biblical motif exactly suited to this point in his theological train of thought. 'Israel is my son, my firstborn; let my people go, that they may serve me'; that was one of the great watchwords of the exodus.[14] And the exodus itself was, massively, the fulfilment of the promise to Abraham, specifically the fulfilment of the promise made in Genesis 15, the chapter where God declared that he would count Abraham's faith in terms of 'righteousness'. *This is the meaning of the covenant,* the single-plan-through-Israel-for-the-world: Abraham's children will be enslaved for a long time, but God will set them free from that slavery, and the means by which he will do it is through the work of the faithful Israelite, through the death of the representative Messiah 'into whom' they are brought in that dying-and-rising moment of baptism, the equivalent of the Red Sea waters. 'You are all children of God through the faithfulness of the Messiah, Jesus, because as many of you as were baptized into the Messiah have clothed yourselves with the Messiah.' Like the 'I' of 2.19f., they have been crucified with him, going down into the water of death and escaping not only the old solidarity of sin but the old solidarity of human, ethnic ties with all the separation from other humans that they entailed. Resistance to the 'new perspective', though utterly understandable granted some of its expressions and some of the spiritual riches that looked for a moment as though they were being jettisoned, is always in danger of putting up resistance to the glorious plan of God *for the rescue of the entire human race* from its fractured, divided, Babel-like existence. 'There is no "Jew and Greek"!' – verse 28, bursting without any connective into the train of thought as the paragraph's sustained climax continues to build, is the initial 'QED' of the argument: this is the point! If you're in the Messiah, you've left behind those old ethnic solidarities along with every other aspect of the 'present evil age'! How can you, Peter, pay any attention to the men from Jerusalem? How can you, Galatians, allow yourselves to be seduced by the 'agitators'? How can you, 'old perspective' diehards, be seduced back into a romantic or existential individualism? *There is a single family,* because this is the whole point: the one God, the creator, always intended to call into being a single family for Abraham. The single plan through Israel for the world has turned out to be the single plan through *Israel's representative, the Messiah,* for the world *including Israel,* and all those who belong to the Messiah now form the one promised family. 'There is no "Jew or Greek"! What's more, there is no "slave or free"! There is even no "male and female"! *For you are all one in the Messiah, Jesus.'* Could it be that, at its lowest level, the 'old perspective' was always wary of this message because it had grown precisely out of a fissiparous Protestantism which was bound to see this challenge as a bridge too far?

Not, of course, that the 'old perspective' hadn't got its finger on something, wasn't in its way necessary as a proper and valid protest against human pride in achievement – and fear when that achievement fell short. But its own internal irony, claiming the scriptures as its sole authority but needing to misread them to force through its central point, has come home to roost, albeit through the oblique and frequently misleadingly stated so-called 'new perspective'. Of course sin matters! Of course salvation matters! Of course the centre of it all is that 'the Messiah died for our sins'! But the point that Paul is ramming home here, in Galatians 2 and 3, one of the very central passages on the whole theme of 'justification by faith', is that 'you are all one in the Messiah, Jesus; and, if you belong to the Messiah, then you are indeed Abraham's "seed", the single family, heirs according to the promise'. You are God's heirs, standing to inherit . . . the world; though Paul will wait until Romans 4 and 8 to develop that point. But if you are God's heirs, don't throw away that inheritance by crawling back under the rule of Torah, as if the cataclysmic, apocalyptic rescue-from-the-evil-age hadn't happened! And that is what you will be doing if you pay attention to the 'agitators' and allow yourselves to be circumcised. Perhaps this is part of the point in the 'no "male and female"' of 3.28: circumcision itself not only divides Jew from Greek, it also puts a wall between male and female, with only the male proudly bearing the covenant sign. It isn't like that in the gospel. Male and female alike believe in the faithful Messiah. Male and female alike are baptized, die and rise with and in the Messiah. Male and female belong side by side as equal members of the single family God promised to Abraham.

Where has this chapter left us in terms of the meaning of 'justification'? The swirling range of themes, whose deep inner coherence we have now explored in terms of the single, if complex and shocking, narrative of God's purposes, provides the setting where the explicit language of 'justification', of *dikaioō* and its cognates, mean what they mean. Actually, considering how important a role Galatians 3 has played within arguments about justification, it is striking that the *dikaios* root occurs comparatively infrequently: in verses 6 ('Abraham believed God, and it was reckoned to him unto/as *righteousness*'), 8 ('God would *justify* the Gentiles by faith'),

11 ('nobody is *justified* in the law, because the *righteous* lives by faith'), 21 ('if a law had been given which could make alive, then *righteousness* would have been by the law'), 24 ('the law was our babysitter, so that we might be *justified* by faith'). That is it: six occurrences in the entire chapter, and no further hint of the *dikaios* root until 5.4f. And the point needs to be made as forcibly as possible, precisely in terms of the exegetical and hermeneutical rule upon which John Piper has insisted: *we must understand Paul in terms of his own context and argument.* The context and argument of Galatians 3.1—4.11, like that of 2.11–21, is all about God's strange but single plan for the family of Abraham, now accomplished in the apocalyptic events of the faithful Messiah's death and resurrection, generating a single family who are characterized by faith, and who through baptism have left behind their old solidarities to discover their inheritance as Abraham's children, God's children.

Nor is this – as critics of the 'new perspective' have said ad nauseam, and I understand why – to replace soteriology with ecclesiology. Ecclesiology matters, of course, and it is impossible to read these chapters without being hit in the face by it. But it isn't an either/or. The whole point of the single-plan-through-Israel-for-the-world always was to deal with the sin and death that had infected humans and the whole creation. Paul takes that for granted throughout this passage, and you can't understand Galatians without likewise assuming it all the way through. The problem of human sin, and the divine answer in terms of the rescue provided by the Messiah, is the presupposition. It emerges gloriously at several points, notably 2.19f. and 3.22. But it is not the main argument. And, yes, you can expound Galatians in terms of its presuppositions about sin and salvation. 'New perspective' theoreticians no doubt need to be reminded of that. But if that is all you do you are being radically unfaithful to Paul's own text, missing the point he is so eager to make to the Galatians and – if you have a high view of scripture – to the church in every age, ours included.

So what can we say about 'justification' in this chapter? Let's take it step by step.

1 The promises God made to Abraham were a *covenant.* Genesis 15 says so, Paul says so (3.15, 17); that is the assumed starting point for the whole passage. The covenant always had in view *the*

liberation of the entire human race from the plight of Genesis 3—11, in other words, God's dealing with the problem of human sin and the consequent fracturing of human community (old perspective and new perspective, but both together Genesis-perspective and Paul-perspective!), which means that God's single purpose through the Abrahamic covenant was to rescue the human race from the present evil age. The calling into being of Abraham's family was always designed as the framework for that deliverance, and it has now been accomplished through the Messiah's faithfulness (as Israel's representative) to that divine plan, in his loving, self-giving, saving-from-sins death. Through that accomplishment, God is now creating a worldwide family where ethnic origin, social class and gender are irrelevant, and where each member receives the affirmation 'you are my beloved children', because that is what God says to his son, the Messiah, and because 'as many as were baptized into the Messiah have clothed themselves with the Messiah'.

2 This overall context compels us to understand Paul's uses of the *dikaios* root in terms of 'membership within God's family', as follows. Remember, throughout, that 'membership in God's eschatological people' *includes as its central element* the notion of having one's sins dealt with: 'family membership' is not *opposed to* 'forgiveness of sins', but is its proper and biblical context. Thus, verse 6: Abraham believed God, and it was reckoned to him as the badge of his membership in, indeed his foundation status within, the covenant family which God was creating. Verse 8: scripture foresaw that God would reckon Gentiles as members of this family, on the basis of faith. Verse 11: nobody receives the verdict 'family member' on the basis of the law, because 'the true family member lives by faith'. Verse 21: if a law had been given which could have made alive, then status within God's people would have been by law. Verse 24: the law was our babysitter up to the coming of the Messiah, so that, on the basis of faith, we might receive the verdict 'member of the family'.

3 Notice how I have introduced the language of 'verdict' into some of these paraphrases. This is to bring out the fact that, though covenant, eschatology and Christology are vital, the lawcourt has not been left behind. But it is not front and centre (as it is, much more obviously, in Romans 3). Paul is *assuming* that those who

have believed in the Messiah and have been baptized into him have thereby been set free from the guilt, penalty and power of 'the present evil age' and their own membership and behaviour within it. He is now, on the basis of that assumption, *arguing* that all those of whom this is true form a single family over which God has already pronounced the verdict 'righteous', 'my people', 'my children', 'seed of Abraham', 'heirs according to promise'. *That verdict, issued in those rich terms, is the fuller meaning of 'justification by faith'.* Take it back to the lawcourt if you want. If you need to know that God has accepted you freely, sinner as you are, because of the achievement of Jesus, so that you are no longer to be classified as 'a sinner' but as a rescued, liberated, adopted child, all that is there for the asking. But do not imagine that by repeating that wonderful, refreshing, liberating message you have even begun to understand the urgent message of Galatians 3. The church needs Galatians 3 as it is, not in the shrunken versions the Western traditions have been satisfied with.

4 To put it in formulae: *righteousness, dikaiosynē,* is the status of the covenant member. Its overtones are, of course, taken from the status that the defendant has after the court has found in his or her favour. *Justify, dikaioō,* is what God does when he declares this verdict. But the verdict of the court, declaring 'this person is in the right' and thus *making them 'righteous'* not in the sense of 'making them virtuous', infusing them with a moral quality called 'righteousness', but in the sense of creating for them the *status* of 'having-been-declared-in-the-right', is the implicit metaphor behind Paul's primary subject in this passage, which is God's action in declaring 'you are my children, members of the single Abrahamic family'. *Righteous, dikaios,* is the adjective which is properly predicated of the one in whose favour the court's announcement has been given, and which, within the covenantal, eschatological and Christological train of Paul's thought, refers to the one who is in good standing within the covenant, despite their background both moral, ethnic, social and cultural.

5 The basis for all this, in theology and eschatology, is the faithful, loving, self-giving death of the Messiah. This is the theological point of reading *pistis Christou* and its cognates in terms of the Messiah's own faithfulness; and this brings us as close as Galatians will let us come to what the Reformed tradition always wanted

to say through the language of 'imputed righteousness'. God always intended that his purposes would be accomplished through faithful Israel. That has now happened – but in the single person of Israel's faithful representative. But this does not mean that he has 'fulfilled the law' in the sense of obeying it perfectly and thus building up a 'treasury of merit' which can then be 'reckoned' to his people. That scheme, for all its venerable antecedents in my own tradition as well as John Piper's, always was an attempt to say something which Paul was saying, but in language and concepts which had still not shaken off the old idea that the law was, after all, given as a ladder of good works up which one might climb to impress God with one's own moral accomplishments. The closest Paul comes to saying anything like that is in 3.21, and he quickly declares it null and void. The law had its divine purpose, and that purpose was to shut up everything under sin. And, as Paul says in the fuller statement of the same point in Romans 7 and 8, drawing on Romans 5.19f., that is the point to which the Messiah came, and was faithfully obedient unto death, even the death of the cross. And that, in turn, is why the Messiah's death under the curse of the law (3.13) is much, much more than a simplistic exchange ('we were under the curse; he took it; we go free'), but rather the rich Pauline logic: God's promises to Abraham were stuck in the Deuteronomic curse, and could not go forward in history to their fulfilment; the Messiah came and bore the covenantal curse in himself, so that the new covenant blessings might flow out at last to the world – and, of course, to Israel as well. It will take all of Romans 10 to explain this more fully, but there should be no doubt that for Paul the Messiah's faithful death is the basis of everything that he says about justification, about the covenant family, about God's purposes for the world.[15]

III

Galatians 4 continues, as I have indicated, in the same train of thought. It does not, however, involve any mention of the *dikaios* root, and so need not detain us long. Justification by faith, as in Galatians 3, is part of the much larger thought-unit of the rescue of God's people and the whole world from the 'Egypt' of slavery, not only to sin and death but to the dark powers that stand behind them. The clear 'exodus' language of 4.1–7, echoed in Romans 8.12–17, is important not least because it is showing how the Abrahamic promises are fulfilled: Genesis 15, we remind ourselves again, spoke both of the coming exodus and of the 'inheritance' in terms of the land. Now, by overlaying that great story across the even greater one of the accomplishment of the Messiah, rescuing his people from the present evil age, Paul is able to say, simultaneously, (a) this is how the Abrahamic promises are fulfilled, how you become Abraham's heirs (3.29), and (b) this is therefore how you are rescued from sin and death.

To make this good, to tell the story of the 'Christian exodus', he reaches for the categories, not of justification by faith, but of what we call Trinity (4.1–7). This was the purpose of the father; this was the accomplishment of the son, sent from the father; this is worked out in you through the spirit of the son, sent likewise from the father. Just as, at the first exodus, the God who had made the covenant with Abraham now made his name and nature known in a whole new way (Exodus 3.13–15), so now, in this greater exodus, the same God reveals himself fully and finally as the God who sends the son and sends the spirit of the son. Justification by faith has a very precise role to play in Paul's theology, but it cannot and should not be made to do duty for the much larger picture of salvation which Paul himself offers. The ultimate charge he makes against the Galatians is not that they have not understood the finer points of 'imputation', but that they are in danger – having been rescued from the present evil age, having been brought into God's new day! – of turning back again to the rulers of the night. This is perhaps the fiercest thing he ever says about Torah: that because it was God's gift to Israel for the time of slavery, of the 'minority' of the young son who has now been brought to maturity (4.1f.), it functioned for Israel as the tutelary deities of the nations had functioned, to keep them in check prior to the coming full disclosure of God's purpose and nature. But now, with the living God having displayed himself in love and power and welcome, how can you turn back to anything that belongs to the period of slavery? You are treating Torah itself as an ethnic 'tutelary deity'! What can have happened to you?

Thus 4.8–11 functions, rhetorically, as the balance to 3.1–5: the highly charged appeal, the 'How can you possibly be doing such a

thing?', within which the more sober, step-by-step argument of
3.6–29, and its extension into 4.1–7, is located. This entire section
thus builds directly on 2.11–21, and of course prepares the way for
the rest of the letter . . .

. . . For which there is no space here, except for a brief glance at
5.1–6. Here, following on from the spectacular (and of course
difficult) allegory of Abraham, Sarah and Hagar (Paul is still trying
to make it clear that the ex-pagan Christians really are Abraham's
children), he issues a stark warning, rooted in 4.1–7. Like the
Israelites in the desert, you have a choice. Either go on to freedom,
and to your inheritance, or go back to slavery in Egypt. Coming
under Torah represents the latter choice, and if you take it you will
quickly find out: because to take Torah on yourself (5.3) means to
take the whole thing on board. Torah does not permit picking and
choosing. You will then find yourself in the situation where Paul
imagined himself, and by implication Peter, in 2.18: set up Torah
again, and it will say, 'You've broken me'. That is why he issues the
sharp warning in verse 4: if you want to be justified in the law, you
are cut off from the Messiah, and you have fallen away from grace.
Of course – because to embrace Torah as your badge of identity is
to say, 'I don't believe that the Messiah has broken through the
barrier, has rescued us from the present evil age, has died as the
faithful Israelite, rescuing people from their sins, and has thereby
transformed Abraham's family from a single ethnic identity into a
multi-ethnic family.' I don't believe it, *and I do not intend to live like
that.* 'Being cut off from the Messiah' is not merely a theological
category. It is something you can see going on when you sit down
and eat. Here are the Messiah's family, this motley crew, eating
together: Peter, Paul and Barnabas, mixed up with Gentile Christians
in Antioch; the Galatian Christians, mostly ex-pagans, prior to the
arrival of the 'agitators'. This is the Messiah's family. And if you
separate yourself from this family, you separate yourself from the
Messiah. That's what's going on.

The explanation Paul offers in verses 5 and 6 underlines this
with a look in a new direction, which is not explained elsewhere
in Galatians but which points ahead to other dimensions we shall
deal with in due course. 'For we, by the Spirit, eagerly await in faith
the hope of righteousness.' The *hope* of righteousness? Has he not
declared in chapters 2 and 3 that those who believe in the Messiah

already have 'righteousness', already hear the verdict in their favour, 'you are my children, my justified ones'? Yes; but Paul has not forgotten that this remains an *eschatological* reality, inaugurated indeed in the Messiah but awaiting its full consummation, and that there is still to come a moment when the secrets of all hearts will be revealed, when the verdict issued in the present will be reaffirmed at last. And the proper stance of the Christian in this interim period, this now-and-not-yet time, is to be one characterized by three things: the spirit, faith, and patient waiting. Thus it is in Romans 8.24f. Thus it is in 2 Corinthians 5.6–10. Paul's theology of 'justification', of the 'righteousness' which is ours in the Messiah and by faith, remains framed, as we shall see far more clearly in Romans, within his overall vision of God's single plan, yet to reach its ultimate denouement.

This in turn is finally explained in verse 6, where Paul points towards that understanding of the Christian life which he will likewise develop in many other places. The Christian looks *back* and celebrates the verdict already issued over faith: 'righteous', 'my child'. The Christian looks *forward* and waits, in faith and hope, for that verdict to be announced once more on the last day. And in between the Christian knows that he or she is not defined by ethnic membership, in Abraham's family or anywhere else, but precisely by the faith *which works through love*. And 'love' here is not simply standing for 'Christian ethics' in general. It is not simply the highest virtue, the surest sign of Christian character. It is the God-given, spirit-driven capacity to live within the new, multi-ethnic family, regarding as sisters and brothers all those who share Messiah-faith. 'Faith working through love': here are Pauline perspectives old and new and much, much more besides. In particular, here are perspectives that re-integrate, as both 'old' and 'new' found it hard to do, the forward look towards the coming day of judgment and the question of who, after all, will inherit God's kingdom, his sovereign rule over the 'inheritance' of the renewed creation (6.14f.): 'those who do such things will not inherit God's kingdom' (5.21), and 'everyone will have to bear his or her own burden' (6.5). How they will do that, and how the final verdict and inheritance will correspond to the present verdict issued on the basis of nothing but faith, will have to occupy us elsewhere. Paul gives at least as many unexplained throw-away hints in Galatians as he offers clear and full arguments. We need the other letters to pick up those hints and explain how they make sense.

There is much more in Galatians which would fill out this picture. In particular, we note the spectacular statement 'God forbid that I should boast, except in the cross of the Messiah, through whom the world is crucified to me and I to the world' (6.14). This wonderful anticipation of the 'no boasting' theme of 1 Corinthians 1.29–31, and particularly Romans 2.17–29, 3.27—4.1, must await treatment later on. But I have said enough, I hope, for the initial point to be made. In this, Paul's first introduction of 'justification', we have examined all the passages in which the relevant language occurs, have set it in its proper Pauline context, and have shown the deep coherence there of a theology of justification which includes all that the 'old perspective' was really trying to say within a larger framework which, while owing quite a bit to aspects of the 'new perspective', goes considerably beyond it. Perhaps Galatians itself is a sign that we should stop thinking in terms of 'perspectives' and start thinking in terms of Paul . . . Well, after working through a robustly polemical letter, why shouldn't we end with a deliberately question-begging and provocative summary?

6

Interlude: Philippians, Corinthians, Ephesians

I

We may be grateful that the other letters do not sustain the frantic, almost panic-stricken mood of Galatians. There are many other moods for Paul to explore. He never settles down in a comfortable armchair to ruminate at leisure. But he has broadened the angle of vision, settled into his stride, and opened up other, yes, perspectives. In particular, he does not have to contend in quite the same way with people who, he is convinced, have turned on its head the very message he taught them. Philippians is positively friendly, not only by comparison with Galatians but in every other way as well.

Philippians 3, the key passage for our present purposes, presents many puzzles which, fortunately, we do not have to worry about here. (For a start, Who are the implied opponents? What is the relation of 3.1 to the rest of the chapter, and the letter as a whole?) We should note, however, as many have done, the way in which the sequence of thought in 3.2–11 picks up, reflects and builds upon the great Christological poem of 2.6–11. It is as though, in the composition of the letter as well as in theology, Paul is determined not only to articulate but also to model the notion of 'being found in Christ' (3.9), being shaped by the Messiah, sharing his humiliation and death in order to share his resurrection and vindication. The structure of the letter, as well as its detailed content, is a clear pointer once more to the fact that, for Paul, 'justification' was something that happened 'in the Messiah'. The status the Christian possesses is possessed because of that belongingness, that incorporation. This is the great Pauline truth to which the sub-Pauline idea of 'the imputation of Christ's righteousness' is truly pointing.

But this is to run too quickly ahead. Our key task is to establish the fundamental flow of the key passage and to discuss the crucial and controversial elements within it. The basic point, directly in line with the dense and emotional statement in Galatians 2.19–20, is that *Paul has discovered in the Messiah the true-Israel identity to which his life under Torah had pointed but which it could not deliver, and he therefore warns the Philippians against being drawn in that false direction.* We shall take these in reverse order.

First, the warnings. 'Look out for the dogs, the evil workers, the "mutilation".' Most writers have agreed that these are highly polemical ways of referring to the kind of 'agitators' whom Paul confronted in Galatia. A case can be made out for a wider reference, with (for instance) 'dogs' referring quite naturally to the 'Cynic' philosophers, whose very name means 'dog', barking at the heels of the respectable. But verse 3 ('the circumcision? That's us!') indicates well enough that 'mutilation', at least, is a contemptuous reference to those who were insisting on circumcision, and whom Paul is designating as no better than those pagans who use body incisions as part of their religious rituals (as, for instance, in 1 Kings 18.28; Leviticus 19.28). Paul, breathtakingly, snatches the phrase 'the circumcision' away from ethnic Israel and claims it for those in the Messiah. The position of the definite article in the Greek indicates that 'the circumcision' is the subject, not the complement, of the sentence, so that the correct translation is not 'we are the circumcision', still less 'we are the true circumcision', but simply ' "the circumcision" is us!' This, by the way, is at the heart of the correct answer to those who suggest that I and others are guilty of imposing something called 'supercessionism' on Paul. If such critics would show that they had read Philippians 3.3, and for that matter Romans 2.25–29 where a very similar point is being made, they might deserve to be taken more seriously.[1] Paul, in other words, is setting out a picture of the believing-in-the-Messiah people as the new reality to which ethnic Israel pointed forwards but to which, outside the Messiah, they could not attain. This viewpoint never wavers throughout the whole paragraph, though of course it broadens to include all sorts of other points within it.

Notice the definition of the church in 3.3b: we are those 'who worship God in the spirit, who boast in the Messiah, Jesus, and who do not trust in the flesh'. That reads again like a summary of elements in Galatians, and for the same reason. But this time, in using his own story, as in Galatians 2.19f., as an index of the transition from Israel according to the flesh to what he now boldly calls 'the circumcision', he sets out much more fully what his former life looked like, in line once again with Galatians (this time at Galatians 1.13f.). 'I have', he says, '[reasons for] confidence in the flesh' (verse 4), indeed, more than anyone else you might think of. There follows the list of those reasons (verses 5, 6): eighth-day circumcision, ethnically an Israelite, from Benjamin's tribe (one of the two that remained after the collapse of the northern kingdom, and then returned after the geographical exile), 'a Hebrew of Hebrews', that is, tracing ancestry back to the earliest times of Israel's story. Then, more specifically, 'as to the law, a Pharisee; as to zeal, a church-persecutor; *as to righteousness within Torah, blameless.*' Ah; there's the rub. What on earth did he mean by that?

Let us first clear away the misunderstanding according to which some of this list designates Paul's 'salvation-historical' situation, while other bits designate his 'attitudinal' stance, quite outside that question of Israel-identity.[2] If there is a sense in which any or all of this is 'attitude' (what Greek word or phrase, I wonder, would that very modern expression render? How would Paul have put such a point, had he wanted to?), there is also a stronger sense in which the whole lot, the entire list, is at every point the self-description of the kind of Jew Paul had been. Yes, no doubt there was 'variegated nomism'. Jewish texts of the period are not parrot-fashion repetitions of one another. But the status which Saul of Tarsus had possessed, and which Paul the Apostle here describes in retrospect, was in every particular (he would have said) the gift of God. God had caused him to be born a Jew, a Benjaminite, to have devout parents who circumcised him on the correct day. God himself had given Israel the law – Paul the apostle was quite emphatic about that! – and the obvious and appropriate response was to keep it with as much care and devotion as one could, yes, even according to the strictest and most zealous Pharisaic interpretation (again, compare Galatians 1.13f.).

What, though, about 'righteousness within Torah', and the remarkable word 'blameless' (*amemptos*)? Does that not indicate Paul's pride in his own achievement, and thus an 'attitudinal' failing, the sort of 'self-righteousness' which the old perspective made its chief target? Well, yes and no. Yes: Paul's very way of telling the story indicates the humiliation of pride, a following in the Messiah-pattern sketched in 2.6–11, which would indicate that he is turning away from something which exalted him personally. Yes, too, in that of course, while Torah is given as a gift to mark out God's people, the distinction Paul is implicitly making is between himself, as someone who became *amemptos* in keeping it, and many Jews who either fell short or, frankly, couldn't be bothered to try. And part of the question of Paul and justification, of Paul's Christian view of (and critique of) his Jewish background, concerns the question: granted the status of 'belonging to God's people', how was that to be filled out? In Sanders's (not always helpful) terminology, having got in, how does one stay in?

Here we have stumbled upon one of the central misunderstandings in current debate, which – to say it again! – it will take all of Romans to help us unscramble. It is vital to distinguish two things: the *status* of God's people, prior to anything they do, and the *life they are called to lead*, which points forward to the eventual judgment. This is not a pre-Christian Jewish distinction which is then left behind in Christian theology. Paul the Christian offers exactly the same double-edged picture, even in the abbreviated form of Galatians: there is, on the one hand, the verdict that is already pronounced, and there is on the other hand, as in Galatians 5.5, the verdict that is still eagerly awaited. The question of the relationship between those two verdicts, and of the account that is given of the Christian life that moves from the first to the second, is important, but not in the present passage.

At first sight, the final phrase of verse 6 ('according to righteousness in the law, I became blameless') looks like a classic statement of 'covenantal nomism' (well, it would, wouldn't it, from a 'new perspective' point of view?). The keeping of the law was not a way of earning anything, of *gaining* a status before God; the status was already given in birth, ethnic roots, circumcision and the ancestral *possession* of Torah. All that Torah-obedience then does – it's a big 'all', but it is all – is to consolidate, to express what is already given, to inhabit appropriately the suit of clothes ('righteousness') that one has already inherited. The 'old perspective' reader will then want to come back and say, 'Yes, but that's the point at which Saul of Tarsus and those like him reckoned it was all up to them; they had to do it, they had to co-operate with God's grace, they were basically synergistic, they approached the final judgment with God's grace in one hand and a pile of their own good deeds in the other.' But at that point a beyond-both-perspectives reader should come back and say, 'A plague on both your houses! You are both failing to see both the parallel and the distinction, in this respect, between second-Temple Judaism and Pauline theology.'

A glance at 4QMMT may help here.[3] There remains quite a bit of confusion as to exactly what that text is saying and how it relates to Paul, but it is still the one place in all extant second-Temple literature where the phrase 'works of Torah' occurs, and in a context moreover where the writer is quoting Deuteronomy 30 and declaring that 'it will be reckoned to you as righteousness'. Put at its simplest, MMT is saying, (a) the covenantal exile is over, and God is at last inaugurating the new covenant; (b) you are members of God's renewed covenant people; but (c) you need to keep *these* regulations (not simply 'Torah' as in the Mosaic law, but these specific post-biblical regulations, interpreting Torah for the new situation), and (d) *this will demonstrate in the present time that you are the people who will be vindicated in the future, on the last day*. Thus (e) 'it will be reckoned to you as righteousness'. In other words, this is how to be 'blameless, according to "righteousness under Torah"'.[4] None of this alters the 'new perspective' way of looking at things. Everything that was being advocated could easily be subsumed under the category of 'response to God's grace', to God's acts in initial election and then in covenant renewal. But that is not quite the point. The 'old perspective' wants to know what account is given of this 'doing the works of Torah' which then follows. Is that, too, all of grace, or does some 'human merit' start to creep in after all?

MMT does not itself answer this question, and nor (by itself) does Philippians 3.6. But my urgent comment is: that's not the point! As I have argued at length elsewhere, MMT is offering a classic statement, admittedly within one particular sectarian framework, for what Paul the Christian referred to as 'justification by works of Torah'. The question is not, 'What must I do to get to heaven?', but *How can you tell in the present who will be vindicated in the future?* The answer of MMT – and, *mutatis mutandis*, of Saul the Pharisee – was, 'You can tell by the fact that they not only possess Torah (that is given in the election of Israel) but that they are doing their best to keep it, more specifically the "works" which mark out the true Israel from the rest, just as Torah in general marks out Israel as a whole from the Gentiles.' The (sectarian) code of MMT is designed to say, 'Do *these* particular "works of Torah", and they will mark you out in the present as the true covenant people.' The 'works' in question in MMT were not sabbath, food-laws, and circumcision; those were designed to mark out Israel from the nations, and were taken for granted at Qumran. Nor were they what we might call 'general moral good works'; these, too, are assumed. Rather, the particular and very specific codes in MMT include various aspects of ritual performance (the calendar, regulations about water, marriage laws, and so on), some of which were markers against Gentiles, but most of which were markers designed to demonstrate membership of the particular sect, the group that believed itself to be the inauguration of God's new covenant people. What the author is saying is: These 'works of Torah' will bring upon you God's 'reckoning of righteousness' here and now, and that verdict will be repeated 'on the last day'. The works in question will not *earn* their performers their membership within God's true, eschatological, covenant people; they will *demonstrate* that membership.

Is this 'ecclesiology' *as opposed to* 'soteriology'? Of course not. It is ecclesiology (membership in God's people) *as the advance sign of soteriology* (being saved on the last day). It is 'justification' in the present, anticipating the verdict of the future. God will declare on the last day that certain people are 'in the right', by raising them from the dead; and that verdict has been brought forward into the present, visibly and community-formingly. For MMT, as for the Pharisee, this happens through 'works of Torah' (though MMT and the Pharisees would have differed about which 'works' these were). For Paul the apostle, this happens 'through Messiah-faith'.

All this helps us to understand Philippians 3.6. Saul the Pharisee believed that God had given Israel the Torah as an act of grace towards his chosen covenant people. He believed, further, that the Pharisaic interpretation of Torah was the correct one. (I have argued elsewhere that Saul must have belonged to the 'strict' party within the Pharisees, i.e. that he was a follower of Shammai, not Hillel.) There is no evidence that any Pharisees thought, as the Qumran sect thought, that God had already inaugurated the renewal of the covenant, with them or with anyone else; but the logic of 'works' in MMT still applies. For Saul, the Pharisaic codification of Torah gave the indication of what Israel's God wanted from his people. He performed the 'works of Torah', attaining a standard that he had regarded as 'blameless'. No doubt this included regular repentance for unintentional sins, and regular offering of sacrifice; 'blameless under the law' is not the same as 'sinless', and the remarkable ascription of the latter to Jesus in 2 Corinthians 5.21 is not something we can imagine even Saul of Tarsus saying of himself. These 'works of Torah' were neither an attempt to earn the covenant membership he already had by God's grace, nor an attempt to add his own merit to the grace he had been given. They were an attempt, he would have said, to do, out of love and obedience to Israel's God, the works *which would function as a sign in the present that he was part of the people who would be vindicated in the future, on the last day, when God would act in his long-promised judgment and mercy*. That is what Paul the apostle referred to as 'justification by works'. That is what he had formerly believed in. And that is what he is now, in Philippians 3.7–11, going to undermine by offering the radical alternative that has pressed upon him, and upon the whole world, in Jesus Christ.

Rubbish! he shouts. (As, no doubt, do some of my critics, still hoping to convince me by their careful observations of the sunrise.) It's all worthless, and you can lose it all, because of something much greater which has now been given to us. Not that it's a contest between varying degrees of theological, moral or soteriological value; rather, the point is that the Messiah has now come, so 'the last day' has burst unexpectedly into the present time, like the owner coming back to reclaim the property he had rented out, and insisting on rearranging the furniture in his own way, to the dismay of the tenants who had made themselves quite cosy as they were. This inaugurated eschatology is the primary driver for Paul's redefinition of what it means to be God's people (which is what he is still talking about, rather than any abstract scheme of 'how people get saved' which ignores the Israel-dimension). If the end has come forward into the present – if the Messiah has arrived in the middle of history; if *resurrection itself* has happened in one case while death still appears to reign all around – then the *verdict of the last day is already known*, and the careful eschatological schemes by which various quite different groups of Jews had organized themselves, their lives and their soteriologies must be seen in a different light. All of that, as becomes clear towards the end of the single long sentence of 3.8–11, stands behind and informs what Paul says, the way he develops it, and the reason why it is important for him to say it like this at this point in the letter.

Thus 3.7 stands as a heading for the sudden, and typically Pauline, flurry that follows. 'Whatever gain I had, I thought it loss because of the Messiah.' Not 'because I discovered an easier way to heaven', or 'because I realized that I could stop worrying about my moral effort and simply trust God', but *because of the Messiah*, and the fact that in him history had turned inside out, the future had landed in the present, 'resurrection' had become a present and not merely future reality and, above all for the present argument, membership in God's people ('the circumcision', as in 3.3!) now had nothing to do with ethnic identity, and everything to do with identity as Messiah-people.

Again, I offer an expanded paraphrase of the long and complex sentence, to help keep the head clear and bring out the full force. This, remember, is the expansion of 3.7, and the explanation of why, despite the boast he had mounted in 3.4–6, 'we' – those in the Messiah! – 'are the circumcision'. 'Well,' he begins, 'but I have regarded everything as loss because of the surpassing worth of knowing the Messiah, Jesus my Lord.' Of *knowing* him: this is the first time in our survey that we have met this notion. It is of course popular to say that, since the language of 'righteousness' is essentially 'relational', 'justification' actually *means* 'the establishment of a personal relationship', a mutual knowing, between the believer and God, or the believer and Jesus. But this is extremely misleading (and made more so by all the loose talk in some Christian circles about 'my relationship with God' as the centre of everything, which then of course becomes problematic when one encounters depression, or enters a 'dark night of the soul'). This 'knowing' is, clearly, *correlated with* the status of 'righteousness' of which he will presently speak, but as so often with Pauline and indeed biblical adjacent technical terms, the two are not the same.

So he continues, repeating himself for emphasis: 'through him I have suffered the loss of all things, and reckon them as rubbish' (3.8) (*skybala*: students usually enjoy being told, which is the truth, that the best translation of this is 'shit' or 'crap', though the word can simply mean 'kitchen scraps' or 'garbage'). This shockingly strong negative language about Paul's Jewish privileges is the mirror-image of the equally strong and shocking positive language about 'the circumcision? That's us!' in 3.3. Political correctness here sometimes leads 'new perspective' exponents to soft-pedal the antithesis, but though the new perspective did indeed gain some early mileage from its perceived political acceptability, there is no reason for the exegete to draw back from telling it like Paul told it. Like the man in the parable who found the pearl of great price, Paul has sold all that he had to buy this one thing. 'It's all rubbish – so that I may gain the Messiah.' Again (here the parable doesn't quite go far enough), it's not a matter of weighing up comparative value and deciding, prudentially as it were, on the better investment. The Messiah has come, and everything else is irrelevant! The sun has risen, and it turns out that we are in its orbit, not the other way around. The conclusion is not 'so that he may be my saviour', but 'so that *I* may be found in *him*' (3.9a), discovering, in my incorporation into the-Messiah-and-his-people, that status, marking me out ahead of the judgment on the last day, which is a status of 'righteousness'.

Paul unpacks the meaning of this status in the four ways we have seen. It is a status of (a) having-the-court-find-in-my-favour-despite-my-unworthiness, (b) 'covenant membership', (c) advanced eschatological judgment (hearing, ahead of time, the verdict which will be announced at the end), and above all of (d) God's verdict on Jesus himself when he raised him from the dead and thereby demonstrated that he really was his son, the Messiah (Romans 1.4; cf. 1 Timothy 3.16). That, we may rightly suppose, is why the resurrection of Jesus Christ looms so large here, rather than his death – which remains at the centre of the gospel, of course, but as usual it is not necessary for Paul to say everything all the time. He highlights, as ever, the points he needs for his present argument.

'Not having a "righteousness" of my own, but that which is "through Messiah-faith"' (v. 9). This status of 'righteousness', Paul insists, is something he has 'in the Messiah'. 'Righteousness' here is not, despite a multitude of attempts to assert such a thing, the status which God himself possesses, and somehow grants or reckons or passes over to the believer. It is 'the righteousness *from* God' (the

Greek is *ek theou*); it is not God's own 'righteousness', but rather the status which is given by, or comes from, God. (The contrasting phrase, *dikaiosynē ek nomou*, hardly denotes a righteousness which the law itself possesses and which is imputed to the law-observant Jew!) Nor is it Christ's 'righteousness', but rather the status which is given through faith.[5] When Paul says, referring back of course to 3.6, that the status he now has is not 'a righteousness of my own, based on the law', he is indeed very close to the similar formulation in Romans 10.3, and is referring to the covenant status which he had had as a Jew, marked out by Torah and hence witnessed to by the keeping of that Torah. But in that passage, as we shall see later, he does not talk about a righteousness *ek theou*, but about God's own righteousness. These distinctions are important if we are to do exegesis rather than force half-understood concepts onto unwilling material.

Thus, Paul declares that he now has 'a righteous status from God', the status which God bestows. And – watch how neatly all this fits, once we understand the context and the exegesis accurately! – instead of Torah as the origin of this status (*dikaiosynē ek nomou*), the origin is God (*dikaiosynē ek theou*); instead of Torah as the marker in the present of this status, it is the faithful Messiah; instead of the works of Torah as the things in the present which demonstrate the already-given status, it is the faith of the believer. Paul now has 'the [righteousness which is] through the faithfulness of the Messiah, the righteousness from God which is [bestowed] upon faith'.[6] The Messiah is the agent (in his death, to which Paul can now refer in this formulaic way); the 'faith' of the beneficiaries, looking away from themselves and to his achievement, is the badge which shows that they are indeed 'in him'. That incorporation is the basis upon which they enjoy the other three elements of 'justification' in the present time: the lawcourt verdict, the covenantal declaration, and the inaugurated-eschatological pronouncement.

What does this mean in detail? And how does it relate to the future? The first word of verse 10, the genitive definite article (*tou*), indicates that what follows unpacks and explains what has just been said. And the primary thing that has just been said is not 'justified' – that is included and vital – but 'belonging to the Messiah': 'that I may know him and the power of his resurrection and the fellowship of his sufferings, becoming conformed to his death, if somehow I may attain to the resurrection of the dead' (vv. 10–11). There we have it. The Messiah's resurrection has inaugurated God's new age. Those who are 'found in him' already know him, they discover his dying and rising at work within them (2 Corinthians 4.7–18 is the obvious commentary on this), and they look forward, from the secure and presently held status of 'the righteousness which is through the Messiah's faithfulness and bestowed on faith', to the final day which can be seen, from one point of view, as 'the resurrection of the dead' (the ontological reality), from another as 'God's vindication of his people' (the covenantal reality), and from another as 'the final day of judgment when God's people will be declared "not guilty; no condemnation"' (the lawcourt reality). This is what Paul means when he says, in an advance shorthand, that 'the one who began a good work in you will complete it unto the day of the Messiah, Jesus' (1.6). And this is the context in which he can then go on to pray for the Philippians, that 'they may be blameless and innocent unto the day of the Messiah, filled with the fruit of righteousness which is through Jesus the Messiah, to the glory and praise of God' (1.10–11). This is the final destination, the outworking in actual holiness and then in final vindication, of the status which is already given, in the present and in advance, to faith and to nothing but faith.

It is highly significant that Paul immediately goes on in 3.12 to point out that he has not already arrived at this point, nor is he already 'made perfect'. Rather, 'I press on to make it my own, because the Messiah Jesus has made me his own' (3.12). This is closely cognate with 2.12f.: 'work out your own salvation with fear and trembling, because God is at work within you, to will and to work for his good pleasure'. And it is at this point, and only at this point, that we start to meet the question which will loom larger as we move forwards towards Romans: how did Paul think about, or describe theologically, what here appears to be straightforward moral effort in the time between initial justification and final judgment?

Clearly he is not talking about the security of justification by faith. That is given, solid, emphatic, unassailable. He is talking about the journey towards the final judgment, the ultimate resurrection. We know from hints here and there something of what he would say, if pressed on this point. 'I worked harder than any of them, yet it was not I but God's grace that was with me' (1 Corinthians 15.10). 'For this I toil, striving with all the energy that he mightily inspires within me' (Colossians 1.29). Or, more dramatically still perhaps, and back in Philippians: 'I can do all things – through the Messiah who gives me strength' (4.13). This sense of God's power at work within him should not be confined merely to vocational tasks; it includes moral holiness. Philippians 3.12–16 puts it on a larger canvas. From the secure base of justification, Paul sets out on a journey which, though its end is in fact secure, always *seems* like something that has to be struggled for, namely the resurrection itself. This demands forgetting what lies behind and straining forward for what lies ahead. It requires pressing on like a long-distance runner with a few miles still to go, tempted no doubt to drop out and rest but urging himself to carry on to the finish line. Somehow, Paul had no difficulty in integrating all this into his theology, and it seems quite clear how he did it: at every point, he says, it is Christ working in me; it is God's grace which is with me; it is God energizing me to will what is good and to do it – and it is God who is pleased with the result. (In other letters he might well mention the spirit at this point, and it is pointless to speculate why he does not do so here in Philippians.) If we, particularly those of us who have been strongly influenced by the Reformation, perceive such language as casting a shadow of doubt over 'justification by faith', the problem is not with this way of putting it – it is after all Paul himself who puts it like this! – but with our traditions. Yes, even our finely motivated pastoral traditions. Paul describes a rich, complex Christian reality, and even the most venerable traditions are capable of forcing the jigsaw of what he says into composite patterns that do not do justice either to the pieces themselves or to the larger picture they are supposed to form.

II

The Corinthian correspondence is a standing reminder, in case any one should suppose that Paul was a one-string fiddle, that he was quite capable of writing at length, with passion, wit and pathos, on a wide range of subjects which (though everything is ultimately interconnected) have little to do with justification by faith. The same point could be made, of course, with reference to the Thessalonian correspondence and Colossians, but the Corinthian letters are so big, so dense, so sprawling, so many-sided, that the omission cannot easily be ignored.

There are just two passages, one in each letter, which must be included for the sake of completeness. The first is a brief flash and exegetically underdetermined; it could mean a variety of things in relation to our present topic, and nothing much hinges on it. The second is equally brief, but (now) highly controversial, and I want to defend the interpretation of it that I have advanced elsewhere, and which has pulled down all kinds of scorn on my head.

One of the leading themes in 1 Corinthians is the contrast between the wisdom of the world and the wisdom of the true creator God, as seen in the high and shocking paradox of the crucified Messiah. This theme, though it informs a good deal of the letter, is set out initially in 1.18—2.5, where 'the word of the cross is folly to those who are perishing, but to us who are being saved it is the power of God'. We note, ahead of our discussion of the parallel, that the idea of something being 'the power of God to salvation' is also made thematic for a letter in Romans (1.16), and that there Paul explains what he means with reference to 'God's righteousness'. Here, however, he explains himself with a different train of thought, by means of a quotation from Isaiah 29.14: I will destroy the wisdom of the wise, and the cleverness of the clever I will thwart.

As usual with Paul, the whole chapter from which he quotes is relevant. Isaiah 29 speaks of God's people surrounded by pagan nations upon whom there falls stupor and slumber, so that God ends up vindicating his people against all those around. This is the picture conjured up in what now follows. The crucified Messiah announced in the gospel tells the Jews that their history has turned inside out, and it tells the pagans that their wisdom is turned to folly. But (as in verse 24, which repeats and expands verse 18) it declares that to those who are called, both Jews and Greeks, the Messiah is God's power and God's wisdom. We note that one can easily imagine a Pauline letter without a mention of justification, but hardly a Pauline letter without a mention of the Messiah.

Paul then applies this to his readers in particular. Most of them were not high up in the world's systems of social and cultural standing. That is because the whole point of the gospel is to put the world – not upside down, because that is where it already is, but the right way up. 'God chose the foolish things of the world to shame the wise, the weak things to shame the strong, and the low and despised things of the world – the non-existent things! – to bring to nothing the things that do exist, so that no human being might boast before God.' Ah: there we have an echo of a theme well known in Romans in particular, already glimpsed in Galatians 6.14: the 'boasting' of social pride and status, a feature of what Paul knew from his own Jewish past which he sees, it now appears, as a reflection of standard pagan self-evaluation. He is talking, then, about status, about discovering all the status you need through the gospel of the cross, about receiving that status as a gift from God in Christ, and about standing firm in it – even 'boasting' in it, paradoxical as that will be – rather than looking for anything that the world and its status-systems might provide.

All this is exactly summed up, though confusingly to later theology because of the sudden rush of previously unannounced theological technical terms, in 1.30. Literally it reads, 'From him are you in Messiah Jesus, who became wisdom for us from God, yes, righteousness and sanctification and redemption.' As frequently in 2 Corinthians (and occasionally elsewhere in this letter too, e.g. 3.21–3), Paul describes the status and (so to speak) the theological location of Christians in terms of the act of God and the fact of the Messiah: 'From God, in the Messiah'. All of grace, by free gift; all in Christ, 'in whom are hid all the treasures of wisdom and knowledge' (Colossians 2.3). What are these treasures?

First and foremost, wisdom, setting the context for the others. But what does it mean that 'he became wisdom for us'? Certainly, that any actual wisdom we need may be had (as James 1.5 promises) by putting in a request to the God we know in Jesus. But there is more. Near the heart of Paul's view of Jesus is the sense, easy to spot but hard to analyse, that like many Jews of his day he saw 'God's wisdom' as a quasi-independent power, as in Proverbs 1—9, Ben-Sira 24 and the Wisdom of Solomon, going out to create a beautiful world, to enable humans to be genuinely and gloriously human, and to live, in particular, in Israel, in the Temple, in and through the Torah (Ben-Sira is particularly clear on this). Unlike other Jews of his day, however, Paul, with this theology in his head and heart, took a flying leap into a view of Jesus, his identity, his mission from the father, and his role in the new creation. This enabled him to draw freely on 'wisdom' ideas, relocating them in and around Jesus, and to invite those who belonged to Jesus to discover in him the personal presence of the Divine Wisdom, God's second self, doing at last what Temple, Torah and 'Wisdom' might have been supposed to do but what they had not succeeded in doing. When Paul looks out at the pagan world with its much-vaunted 'wisdom' of various sorts, leading people to puff themselves up and give themselves airs (a favourite theme in 1 Corinthians), he looks at the creator God who has unveiled in Jesus the Messiah his wisdom-in-person, the one through whom the worlds were made (1 Corinthians 8.6), the one in whom believers are therefore to discover in every possible way what it means to be genuinely human. That, indeed, is the foundation for everything else that follows in the letter.

It is in that context that Paul adds the other three terms, 'righteousness', 'sanctification' and 'redemption', without advance warning or subsequent explanation. In the light of all we know about them from elsewhere in his writings, we can say this much about them. 'Righteousness' is the status of all believers, in the various senses we have described it already; 'sanctification' is in one sense their *status* as God's holy people, but is also, and more particularly, their *actual life* of holiness through the power of God working in them by the spirit; 'redemption' is a rather different thing, neither a status that Christians possess nor an element of the life that they live, but the accomplishment of God on their behalf, the great new exodus through which they have been set free from the slavery of sin (compare Romans 3.24: 'the redemption which is in the Messiah, Jesus').

The fact that the three nouns not only carry different meanings but are also different sorts of things – broadly, a status, a process and an event – indicates that Paul is not here trying to make a precise theological statement about what exactly it means that the Messiah has 'become for them' any of these things, or how each of them relates to the primary attribute, 'wisdom'. Nevertheless, there is no problem, granted what we have already seen in Galatians and Philippians, about saying with confidence that here, as there, 'righteousness' is something that believers have because they are 'in Christ' – though it is quite illegitimate to seize on that and say that therefore they have something called 'the righteousness of Christ' imputed to them, in the full sixteenth- and seventeenth-century sense so emphasized by John Piper. There is, as we have already glimpsed, a great truth underneath that Reformation claim, and I shall try to expound it in due course. But we cannot press this verse into service as a primary vehicle of it, not least because, were we to do so, we should also have to speak, presumably, of 'imputed wisdom', 'imputed sanctification' and 'imputed redemption'. For the moment, the point can be put thus, giving attention to the four different *kinds* of things being predicated of Jesus, and, in him, of Christians.

1 He is God's wisdom incarnate: that is primary, and that means that the way to become a wise human being is not to follow the world's fashions, but to live in him so to discover genuine human existence.

2 He has become for us 'righteousness': that is, God vindicated him, like a judge in a lawcourt finding in favour of one who had previously appeared condemned, when he raised him from the dead. God vindicated him as his own son, the Israel-in-person, the Messiah, anticipating at Easter the final vindication of all God's people in their resurrection from the dead. Those who are 'in Christ' share this status, being vindicated already in advance of that final vindication. (In other words, it is not the case that Paul is suggesting here that Jesus Christ has perfectly obeyed the moral law and thus possesses in himself 'moral righteousness' – that would be to change the meaning of the word entirely at this point – which can then be 'credited' to those who are 'in him'. Jesus was not a legalist! That was not why God gave the law in the first place.)

3 He has become 'sanctification': at a guess, based on several other passages, Paul means by this that God has put to death all that is 'fleshly' in him, and has raised him up in a new body which sin and death cannot touch, so that those who are 'in him' now possess, as a reality and a possibility, the putting-to-death of sin and the coming-alive-to-God which plays such a strong role later in the letter, not least in chapter 6.

4 Finally, he has become 'redemption' for us: that is, in him God has accomplished the great new exodus, the crossing of the Red Sea of death, leaving behind the hordes of Pharaoh who had

enslaved God's people, so that those who are 'in Christ' are now the people already rescued from that slavery (see Colossians 1.12–14). In all these ways, which overlap and interlock at many different levels, God has provided in Jesus the Messiah everything that his people need. They do not need to compete with the world around them for status or prestige. They can boast in the Lord, knowing that in him they are complete (Colossians 2.9f.).

In other words: a wonderful summary of a great deal of Paul's theology – but not a ringing endorsement of the Reformed doctrine of 'imputed righteousness'.

III

The brevity of the reference to 'righteousness' in 1 Corinthians 1 does not, then, allow us to draw absolutely hard and fast conclusions. But many – almost all – exegetes have supposed that we can do just that from the other Corinthian reference, 2 Corinthians 5.21: 'Him who knew no sin, on our behalf God made him sin, so that in him we might become the righteousness of God.' There you have it, exclaim everyone from Luther to John Piper: the wondrous exchange! He takes our sin, we take his righteousness. The righteousness of Christ is imputed to us, just as our sin was imputed to him when he died on the cross. What could be more straightforward?

Part of me recoils from having to question this traditional reading of the text. This is not just nervousness at spitting in the strong wind of a powerful and (I have to say) appealing tradition. Because I can see a great truth underneath the claim that is being made, the truth which anchors Christians in the love of God rather than anything in themselves, I am loth to say that I disagree with this reading of the text. But the double rule of good exegesis drives me on. First, we must pay attention to the text against all our traditions, however venerable their provenance and however pastorally helpful we find them. Second, if we do not do this, but rather (even unwittingly) allow our traditions to force us to read the text in a way which it does not in fact support, that means that there is something the text really does want to tell us which we are muzzling, denying, not allowing to come out. And in this case I think that is precisely what is going on.

Once again, the important thing is to read what Paul says exactly in context. Anyone who is tempted at this point to skip a few pages and cut straight to the 'answer' is warned against such folly – in this book, or indeed in 2 Corinthians. The crashing chord we call 2 Corinthians 5.21 comes at the end of *this* symphony, not another one, and it means what it means there and nothing else. You will only understand it when you listen to the whole tune and see the harmonic and rhythmic build-up.

Watch what happens when we do. For a start, we recognize that the entire section of 2.14–6.13 is a long apologia for Paul's apostleship. True, it takes in many twists and turns. But Paul has been challenged by the super-apostles who have muscled their way into the Corinthian church and persuaded many believers that he is not really up to the job, not really the kind of apostle they ought to acknowledge. If he wants to come back to Corinth, he's going to need letters of recommendation from someone (3.1). They are goading him: he needs to commend himself (3.1; 4.2; 5.12; 6.4; cf. 10.12, 18), and so he will, but it will be a self-commendation of an extremely paradoxical sort. He will insist that he, and the other apostles, are completely insufficient for the tasks laid upon them, the tasks not merely to tell people about Jesus but to embody the gospel in their own lives, their own sufferings, their own paradoxical triumphs (2.14–17). Who indeed is sufficient for these things (2.16)? (Again: anyone reading this who is thinking, 'What has this to do with chapter 5 verse 21?' is urged to stick with the argument and think it through.)

Paul answers his own question in various ways. Our 'sufficiency' is from God (3.5f.): God has 'made us sufficient' to be 'ministers of the new covenant, not in the letter but in the Spirit'. And he writes another dozen verses to explain, in great detail, what he means by that. We do not proclaim ourselves, he says in the next chapter (4.5), but Jesus the Messiah as Lord, and ourselves simply as your servants through Jesus. *This entire section is about Paul's servant-ministry, and the way it works out in practice*: the apostles are to be 'the smell of the Messiah' (2.15), and the light that shines in their hearts has done so in order that, when other people see them, they may see that light shining (4.6).

What will this look like? Not at all what the Corinthians want or imagine (assuming, with most commentators, that the problem, loosely speaking at least, was to do with Paul's shabby and unprepossessing outward character over against the more flashy super-apostles). 'Servants through Jesus' will mean suffering all kinds of things as the message goes out, because that will mean 'carrying about in the body the death of Jesus, so that the life of Jesus may also be revealed in our mortal body' (4.10), knowing that this embodiment of the dying and rising of Jesus, this fresh apostolic incarnation of the Messiah, is actually itself *part of the revelation of the gospel*, part of the way the good news gets out and about and goes to work in the world. All this is then set (because otherwise one might wonder how an apostle, faced with this awful vocation, could bear to continue) within the larger eschatological framework which Paul everywhere assumes and only occasionally spells out. Present life is lived in the light of the coming fact of resurrection, which itself is set in the context of the coming great day of judgment (5.10). Then everyone, not least apostles themselves, must stand before the Messiah's judgment-seat, so that each 'may receive what has been done through the body, whether good or bad'.

Any sense that this does not apply to Paul himself, or that he is in any way complacent or cocky when faced with such a prospect, is immediately dispelled by 5.11. It is because we know the fear of the Lord that we persuade people. Here he draws together the threads of his argument so far. To say it again: it is about his apostleship; his apostleship as the embodiment of the gospel he preaches; his apostleship as the whole-person activity of persuading people. We want you, he says to the Corinthians, to see just who we really are, open to God, open to you. Indeed, we want you to be proud of us for the right reasons, as opposed to being ashamed of us for the wrong ones (5.12). We apostles are, after all, people controlled by the love of the Messiah; *he died for all, so that those who live should live not for their sakes but for his sake who died for them and rose again* (5.14f.) – a direct allusion once more to the 'gospel message' of 1 Corinthians 15.3f., and a direct mapping of his own ministry on to that of the gospel. Paul is not just someone who tells people about the gospel; he is someone who embodies it.

Paul has hereby staked out the ground for the argument he will now develop. Remember, he is talking primarily about his own ministry, and trying to explain to the Corinthians that the very features of his life of which they have been persuaded to be ashamed are actually the features of which they should be proud. He now develops a two-step statement of this, starting here in verse 15:

a. Christ died for all;
b. we live for him, who died and was raised.

– (a) a statement of the death of Jesus, followed by (b) a statement of the ministry which results. This is the pattern of several two-pronged statements that follow, of which 5.21 is the climax.

Verses 16–21 then follow with an exalted, celebratory statement of the way in which the whole world has changed, so that all human evaluations, particularly of other humans and also, even, of the Messiah himself, need to be stood on their heads. Don't judge me by the ordinary human standards, he is saying; what is going on here, in the Messiah, is nothing short of new creation (5.17), and that's the light in which you have to think about everybody and everything. So here (5.18) comes the second two-step statement, enfolded in the larger comment (so frequent in 2 Corinthians) that 'all this is from God':

a. God reconciled us to himself in the Messiah;
b. God entrusted to us the ministry of reconciliation.

Again, a statement of the effect of Jesus' messianic death, followed by a statement of 'the ministry' which the apostles have received from God as a result. (This is only what we should expect, granted that the whole passage from 2.14 to 6.13 is all about this very same thing.) This is immediately (5.19) expanded, in typical Pauline fashion, into a third, fuller version of the same thing:

a. God was in the Messiah, reconciling the world to himself, not counting their trespasses against them;
b. [God was in the Messiah, doing all this and] entrusting to us the word of reconciliation.

– once more, a double statement: (a) the cross as God's act of reconciliation and forgiveness; (b) the apostolic ministry through which that act is put into effect.

Verse 20 is routinely misunderstood because it is routinely mistranslated. Those who do not follow carefully what Paul has actually been talking about are sometimes so dazzled by the high rhetoric and the complex and compelling theological themes that they have forgotten that Paul is still *describing the ministry which he holds from God*. He is not, now, addressing the Corinthians themselves, as though to say 'this applies to you; you, too, need to be reconciled to God'. That is an evangelistic message. Although, God knows, the Corinthians were an extremely muddled lot, they had already responded to the gospel, had come to be in Christ, had received reconciliation, had had the spirit at work in their hearts. Otherwise Paul could not have written chapter 3. So it makes no sense to import the little word 'you' into verse 20, where it occurs in no Greek text. Paul is not appealing to *the Corinthian Christians* to be reconciled. He will shortly appeal to them (6.1) to make proper use of the grace they have already received, but 5.20 is not an appeal. It is a *description* of what Paul characteristically does, an explanation of how the thrice-repeated two-pronged formula works out ((a) the Messiah died for us, (b) we have this ministry). As in 5.11, where he says simply 'we persuade people', so in 5.20 he says 'we make our appeal'. Watch, he says to the Corinthians: this is how I spend my time. This is what I get up in the morning to do. I appeal to people, *on behalf of the Messiah*, 'be reconciled to God'. That's what I go about telling people. And, as a result, I am in the position of a royal ambassador, a plenipotentiary, one in whom, when people look at me, they see the King whose message I bring; one from whom, when they listen to me, they hear the word of the King; one in whom, in other words, when I am present and doing my job, they are confronted not only with the King but also with the God whose son he is, the God who was 'in the Messiah reconciling the world to himself', the God from who all this comes (5.18), the God who is now 'making his appeal through us'.

How should he summarize all this? How better than in the way that he has? A fourth, climactic, breathtaking two-pronged statement of the Messiah's death on the one hand and his own ministry as God's plenipotentiary, the Messiah's loyal ambassador, the one in whose life, heart and body the faithfulness of God – that is, the death and resurrection of the Messiah – had come to dwell in order that through him the church and the world might smell the Messiah's smell (2 Corinthians 2.16), see the Messiah's glory, hear the Messiah's message. Thus, one last time, a statement of the death of Jesus followed by a statement of the apostolic ministry:

a. The one who knew no sin, God made sin for us;
b. so that in him we might become the righteousness of God.

– in other words, that, in the Messiah, we might *embody God's faithfulness, God's covenant faithfulness, God's action in reconciling the world to himself.*

Yes, I know. This is not the way the great tradition has read this verse. And not everyone will be convinced by the argument I have now used, which is that 5.21 forms the climax of a three-chapter build-up of sustained exposition of the nature of apostleship as the embodiment of the gospel, the gospel of God's faithfulness in the Messiah, and also the climax of a thrice-repeated sequence of just such a double statement about the Messiah's death on the one hand and the apostolic ministry on the other. Before continuing with other arguments, I do want to ask anyone in that position whether they are rejecting this argument because they find it unconvincing (Why should Paul mount such a careful argument? Why shouldn't he just toss words around and let them fall in neat soundbites unrelated to the subtle and sustained line of thought he has been following?) or because they are sorry to see a favourite text snatched from their grasp, to be replaced merely (!) by a text about the wonderful but paradoxical nature of apostleship. Who needs that, after all? Nobody wants to hear sermons about apostleship.

Well, perhaps they should. Perhaps it has been a problem in the Western church since long before the Reformation that its leaders have not paid sufficient attention to the deeply subversive theology of Christian ministry which is the backbone of 2 Corinthians. And yes, I speak with feeling, as myself heir to part of that ambiguous tradition (and, at the time of revising this chapter, present at a Lambeth Conference where precisely these questions are coming into worryingly sharp focus). But let us proceed. What other signs are there of the reading I am proposing?

First, the meaning of 'the righteousness of God' itself. Clearly this has to wait until we have got our teeth into Romans, or perhaps allowed that great bear of a letter to get its teeth into us. But, anticipating the later argument – though building on the one we offered in chapter 3 above – we can say with extremely solid assurance that 'God's righteousness', in Paul as in the Psalms and Isaiah, regularly refers to God's own righteousness, not in the mediaeval senses which *iustitia Dei* generated, but in the Old Testament and intertestamental sense of 'the covenant faithfulness of God, through and because of which God is faithful to the promises to Abraham, the promises through which the single-plan-through-Israel-for-the-world can come into operation, the promises through which, ultimately, all creation will be set right'. 'Righteousness' carries the overtones both of 'justice' – the creator's passion to put things right – and of 'faithfulness' – YHWH's faithfulness to the covenant which he established so that through it he might indeed put all things right. That 'righteousness', in Romans, is what is revealed in the gospel (1.16), unveiled in the events concerning Jesus (3.21), ignored by Israel (10.2) but active none the less in creating, in Christ and by the spirit, the promised worldwide family (3.21—4.25) and, out beyond that, in renewing the whole creation (8.18–26). That is 'the righteousness of God'.

2 Corinthians 5.21 is, in fact, the climax of a long argument in which Paul has set out how it is that God has renewed the covenant in Jesus the Messiah, making him, Paul, a minister of that new covenant (3.6–18),[7] and thereby a minister of the new creation (5.17), while doing so through putting Paul in the uncomfortable but gospel-revealing position of re-embodying the Messiah's dying and rising, the very events which in Romans 3 Paul declares to be the revelation of God's righteousness. How, one might ask, can 2 Corinthians 5.21 mean anything else than just that?

But there is more. The little word *genōmetha* in 5.21b – 'that we might *become* God's righteousness in him' – does not sit comfortably with the normal interpretation, according to which 'God's righteousness' is 'imputed' or 'reckoned' to believers. If that was what Paul meant, with the overtones of 'extraneous righteousness' that normally come with that theory, the one thing he ought not to have said is that we 'become' that righteousness. Surely this leans far too much towards a Roman Catholic notion of *infused* righteousness? How careless of Paul to leave the door open to such a notion! But if Paul means 'so that we apostles embody in our own lives the fact that, in Christ, the God of the covenant has been faithful to his single-plan-through-Israel-for-the-world', is this not an exact and accurate way of saying just this?[8]

All this is further supported by the way in which, throughout these chapters and indeed throughout 2 Corinthians, in a way unique among Paul's letters, we find again and again that Paul is talking about what God is doing in Christ and thereby in and through the apostle and his work. We may cite, for instance, 1.18–22, of which the following is a fairly literal translation:

> God is faithful: our word towards you was not 'yes' and 'no'. For the son of God, Jesus the Messiah, who is preached among you through us, that is, through myself and Silvanus and Timothy, has not become 'yes' and 'no', but in him it has always become 'yes'. For all the promises of God are 'yes' in him; that is why, through him, we speak the 'Amen' to God, for his glory, through us. [The strange and convoluted Greek here, flattened out in many translations, should be noted as making precisely my point.] The one who confirms us with you unto the Messiah, and anoints us, is God, who also sealed us, and gave us the pledge of the Spirit in our hearts.

This kind of thing is repeated throughout the letter. It is as though Paul cannot get tired of saying it: if you want to know who we are, we are people in whom God is at work, because of and according to the pattern of the Messiah, for the benefit of you and of the wider world. How might we expect Paul to summarize all this? What about this: 'In him we embody the covenant-faithfulness of God.'

There are two further important arguments as well. Chapter 6 opens with an appeal to the Corinthians to see where they are in the divine timetable, to recognize that this is the day of grace, the day when God's promises are fulfilled, the day when the world is turned the right way up – the day, in other words, when they should expect everything to be different. The appeal opens, reflecting exactly the end of chapter 5 as we have understood it: 'working together, then' – in other words, 'working together with God'. God is appealing 'through us' (5.20); he is at work within us, enabling us to *become*, to embody, his covenant faithfulness, so that we are his fellow-workers. (We note in passing that, though of course Paul has said plenty about the meaning of Jesus' death in 5.11–20, that has not been his main theme, but rather the key to understanding the thing which *is* his main theme, namely his apostolic ministry. That being the case, it would be strange if, as the obvious rhetorical climax to the chapter, he came out with as it were a detached statement of what we might call atonement-theology, such as would be the case on the traditional reading. Had that been so, he might have had to open up chapter 6 in a different way, to get back to his main theme. As it is, the flow is perfect.)

But there is one more point. In 6.2 he appeals to the Corinthians not to 'receive God's grace in vain'; in other words, not to sit there as recipients of the grace of God in the gospel while denying its real power to turn the world the right way up through Jesus' death and resurrection. He does so with a quotation from Isaiah 49.8: 'I heard you at an acceptable time; I helped you on the day of salvation.' He stops the quotation there, because his rhetorical punch derives directly from it: *now* is the acceptable time, *now* is the day of salvation. But had he gone on – and, as we have seen, one of the great gains of Pauline research in recent years has been the awareness that Paul has larger segments of scripture in mind than he quotes at any one time – we would have found the following:

> Thus says YHWH:
> In a time of favour I have answered you;
> On a day of salvation I have helped you.
> I have kept you and given you
> *as a covenant to the people,*
> to establish the land,
> to apportion the desolate heritages;
> saying to the prisoners, 'Come out,'
> to those in darkness, 'Show yourselves.'
> (Isaiah 49.8f.)

Yes: Paul is referring to the so-called 'second servant song', locating himself and his ministry within that great prophetic word of light for the nations. Hardly surprising: the servant songs speak again and again of the paradox of being God's mouthpiece, of facing despair and frustration (49.4) and yet continuing to speak God's word to a wider audience, knowing that 'YHWH has comforted his people, and will have compassion on his suffering ones' (49.13). And here, in the middle of the passage, Paul quotes a line whose immediate sequel, if I am right, simply repeats the exact meaning of 2

Corinthians 5.21b: *I have given you as a covenant to the people.* Or, in Paul's language, 'That we might, in him, become the righteousness of God'. There is the pain, and there is the glory, of the apostolic ministry to which Paul is called, as are all who announce the crucified and risen Messiah.

IV

Ephesians is not, of course, considered kosher by many Pauline scholars. As we noted before, it is often held at arm's length, reckoned as 'deutero-Pauline', a representative of 'early Catholicism', or, in one remarkable piece of non-insight, 'a fading vision'. On the contrary: this is one of the most visionary texts ever written, and part of that vision is the clear-eyed description of the apostolic ministry in its many-sided significance, holding together and expounding at length themes which many of Paul's interpreters have been eager to hold apart and expound over against one another. Thus, whether it be by Paul or someone writing in his name does not particularly concern me at the moment (though my instincts and judgment, like those of my teacher George Caird, incline in the former direction). Even if this text is secondary, it was written by someone who knew Paul's mind very well and stood close to him in many important respects.

And it is of course in Ephesians that the two 'halves' of Pauline gospel emphasis are laid out side by side. Ephesians 2.1–10 is the 'old perspective': sinners saved by grace through faith. Ephesians 2.11–22 is the 'new perspective': Jews and Gentiles coming together in Christ. Does this mean that they are after all two different things, only joined together by a 'therefore' which could mean that one is primary, the other secondary?

By no means. The larger context of the letter shows that they belong intimately together. The great opening prayer of thanksgiving (1.3–14), praising the father for what he has done in the son and the spirit, sets out the redemption which is the main feature of the good news, and then already applies it to the two groups, Jewish and Gentile Christian, who have come together in Christ. 'In him we were called . . . we who had first hoped in the Messiah; and in him you too, having heard the word of truth and having believed, were sealed with the Spirit.' 'We' and 'you', Jew and Gentile, coming together, and all to the praise of God's glory. Nor is this incipient ecclesiology merely a pleasing decoration, a side-comment on what a fine thing the gospel is. Paul's prayer in 1.15–23, for the church in the areas to which this (probably circular) letter will go, is that God will enlighten the whole church in mind and heart, to understand what it is that has been accomplished in Christ in and for them, and through them for the world. The church is the Messiah's body, 'the fullness of the one who fills heaven and earth' (1.23). This is the *united* church, not as an optional extra when the work of redemption has been celebrated, but as itself *part of the reality of the gospel*, the way in which God is taking forward his plan for the whole cosmos. The reunion of the scattered fragments of humanity in the Messiah is the sign to the world that here we have nothing short of new creation. Ecclesiology – so often scoffed at by those who see it as merely 'horizontal' rather than the really important thing, the 'vertical' dimension of soteriology – is non-negotiable. In Christ there is no vertical and horizontal. Paul was not a Platonist. 'God has put all things under his feet' (1.22, quoting a favourite Pauline text, Psalm 8.7), and ecclesiology – the fact of the church and the true understanding of its life – is the immediate result.

This brings Paul (let us call the author that for the sake of the argument, even if it was in fact a cousin of the apostle who happened to have the same name) back again to the distinction between 'we' and 'you', though now the other way round. Notice how, in 2.1–10, this feature of the structure already anticipates the coming-together of 2.11–22: the 'old perspective' bit contains the 'new' within it! 'You were dead in trespasses and sins' – but so were we! 'We too followed the desires of flesh and mind: we were children of wrath, just like the rest' (2.3) (this is of course straightforwardly parallel to Romans 3.10–20: Jews join Gentiles in the dock, with no defence against the charges). 'But God' – if this is not by Paul, it is by someone who has got one of his favourite phrases off pat – has acted in the Messiah. His death, resurrection and ascension have now become ours, and all so that 'in the ages to come God might show the surpassing riches of his grace in kindness towards us in the Messiah, Jesus' (2.7). We have come together: as Jew and Gentile were brought to the same point of helpless guilt, so together they have been raised to glorious heights in Christ.

And so to the statement which rings so many bells with Romans and Galatians, even though it has its own subtly different way of putting things. 'For by grace you have been saved through faith': this is in fact the *only* place in Paul where we are told in so many words that we are *saved*, as opposed to being justified, through faith (see below on Romans 1.16f.). There has been so much slippery thinking and writing down the years, in both old and new perspectives and many others besides, in which 'salvation' and 'justification' have been tossed around as mere synonyms, both being thereby denied their proper force. Paul is here talking of *salvation*, that is, rescue from death and from the sin which causes it. This is of course closely correlated with justification, though not in the simplistic way some imagine (justified in the present, saved in the future): salvation in Paul is past, present and future, and as we shall see, so too is justification. Rather, justification is God's declaration that someone is in the right, is a member of the sin-forgiven covenant family, while salvation is the actual rescue from death and sin. We will return to this, but it is important in 2.8–10 not least because, as Paul will go on to stress in 2.11–22, the Gentiles in particular have been rescued from a terrible plight: not only sinful as the Jews themselves were, but outside all hope, all promise, all possibility. It is the *rescue* from the powers of sin and death that Paul needs to stress here, even though the close correlation of that with his more frequent justification-discussions means that he draws on the same language: by grace, through faith (compare Romans 3.21–26), so that nobody can boast (Romans 3.27–31). (Who knows how frequently or infrequently Paul actually talked about all these topics? The letters are such a small photograph album from such a crowded career.)

But the emphasis then falls, not on the present status, nor even on the enormity of the rescue operation which has brought them to this place, but on the task that lies ahead: for we are his workmanship, his *poiēma*, God's artwork, his 'poem': created in the Messiah, Jesus, for good works, which God prepared beforehand for us to walk in. There are echoes, here, of 1 Corinthians 1.30: 'Of him are you in Christ, whom God made for us wisdom . . .'

But what are these 'good works'? The Reformation legacy, eager to deny that 'good works' in the sense of morally virtuous deeds can play any part in commending us to God, was happy to cite this passage by way of answer to the normal charge that 'justification by faith alone' would cut the nerve of all Christian morality. No, they said: we are not saved (or justified; but they often coalesced the two) *by* good works, they said, but we are saved (and justified, for that matter) *for* good works. They follow from grace. They neither prepare for it, earn it, nor co-operate with it when it is doing its sovereign job.

Well and good. This is not far, of course, from what the 'new perspective' would say about Judaism: rescued by grace then given Torah as the way of life. But I do not actually think that that is what Paul is talking about here. Yes, 'good works' will undoubtedly include 'moral behaviour'. But Paul is more interested, as he is in Philippians 1.27–30 and 4.8f., in the public face of the church in the world, in Christians shining in the world as lights in a dark place (4.17–5.20; compare Philippians 2.12–18). This will involve Christians behaving according to radically different standards to the world, but the point of this is not simply 'because you now need to be virtuous' but 'because the church is the body of Christ in and for the world'. The point is not of great importance for our present discussion, but it is extremely significant for wider issues facing the church in our own day.

All this brings us directly to the 'new perspective' bit: 2.11–22. Just as there were signs in 2.1–10 that Jews and Gentiles were coming together, even though the basic discussion was about sin and salvation, so here it is the other way round, still indicating the close linkage of the two themes. The sacrificial blood of the Messiah is not just shed so that sins may be forgiven; it is also powerful to bring Gentiles into the place where the Jewish people already were (albeit at dire risk through sin, as in 2.3). The Messiah has reconciled both Jews and Greeks to God in one body through the cross, giving both of them access to the father (2.16, 18). There is an interesting parallel here with Galatians 3.10–14, where the cross enables the promise of Abraham to go out to the Gentiles, and enables Jews, already within the covenant but needing to be renewed, to receive the spirit. But we note, as of particular importance for our whole study, the role that the law played in the separation of Jew and Gentile, and the role that the cross plays in overcoming it:

> He [the Messiah] is our peace; he has made the two into one,
> and has destroyed the dividing wall that partitioned us off in mutu-
> al hostility. He has abolished, in his flesh, the law of commandments
> and regulations, so that he might create the two in himself into one
> new person, so making peace, and so that he might reconcile both
> in a single body to God through the cross, killing the enmity by
> means of it. (2.14–16)

Here is the point – large as life, in the pages of the New Testament –
that was one of James Dunn's major breakthrough moments in
the development of the 'new perspective'. The 'works of the law'
against which Paul warned were not, he suggested, the moral good
deeds done to earn justification (or salvation), but the particular
commandments and ordinances which kept Jew and Gentile separate from one another.[9] We do not need to study the various types
of first-century Jewish attitudes to the law to see that here in
Ephesians 2 someone at least thought that was how those commandments functioned – and that the cross of Jesus Christ not
only rescued sinful human beings from their eternal fate but
also rescued fractured humanity from its eternal antagonism. *And
the author of Ephesians clearly thought that those two were part
of the same act of redemption, intimately linked aspects of the
single purpose of the one God, aimed at the healing of creation.* The
image of the dividing wall is, pretty certainly, taken from the
Jerusalem Temple, with its sign warning Gentiles to come no further. That has gone in Christ, because in him a new Temple is
constructed.

The result is exactly as in Galatians 3.28f.: you are all one in the
Messiah. This time, however, it is expressed through the controlling
image of the Temple which has been implicit all through the paragraph. The point about the single Jew-plus-Gentile family, exactly
as in 1 Corinthians 3.10–17, is that this people, this family, this
church, is the place where God dwells by the spirit. Is resistance to
ecclesiology in Paul bound up with resistance to finding too much
for the spirit to do as well? Or is it merely that a residual Protestant
fear of anything that looks like a 'high' ecclesiology might lead the
vulnerable flock back to the wrong sort of church? But supposing
a 'low' ecclesiology, a mere individualism with saved individuals
getting together from time to time for mutual benefit, were to turn

out to be a denial of some of the key elements of Paul's mission-
ary theology?

The result of all this, set out with great excitement in the next
chapter, is to say (3.1–7): this is the revelation of the mystery! This,
the coming together of Jews and Gentiles, reduced to a sociological
trick in some versions of the new perspective, ridiculed as a mere
avoidance of hassle by some in the old perspective, ignored by many
Pauline interpreters for many years as an irrelevant side-issue – this
coming together of Jews and Gentiles is, for the author of Ephesians,
the very heart of the mystery of the Messiah, the secret which had
not been revealed before but now is on public display. The Gentiles
are fellow-heirs! They are part of the same body! They are co-sharers
in the promise through the gospel! And, tellingly, this bringing-the-
world-together gospel was the main aim of God's grace in calling
Paul to be an apostle . . .

Why? What's the point? Yes, say the scoffers, ethnic divisions are
broken down, we know that, but why make such a fuss about it?
The answer is that the church, thus united through the grace of God
in the death of Jesus, *is the sign to the principalities and powers that
their time is up.* Ephesians is not about the ordering of the church
by the gospel for its own sake. 'Ecclesiology' may sound secondary
and irrelevant to some ardent enthusiasts for the 'old perspective',
but that could just be because they are unwilling to face the consequences of *Paul's* ecclesiology. For him, the church is constituted,
and lives its life in public, in such a way as to confront the rulers
of the world with the news that there is 'another king, this Jesus'
(Acts 17.7). Paul says it again: this was the grace given to me, this
was the mystery revealed of which I became a servant, the mystery
lodged since all eternity in the creator's single plan: 'that now the
many-splendoured wisdom of God might be made known to the
rulers and authorities in the heavenly places, through the church,
according to the eternal purpose which he has accomplished in
the Messiah, Jesus our Lord' (3.10). How can 'ecclesiology' be a
secondary topic, unworthy to be associated with the great doctrine
of justification, when scripture itself gives it this high a place? Why
should not the point of justification itself be precisely this, that, in
constituting the church as the single family who are a sign to the
powers that Jesus is Lord and that they are not, it serves directly the

mission of the kingdom of God in the world? It cannot be, can it, that part of the old perspective's reaction to the new is the tacit sense that once we associate ecclesiology with the very centre of the gospel we will have to go all the way and rethink the political role and task of the church? Surely the wonderful 'objective' scholarship of so many 'old perspective' exponents would not allow such a motive to affect exegesis! And yet . . . Luther's 'two kingdoms' theology may have more bearing on this than we might like to think. Not to mention the deep resistance, in some of the same circles where the old perspective still flourishes, to any attempt to articulate a gospel-based 'kingdom'-theology to complement and illuminate Paul's soteriology . . .

But these are of course unworthy reflections. Back in Ephesians, we find – as with the old perspective – that this Jesus, who unites Jew and Gentile and thereby confronts the powers, is the one (3.12) through whom, as in Romans 5.1–2, we have 'boldness and confidence of access, through his faithfulness' (or 'through faith in him'; here, both are equally true). Paul thus ends the first half of the letter the same way he began it, in prayer, but prayer now to the one universal father (3.15), for the strengthening of the church through the indwelling of the spirit and of the Messiah himself (one of the rare places where 'Christ in you' complements 'you in Christ'; compare Galatians 2.20), and so that, as in Philippians 3.7–11, and again in Galatians 2, they may know the love of the Messiah, even though it goes beyond anything that can be known, and so may be filled with all the fullness of God. If the church is 'Christ's body, the fullness of him who fills all in all' (1.23), it too needs to be filled with God's own fullness. Old and new perspectives on Paul come together and, though tossed and tumbled about in the process, they are transformed and transcended, and together they give rise to prayer and praise in what was either Paul's own majestic synthesis or that of his most sincere flatterer.

Ephesians thus leaves us, breathless perhaps, with a sense that there are indeed properly Pauline perspectives out beyond the antithesis of the old and the new. It isn't just a matter of getting the two of them in proper balance. Rather, when they are allowed to come together and knock sparks off one another, or perhaps when they are allowed to grow together within their full exegetical context, they belong within a larger vision of Paul's gospel and theology than much of the discipline of Pauline studies, and much of the preaching of Paul in a variety of churches, had ever envisaged.

Claims of even this magnitude have a habit of growing pale before one of the greatest documents ever written by a human being. We turn at last to Romans.

7

Romans

Never mind the old and the new: how do we keep Romans in *any* kind of perspective? It bestrides the narrow worlds of scholarship and church like a Colossus, and we petty exegetes walk under its huge legs and peep about . . . no, let's not go there. That was, after all, said of Caesar, and part of the point of Romans is that it is written to Caesar's city but with a message very different from that of Caesar himself. And, if I am right (though this is a different topic), part of its aim is to challenge, at several levels, the ideological foundations of Caesar's empire.

Nevertheless, all roads led to Rome in the ancient world, and all roads in biblical exegesis lead to Romans sooner or later – especially when it comes to justification. The problem I now face is of compression and omission: how to squash what needs to be said into the space available without shrinking the argument beyond what it can bear, and how to leave out that for which there is no room – which favourite passages to avoid, which key debates to short-circuit, which supporters not to quote, which opponents not to take on – without damaging the argument I wish to put forward. The only possible strategy is to head for the absolutely vital passages, to do my best once more to expound them, and to deal with such objections as I can. And there is only one place to begin.

'I am not ashamed of the gospel, for it is God's power for salvation to all who believe, the Jew first and also the Greek. For God's righteousness is unveiled in it, from faith to faith, as it is written, The righteous shall live by faith' (1.16f.).

There is, of course, a sense in which we only know what Paul's dense introductory sentences mean when we have read the fuller statements into which they grow as the argument proceeds. But let me start with a bold double claim. Unless there had grown up in

153

the Western church a long tradition of (a) reading 'God's righteousness' as *iustitia Dei*, then (b) trying to interpret that phrase with the various meanings of *iustitia* available at the time, and (c) interpreting that in turn within the categories of theological investigation of the time (especially the determination to make 'justification' cover the entire sweep of soteriology from grace to glory) – unless all this had happened, nobody would ever have supposed that the 'righteousness' in question in Romans 1.17 was anything other than God's own 'righteousness', unveiled, as in a great apocalypse, before the watching world. And unless the scholars of any time had lost their moorings completely, drifting away from the secure harbour of ancient Jewish thought, not least the biblical thought where both Paul and his contemporaries were anchored, and had allowed the little ship of exegesis to be tossed to and fro with every wind of passing philosophy, nobody would have supposed that 'God's righteousness' was anything other than his faithfulness to the covenant, to Israel, and beyond that again to the whole of creation. It would have been taken for granted that 'God's righteousness' referred to the great, deep plans which the God of the Old Testament had always cherished, the through-Israel-for-the-world plans, plans to rescue and restore his wonderful creation itself, and, more especially, to God's faithfulness to those great plans.

That, in short, is the conclusion I draw from the evidence I referred to earlier, and which I have set out more fully elsewhere. I am at this point by no means alone.[1] But, despite many attempts by myself and others to make the position clear, the counter-suggestions seem to indicate that the point has still not got across. John Piper really does seem to think that to stress 'covenant faithfulness' is to shrink the notion to quite a small compass, whereas in the Psalms and Isaiah, in Daniel 9 and a good deal of second-Temple literature (not least 4 Ezra), the belief that God is, and will be, faithful to his covenant is absolutely foundational both for Israel's hope of rescue and, out beyond that, for the hope of a restored creation.

But – still remembering Piper's own statement about how Paul's terms must ultimately be understood with reference to the actual contexts in which he uses them – the best argument for taking *dikaiosynē theou* in 1.17, 3.21 and 10.3 as 'God's faithfulness to the covenant with Abraham, to the single-plan-through-Israel-for-the-world', is the massive sense it makes of passage after passage, the way in which bits of Romans often omitted from discussion, or even explicitly left on one side as being irrelevant to the main drift of the discourse, suddenly come back into focus with a bang. There are many passages which have been thus treated and which now come up in three dimensions. Romans 9—11 itself, of course, for so long treated as essentially irrelevant (except as a happy hunting ground for theories about predestination); 3.1–8, which always shares the fate of its grown-up cousin, chapters 9—11; and, smaller but equally significantly, 2.1–16 and 2.17–29, both of which are regularly treated as though *all* they were was part of a general blanket condemnation of the human race, rather than an advance exposition of the larger picture which will be developed as the letter progresses. And, notoriously now, there are passages which, within an 'old perspective' framework and without the strong view of 'God's righteousness' to guide the way, simply fall apart.

To mention only the obvious exegetical casualties of the 'old perspective':

(a) The tight little paragraph 3.27–31 regularly comes unglued at its crucial joint, the *ē* at the start of 3.29.

(b) Abraham in chapter 4 is treated as an 'example' or 'illustration', and the point of the chapter is thereby completely missed, resulting in the oddity of placing within parentheses phrases in verses 16 and 17 which are actually the main point of the whole discussion.

(c) Within 9—11 itself, even when Paul structures his argument by questions about the word of God having failed, about God being unjust, about God's rights as judge, about his revelation of wrath and power, and then about his mercy (9.6, 14, 19, 22, 23) – all of which, to the eye trained in scripture and Jewish tradition, should say, 'This is all about God's own righteousness' – the point is simply not seen, let alone grasped. Such is the effect of the late-mediaeval blinkers still worn within the post-Reformation traditions.

(d) Then, of course, 10.6–13 falls as well. If one is not thinking about God's faithfulness to the covenant, one might well miss – and the vast majority of exegetes have missed! – the crucial significance of Deuteronomy 30 within its own biblical context and within the re-readings of scripture in Paul's day, and the way in which that passage, and the various second-Temple re-readings of it, including Paul's, all point to the foundational belief that God is faithful to the covenant and will therefore bring about its renewal at last.

(e) Finally, the climactic statements about God in Romans 11 (verses 22, 32 and of course 33–36) still fail to alert those whose minds are steeped in the theology of a different age to the fact, which even the bare verbal statistics will tell you, that Romans is a book about God, and that the primary thing it is saying about God is that he is the God of faithful, just, covenantal love, that this has been unveiled in the gospel message about Jesus of Nazareth, the crucified and risen Messiah, and that through this gospel message, and the radical unveiling of God's covenant justice and faithfulness, God's saving power is going out into the world, and will not rest until creation itself is set free from its slavery to corruption and decay and shares the liberty of the glory of God's children. Does the letter fit together well on this account, or does it not?

Even a short reflection, therefore, suggests that the best argument for the 'righteousness' in 1.17 being God's own, and referring to his (albeit strange and unexpected) faithfulness to the covenant, is the argument of Romans itself. How then does the rest of the opening summary play out?

First, we note once more that verses 16 and 17 are not a statement of 'the gospel'. I am aware that some of the things I have sometimes said at this point have been too truncated, and I am sorry for giving wrong impressions. Paul has various ways of summarizing his 'gospel'. In Romans itself, he does it in 1.3–5, where it is the proclamation that Jesus, the Messiah, is the risen Lord of the world, summoning the whole world to believing allegiance. In 1 Corinthians 15.3–5 he does it in terms of the Messiah dying for our sins in accordance with the scriptures, and being raised again also in accordance with the scriptures. But the important point to note is that 'the gospel' is a message primarily about Jesus, and about what the one true God has done and is doing through him. By contrast, 1.16–17 is a claim about the *effect* of the gospel: when it is preached,

God's power goes to work and people are saved. 'I am not ashamed of the gospel', followed by an explanation of what the gospel *does*, is not the same thing as 'here is the gospel itself'.

Second, the people who experience this 'salvation' are 'all who believe, the Jew first and also the Greek'. (I said above, when discussing Ephesians, that Ephesians 2.8 is the only passage where Paul specifically says 'saved by faith'; here he says that the gospel is God's power for salvation to those who have faith, which amounts to very much the same thing.) Notice how the two come so close together: (a) 'to all who believe', (b) Jew first and also Greek. Old perspective and new; except that the 'all' in the first phrase is itself a pointer to the second. The two are not divided for Paul, but only in our presentations of him.

Third, 'from faith to faith' is even denser than the rest of the statement, and can only be interpreted in the light of data from elsewhere. But, anticipating my discussion of 3.22, I will just say that I think Paul intends to hint that when God's covenant faithfulness/justice is unveiled, this is done *on the basis of the faithfulness of Jesus the Messiah*, on the one hand, and *for the benefit of those who believe*, on the other. One would never, of course, guess this from 1.17 itself, but that holds true for a great many of Paul's advance summary statements. That is how he writes: symphonically, hinting at themes yet to be stated in full.

Finally, Paul quotes Habakkuk 2.4: 'the righteous shall live by faith' (all translations of the clause are tendentious, and depend on what you think he means by it). There is a large nest of interlocking problems at this point, which many scholars have had great fun disentangling, discussing, sometimes actually clarifying, and sometimes even solving – though that will always remain moot. The beginning of the view to which I have come (which I think was first whispered to me by my friend Peter Rodgers in a seminar in Keble College, Oxford when we were young graduate students together) is that Paul is aware of the entire context in Habakkuk, in which God's covenant faithfulness, his loyalty to his people, appears to be called into question by the awful events going on all around. In that situation, what is called for is faith; and faith will be the badge of God's true people in and through that turbulent time of terrible judgment and hoped-for mercy. (In the Septuagint, the connection is even stronger, since there the verse refers to God's own faithfulness as the means of life for his 'righteous' people.) The quotation thus rounds off the introductory formula, not simply by referring forwards to the exposition of 'justification by faith', but by alluding to the great crises of Israel's past, and to the way in which, when God's faithfulness was being put to the test, God's people were marked out by, and found life through, their faith. Paul's quotation of this passage here has nothing to do with Paul merely running through a mental concordance of biblical passages which linked 'righteous' and 'faith' and, finding Habakkuk 2.4 along with Genesis 15.6, deciding here and in Galatians to drop them both into his argument.[2] It has everything to do with his sense that, at a time when divine judgment seems called for on the wickedness of the nations and on the backsliders within Israel, that judgment will itself be rooted in the divine faithfulness to which the only appropriate response is human faith.

II

This brings us directly to 1.18–3.20. This is obviously a single section, framed by Paul's references to 'God's righteousness' in 1.17 and 3.21, setting out the ground for the fuller treatment of the stated theme. But treating the passage simply *as* a single section carries considerable risks, notably that of short-circuiting the exegesis of the particular parts in order to make the point which Paul is undoubtedly making overall (that all people are sinful) while ignoring the many other things he says on the way. This, in fact, is one of the few cases where a failure in exegesis is caused by *too much* attention to the overall scope of a passage, and not enough to the small details and sub-sections.

In particular, three of the sub-sections are extremely important for the topic of justification. To begin with, 2.1–16 sets out, clearly and dramatically, a picture of the last judgment. This picture is rooted in Jewish thinking about the final Assize. It is angled rhetorically to springing the trap (following the sobering indictments of 1.18–32) on the superior-minded pagan moralist, and perhaps also (this is controversial, but irrelevant for our purposes) on the equally superior-minded onlooking Jew.[3] But neither of these should make us imagine that Paul means anything other than what he is saying. Some have suggested, for instance, that the whole thing is an elaborate charade, in which, while he suggests that some people will be found at the last to have 'done good' and so receive glory and honour and peace, this is merely a mirage, since he is going on to prove that nobody actually does this. This is a fairly desperate suggestion exegetically, gaining its only (but spurious) apparent support from the fact that most preachers on Romans have skipped rather hastily over chapter 2 in order to hurry on to 'the gospel' in chapter 3, so that the reception-history of Romans has undoubtedly encouraged a sense that Romans 2 is not a particularly serious part of the book – a very odd thing to conclude for anyone who knows Paul.[4] Rather, unless we are absolutely forced to deny it, we should assume that when Paul appears to be laying down first principles about God's future judgment, he truly is laying down first principles about God's future judgment.

The main reason, of course, for embarrassment on this topic is that here Paul, in the first mention of 'justification' in the letter, states openly and cheerfully that 'the doers of the law will be justified' (2.13).[5] It is, by the way, clear throughout chapters 2 and 3 that the lawcourt is one of the primary 'home base' points of what Paul is saying. Here, quite obviously, he has in mind a lawcourt in which God is the judge and humans are appearing before him to have their cases tried. Some, declares Paul, will hear the verdict '*dikaios*', 'in the right'. These will not be the people who only hear the Torah but do not perform it; they will be those who 'do the law'. This is in line with the straightforward statement in 2.6, quoting Psalm 62.13, that God will 'render to each person according to their works'. What Paul means by this will of course remain puzzling for a little while. But it will gradually become clear for those who note the question and keep their eyes and ears open as the argument proceeds.

So it is indeed a Jewish 'final-assize' scene – with one difference: we now know the name of the judge. Just as in the Areopagus address,[6] Paul sees Jesus as the Messiah, marked out as such by his resurrection (Romans 1.4) and therefore holding the office which in some biblical and some post-biblical texts the Messiah would hold, that of eschatological judge.[7] And his judgment, as one would expect from a well-run biblical lawcourt, will be without favouritism (2.11), so that Jew and Greek will appear on an even footing before him. Possession of Torah, as we just saw, will not be enough; it will be doing it that counts (whatever 'doing it' is going to mean). Paul cannot deny this without undermining the very foundation of all Jewish theology, namely God both as the creator and as the just judge who will put things right at the last.

But, though the idea of a final judgment is common to most Christian theologians, the idea that Paul would insist on such a judgment at which the criterion will be, in some sense, 'works', 'deeds', or even 'works of the law', has naturally been anathema to those who have been taught that his sole word about judgment and justification is that, since justification is by faith, there simply cannot be a final 'judgment according to works'. I am frequently challenged on this point in public, after lectures and seminars, and my normal reply is that I did not write Romans 2; Paul did.

Nor did I write Romans 14.10–12:

> You, why do you judge your brother? Or you, why do you despise your brother? For we must all come and stand before the judgment seat of God.[8] For it is written, 'as I live, says the Lord, to me every knee shall bow, and every tongue shall confess God'.[9] So each of us must give an account of ourselves to God.

Nor did I write 2 Corinthians 5.10, at which we looked in the previous chapter: we must all appear before the Messiah's judgment seat, so that we may each receive the things done in the body, whether good or bad.

We might add other passages as well. Galatians 5.19–21 speaks of people who follow 'the works of the flesh' being excluded from 'the kingdom of God', in a similar way to 1 Corinthians 6.9. Also in 1 Corinthians we find a final judgment scene in 3.12–15, where it appears that Christian workers will be judged on the quality of their work, with some finding that they suffer loss at one level though themselves still being saved, 'but only as through fire' (3.15). In the next chapter Paul speaks of the coming judgment that he too must face. This, he says, will be the real thing, in contrast to any judgments that human courts (including the 'court' of the Corinthian church!) might pass on him (4.4). He speaks there (4.5) of that coming judgment in language reminiscent both of Romans 2.15f. (the secrets of the hearts being disclosed) and also 2.28f. (people who receive praise from God). He speaks of the coming 'day of the Lord', at which there will of course be a judgment, in 1 Corinthians

5.5, and quite frequently elsewhere.[10] Back in Galatians, we find the two final destinations spelt out: some sow to the flesh and reap corruption, others to the spirit and reap eternal life (6.8). And Ephesians 6.8 speaks of a time when each will receive a reward for good work performed, whether slave or free. Finally, back in Romans, in the centre of the very chapter where Paul has declared that 'there is therefore now no condemnation for those who are in Christ Jesus', he also writes, 'for if you live according to the flesh, you will die, but if by the Spirit you put to death the deeds of the body you will live' (Romans 8.1, 13).

There is simply far too much of this material for it all to be swept aside. Romans 2.1–16 must take its place, not as an odd aside which doesn't fit with what Paul says everywhere else, but as a central statement of something he normally took for granted. It is base-line stuff. Unless we offer a reading of Paul within which all this makes sense, not just as a grudging theological concession on the side but fitted properly into the overall structure, we have not done our job as exegetes, still less as theologians.[11]

I am aware that some have made a sharp distinction between (a) the notion of 'reward', a specific grant of favour (of whatever sort, who knows) at the final Assize, and (b) the notion of an actual judgment according to works, where all, including Christians who have been 'justified by faith', must present themselves, render account, and be assessed. Some of my critics are keen to deny the latter, in order to insist on ruling out 'works' as having any part in justification itself. They therefore assert the former ('reward') as a way of doing justice to the passages I have listed and similar ones elsewhere, not least in the gospels.[12] This is a way of maintaining the belief that 'justification by faith without works' carries on, as it were, all the way through: in other words, that the only justification the Christian will ever have is because of the merits of the Messiah, clung to by faith, rather than any work, achievement, good deeds, performance of the law, or anything else, even if done entirely out of gratitude and in the power of the spirit.

I understand this anxiety. It grows, not least, out of pastoral concern for those who torture themselves mentally and spiritually with the fear that they may not, after all, have 'done enough' to satisfy God at the final judgment. It is supported by passages like Galatians 3.4f.: 'having begun with the spirit, are you now ending with the flesh?' Having begun, in other words, with 'faith alone', are you now determined (through human pride, or fear, or whatever) to end with 'works alone', or perhaps some 'synergistic' mixture of faith and works? And is this not – however much one says one believes in grace – a way of taking back, with the Pelagian left hand, what one had just given with the Augustinian right?

Put like that, it might well be. There have undoubtedly been many Christians down the years who have genuinely believed that 'the Lord helps those who help themselves' (some, indeed, who have supposed that that bit of cheerful Pelagianism was found in the Bible!), and who have stumbled on all their lives with just that revolving-door spirituality, sometimes proud of having put God in their debt, sometimes afraid that they had failed to do so, never realizing the glorious truth that we can never put God in our debt and that, according to Jesus himself, we don't have to. 'When you have done all you were commanded to do, say, "We are unprofitable servants; we have merely done our duty" ' (Luke 17.10). Nothing that I am now going to say takes away from this glorious truth by one milligram.

The problem is – at the level of formal theological method, at least – that those texts about final judgment according to works sit there stubbornly, and won't go away. Even that line in Luke 17 points out that you *are* 'commanded to do' certain things, and you must do them. And to the rather negative point made there – as though the best we can do merely brings us back from an overdraft to a zero balance, with no hope of ever getting in credit – one might add the more positive one: there are several passages, not least in key places in Paul himself, where it is clear that the things the Christian is commanded to *do* are not meant to be a grudging duty only, nor are they meant merely to bring us back into a zero balance before an unsmiling Judge. What the Christian is to do is *to please God*, to bring a smile to the father's face, to give him delight, to gladden his heart. 'Well done, good and faithful servant!' says the master in Jesus' parable. So too in Paul:

> Present your bodies as a living sacrifice, holy *and well-pleasing to God*. (Romans 12.1)

> One who serves the Messiah in this way is *pleasing to God* and approved by men and women. (Romans 14.18)

So we make it our aim, whether at home or away, to be *pleasing to him*. (2 Corinthians 5.9 – leading directly, with the word 'for' to show that this is an explanation, to the great and solemn statement about standing before the Messiah's judgment seat, which leads in turn to the phrase, 'knowing therefore the fear of the Lord'.)[13]

Figure out what is *pleasing to the Lord*. (Ephesians 5.10)

Work out your own salvation with fear and trembling, for it is God who is at work in you, to will and to work *for his good pleasure*. (Philippians 2.12b–13)

That you may behave in a manner worthy of the Lord, so as *to give him pleasure in all respects*, bearing fruit in every good work and growing up in the knowledge of God. (Colossians 1.10)

Just as you have received instructions from us as to how you should behave, *and please God*, as you are doing, you should do so more and more. (1 Thessalonians 4.1)

That God may make you worthy of your calling, and may fulfil in you *every good pleasure of goodness* (*pasan eudokian agathōsunēs*) and work of faith by [his] power. (2 Thessalonians 1.11)

Please note: this is not the logic of merit. It is the logic of love. Part of the problem with seeing everything in terms of merit (as some mediaevals did, thereby conditioning the thought-world of the Reformation as well), whether it be the merit we should have and can't produce, the merit which God reckons to us, or whatever, is that even if we get the logic right we are still left with God as a distant bank manager, scrutinizing credit and debit sheets. That is not the heart of Paul's theology, or that of any other New Testament writer, as it was not the vision of God which Jesus himself lived and taught. Not that saying 'love' is a cheap-and-cheerful way of avoiding theological problems, or indeed moral ones. That tendency, granted, is one of the tragedies of our own times. But we should not, because of it, turn away from what scripture actually says.

Within the logic of love is the rich, theological logic of the work of the holy spirit. This brings us back to a point made much earlier. When, by clear implication, I am charged with encouraging believers to put their trust in someone or something 'other than the crucified and resurrected Savior',[14] I want to plead guilty – to this extent and this extent only: that I also say, every time I repeat one of the great historic creeds, that I trust in the holy spirit.

Of course, within Trinitarian theology one is quick to say that this is not something other than trusting in Jesus the Messiah, since it is his own spirit; the Father who sent Jesus is now sending 'the Spirit of the Son' (Galatians 4.4–7). But the point about the holy spirit, at least within Paul's theology, is that when the spirit comes the result is human freedom rather than human slavery.[15] When God works within a community, or an individual, the result is that they 'will and work for his good pleasure' (Philippians 2.13). The pastoral theology which comes from reflecting on the work of the spirit is the glorious paradox that the more the spirit is at work the more the human will is stirred up to think things through, to take free decisions, to develop chosen and hard-won habits of life and to put to death the sinful, and often apparently not freely chosen, habits of death. Sin is what bubbles up unbidden from the depths of the human heart, so that all one has to do is go with the flow. That has the appearance of freedom, but is in fact slavery, as Jesus himself declared.[16] True freedom is the gift of the spirit, the result of grace; but, precisely because it is freedom *for* as well as freedom *from*, it isn't simply a matter of being forced now to be good, against our wills and without our co-operation (what damage to genuine pastoral theology has been done by making a bogey-word out of the Pauline term *synergism*, 'working together with God'), but a matter of being released from slavery precisely into responsibility, into being able at last to choose, to exercise moral muscle, knowing both that one is doing it oneself and that the spirit is at work within, that God himself is doing that which I too am doing. If we don't believe that, we don't believe in the spirit, and we don't believe Paul's teaching. Virtue is what happens – I know many in the Reformation tradition shudder at the thought of the very word 'virtue', but there is no help for it if we are to be true to scripture and to Trinitarian theology – when the spirit enables the Christian freely to choose, freely to develop, freely to be shaped by, freely to *become* that which is pleasing to God.

We seem to have moved quite a way from Romans 2, but this is the discussion we needed to have in order to make sense of what we are presented with, both in Paul's text and in the writings of those who have been naturally and rightly anxious about 'adding our own merit' to 'the finished work of Jesus Christ'. This is where, to come back to where we started, a fully Pauline doctrine of justification needs two things which many discussions have regularly screened out (back to the jigsaw with half the pieces deliberately kept in the box) but which Paul emphatically puts back in: eschatology and the spirit.

In a nutshell:

(a) the judgment of which Paul speaks in Romans 2.1–16 is of course the *future* judgment, that which will take place on the last day. When, on that day, God issues through the Messiah the positive verdict spoken of in 2.7, 10 and 13, it corresponds to the *present* verdict which, in 3.21–31, is issued simply and solely on the basis of faith.

(b) How do these two verdicts correspond? The answer has to do with the spirit. When Paul returns triumphantly to the future verdict in chapter 8 ('there is therefore now no condemnation for those who are in the Messiah, Jesus'), he at once explains this with a long discourse about the work of the spirit (8.2–27). What Paul says about Christians could be said about the doctrine of justification itself: if you don't have the spirit, you're not on the map (8.9).

The spirit is not, of course, mentioned in 2.1–16. But that is Paul's way: to introduce a theme quietly, symphonically, with hints and suggestions. He does the same throughout Romans with his statements about the Torah, which only make sense when seen all together and in the light of the argument as a whole. Indeed, these two go together. When Paul speaks of 'doing the law' in 2.13, he is thereby setting up a long train of thought which will run through several passages until, in 8.5–8, he explains, and even then obliquely, that it is the mind of the flesh that does not and cannot submit to God's law, so that by implication the mind of the spirit can and does make that submission. This, in turn, points on to 10.5–13, where the 'doing the Torah' spoken of in Leviticus is explained in terms of Deuteronomy 30, and, further, in terms of Joel 2.32, the passage about the outpoured spirit.

And, coming back once more to chapter 2, when we read Romans as a whole we can see quite clearly that the description in 2.26–29 of those who 'keep the commandments of the law' even though they are uncircumcised (2.26), who actually 'fulfil the law' (2.27), are *Christian Gentiles*, even though Paul has not yet developed that category.[17] As in Philippians 3.3 ('the circumcision? That's us'), Paul has the temerity to say that 'the Jew' (not 'the true Jew', we note, but simply 'the Jew') is the one 'in the secret', that is, inwardly as opposed to the outward mark of circumcision, and that 'circumcision' (again, he doesn't say 'true circumcision') is a matter of the heart, of the spirit rather than the letter. The obvious cross-reference here to 2 Corinthians 3.4–6, and with it to Paul's entire theology of Christians as members of God's 'new covenant', would have made all this clear long ago had that whole theme not been marginalized in so many of the de-Judaized and de-historicized presentations which have squashed Paul's thought into frameworks it was not designed to fit.

But if we thus read 2.26–29, rightly, in the light of the rest of the letter and of Paul, we must also read in this light 2.1–16, particularly 2.6–7, 10 and 13–16:

> [God] will 'render to each according to their works': to those who through patience in good work seek for glory, honour and immortality, he will give the life of the age to come . . . glory, honour and peace to all who work what is good, to the Jew first and also the Greek . . . When Gentiles, who by birth do not possess Torah, do the things of the Torah, they are a 'law' to themselves, even though they do not have the law. They show that the work of the law is written on their hearts, with their conscience also bearing witness and their conflicting thoughts accusing or perhaps excusing them on the day when God judges human secrets according to my gospel through the Messiah, Jesus. (2.6–7, 10, 13–16)

There are, of course, some good reasons for thinking that Paul might after all be referring here to the 'moral pagan'. He may indeed be quite deliberately teasing at this point, wooing a reader on from the challenge in 2.1 to the possibility of a different way of approaching the whole moral task. But the forward echoes to 2.26–29 and

2 Corinthians 3 must be regarded as decisive. These people are Christians, on whose hearts the spirit has written the law, and whose secrets, when revealed (see 2.29 again), will display the previously hidden work of God.

The point of *future* justification is then explained like this. The verdict of the last day will truly reflect what people have actually done. It is extremely important to notice, in line with that sense of sudden anxiety in 2.15, that Paul never says Christians *earn* the final verdict, or that their 'works' must be complete and perfect. He says 'those who by patience in well-doing' (echoes here of 5.3–4) 'seek for glory and honour and immortality'. They are seeking it, not earning it. And they are seeking it through that patient, spirit-driven Christian living in which – here is the paradox at the heart of the Christian life which so many have noticed but few have integrated into Paul's theology of justification! – *from one point of view* the spirit is at work, producing these fruits (Galatians 5.22f.), and *from another point of view* the person concerned is making the free choices, the increasingly free (because increasingly less constrained by the sinful habits of mind and body) decisions to live a genuinely, fully human life which brings pleasure – of course it does! – to the God in whose image we human beings were made. As long as theologians, hearing this kind of proposal, shout 'synergism' and rush back to the spurious either/or which grows out of a doctrine that has attempted to construct the entire soteriological jigsaw on the basis of a mediaeval view of 'justice', and with some of the crucial bits (the spirit, eschatology, not to mention Abraham and the covenant) still in the box, or on the floor, or in the fire, we shall never get anywhere. And at this point it is *my* instincts as a pastor that are aroused. I want my people to hear and understand the whole word of God, not just the parts of it that fit someone's system.

I am not saying for one moment that 'God does part of it and we do part of it' (one classic form of 'synergism', but not Paul's). Paul's regular paradoxes, which we already noted, remain the best way of putting it: 'striving with all the energy which he mightily inspires within me' (Colossians 1.29); 'I worked harder than all of them, yet it was not I but God's grace that was with me' (1 Corinthians 15.10). Of course, Paul is referring in those passages to his specific work as an apostle, not to the life of Christian character and moral virtue, though from all we know of him (not least in 2 Corinthians) it is safe to say that he would not have separated those two things. And when we put his repeated and developed teaching about the place of the spirit and the place of future judgment side by side, we find that it all fits. Humans become genuinely human, genuinely free, when the spirit is at work within them so that they choose to act, and choose to become people who more and more *naturally* act (that is the point of 'virtue', as long as we realize it is now '*second* nature', not primary), in ways which reflect God's image, which give him pleasure, which bring glory to his name, which do what the law had in mind all along. That is the life that leads to the final verdict, 'Well done, good and faithful servant!'[18] The danger with a doctrine which says 'you can't do anything and you mustn't try' is that it ends up with the servant who, knowing his master to be strict, hid his money in the ground.

And if, as a late-flowering but spurious post-Reformation romanticism and existentialism has conditioned people to think, we simply 'wait for the Spirit to do it within us', so that we only think it right to do that which 'feels natural', we have missed the point entirely and are heading for serious trouble. If the 'fruits of the Spirit' happened without human thought and moral effort, why did Paul bother to list them and urge the Galatians to develop them? Why not sit back, put your feet up, and wait for them to emerge by themselves? The spirit and human freedom! At this point – surprise, surprise – the great traditions come together. Augustine's *De Spiritu et Littera* and Luther's *Freedom of a Christian Man* come to mind, not (of course) that I am agreeing with all that either of them say.

There is, then, for Paul, a final judgment, and it will be 'according to works'. How does this relate to 'justification by faith'? That, of course, is the question; and – again, surprise, surprise! – it is the question which Paul himself will address in 3.21—4.25. But before we can get there we must pause and look, more briefly, at the massive theme which is woven deep into the structure of 2.17—3.8, which is normally not just marginalized but completely ignored, but without which any perspective we may get on Paul will be at best through a glass darkly.

III

'If you call yourself a Jew'. Paul's challenge in 2.17, picked up then in 2.29 ('let me tell you who "the Jew" is!'), is far more than the simple argument that Jews, too, are sinful, though that of course is where the larger argument is going (3.9, 19–20). It is the first statement of the theme which we saw so markedly in Galatians, and which continues unbroken, though in different modes, through most of the rest of the letter. It is the story of the single-plan-through-Israel-for-the-world. It is, in short, the covenant: not a romantic notion, not a catch-all or cure-all to avoid dealing with other soteriological issues, merely the central narrative of most of scripture, though not, sadly, most of Christian tradition.

When Paul lists all the things that 'the Jew' might want to say – and he should know, since he is addressing his own former self – he does not do so scornfully, as though to say 'what a silly set of ideas'. He is agreeing. 'The Jew' does indeed bear that proud name, meaning 'praise', as we see in the implicit pun in 2.29.[19] The Jew does indeed rest upon Torah; does indeed 'make his boast in God all the day';[20] is indeed called (and, through Torah, equipped) to 'know God's will, to work out things that differ'; is able to take on the role (remember, the plan through-Israel-for-the-world) of being the guide to the blind, the light for those in darkness; is truly called to correct the foolish, to teach the young – and all because in Torah 'the Jew' possesses the very embodiment, the actual expression, of knowledge and truth. None of this is said in sarcasm. None of it is said in order to mimic the claims that 'the Jew' would make but which Paul, the Christian, now believed to be false. He says it all sincerely. This is God's single plan, through Torah-equipped Israel, for the world.

It follows (this is enormously important, not least for 3.1–8 and with it for the whole of 9—11) that Paul is not primarily talking here about the salvation *of* 'the Jew'. He is talking about God's plan for salvation to come *through* 'the Jew', as Jesus himself put it (John 4.22). That is how the over-hasty compression of 1.18—3.20 into 'that's that, all are guilty, none can be justified or saved as they stand' has become a way of ignoring what the text is actually about. The boast of 'the Jew' in 2.17–20 is not 'well, look, I'm an exception, the Gentile world may indeed be in a mess but I'm all right, I will be saved, because I've got the Torah and I practise it.' That is precisely not what 2.17–20 is saying. The boast is 'Well, but *I am the solution to this problem.*' God's plan was through-Israel-for-the-world. The light for those in darkness, the teacher of the foolish, and so on: this is not a statement of 'therefore I will be saved', but 'therefore this is how God will solve this problem'. This, by the way, shows that one frequent response from puzzled commentators to what Paul says in verses 21 and 22 (surely, Paul, people have often said, not *all* Jews commit adultery and rob temples?) misses the point entirely. He is not here demonstrating that all Jews are sinful. He is demonstrating that the boast of Israel, to be the answer to the world's problem, cannot be made good. If the mirror is cracked, it is cracked; for Israel's commission to work, Israel would have to be perfect. It is not. It is pretty much like the other nations.

The trouble with Israel's claim, then, is (as Bernard Williams once said about pragmatism): it's true in theory but it doesn't work in practice. Here we meet exactly the same problem which Paul was addressing in Galatians 3.10–14: not that 'Israel is guilty and so cannot be saved', but 'Israel is guilty and so cannot bring blessing to the nations, as Abraham's family ought to be doing.' This is not simply a problem for Israel; it is not simply a problem for the world (though it is of course both of those as well). It is a problem for God, as 3.1–8 makes clear. God's single saving plan has apparently been thwarted. How is he then going to be faithful not only to the promises made to Israel but to the promises made *through* Israel? All this only makes sense within the Jewish belief in God's-plan-through-Israel-for-the-world, which Paul does not undermine but rather reaffirms. And all this points massively to an understanding of 'God's righteousness' in terms precisely of that through-Israel-for-the-world plan, the covenant plan, the plan now unveiled in action in Jesus the Messiah. Hence 3.21—4.25.

Dare I say what stirs in my mind at this point? Part of the problem with the 'old perspective' on Paul is that it has followed the long mediaeval tradition (to which it was never more thoroughly indebted than when reacting to some of its particulars) in this respect particularly: it has *de-Judaized* Paul. It has snatched him out of the context where he lived, where he made sense, out of his God-given theological context, rooted in Israel's scriptures, according to which God made promises to Israel and never went back on them because they were promises *through* Israel for the world. And part of the point of the new perspective, though deeply flawed in other ways, is that, from its roots in Schweitzer, Wrede, G. F. Moore and W. D. Davies through to its further expressions in Stendahl and Schoeps and finally its new flowering in Sanders, it has lodged a sustained protest against just this de-Judaizing. Of course – and my critics will no doubt have fun pointing this out – those of us, like Jimmy Dunn, Richard Hays, Douglas Campbell, Terry Donaldson and myself, who have tried to listen to the force of this point, have not always followed either history or exegesis perfectly. We have been so eager to think through the implications of the alternative, and deeply Jewish, readings of Paul that we in our turn may well have ignored elements (not non-Jewish elements, of course, but elements of Paul's inner dialectic) that the 'old perspective' was right to high-light and which it has been right stubbornly to insist on, even if sometimes feeling like Canute with the waves of the sea washing around his throne. But if we are to listen to what Paul says, in a vital and overlooked passage like 2.17–20, we may yet achieve the proper balance.

The problem with the single-plan-through-Israel-for-the-world was that Israel had failed to deliver. There was nothing wrong with the plan, or with the Torah on which it was based. The problem was in Israel itself. As we shall see later, the problem was that Israel, too, was 'in Adam'. This lies deep at the heart of Paul's theological insight, and it is the reason why so much of his theology appears so intractably complex to those who have not even grasped its first principles. *God's single plan was a plan through-Israel-(even-though-Israel-too-was-part-of-the-problem)-for-the-world.* Miss this point, and (like C. H. Dodd, famously, and a thousand other commentators, less famously) you will wish Paul had never written 3.1–8. Or, for that matter, 9—11.

Thus: Israel has failed to deliver on the divine vocation. It isn't just Paul who says so, it is the Old Testament itself. 'The name of God is blasphemed among the nations because of you.'[21] Instead of the nations looking at Israel, listening to God's word and learning his wisdom, they have looked at Israel and said, 'We don't want a god like theirs.' The promise has not only not been fulfilled; it has been stood on its head. Israel still has a role vis-à-vis the nations, but now, according to Isaiah and Ezekiel, it is a purely negative one.

This prophetic judgment, echoed by Paul, is thus not about 'proving that all Jews are sinful'. It is not based on Paul's or anyone else's contemporary observations of how actual Jews actually behaved – though no doubt Paul could tell tales of sinners as well as saints. The point is that the Old Testament itself declares that things hadn't worked out; that the single-plan-through-Israel-for-the-world had run into the sand. Ah, but, says someone, Isaiah 52 and Ezekiel 36 are texts which go on to speak of God's rescue operation for Israel, of a new work which will deliver Israel from the awful situation of . . . yes, exile. Well, precisely. Exile is the massive demonstration, carved in the granite rock of Israel's history, that the promise-bearing people are themselves in need of the same redemption that they were supposed to bring to the world. Isaiah 52 leads straight into the promise of the Servant who will be 'handed over for our transgressions', and Ezekiel 36 goes on to speak of God's new work, transforming the heart by the spirit, so that Israel will be able to keep his commandments, and so that the nations will know that he has done it.[22]

And that is precisely what Paul is talking about in 2.25–29. He is not simply saying, 'Well, but supposing some Gentiles do the Torah – they will be saved, won't they?' He is saying, 'Supposing God does what he promised, transforming people's hearts so that they keep his commandments, so that they become "the Jew" and "the circumcision" – what then?' He does not at the moment answer his own question. But what we see, looming up from a close reading of what Paul actually says, is the prospect of a new ecclesiology, a mission-oriented people, a people based on the work of the Servant and the work of the spirit, who now carry God's light, truth and teaching to the waiting nations. This is, fundamentally, Ezekiel-36 theology. It is return-from-exile theology. Why? Because that is what Paul thinks has happened, at last, after Daniel 9's putative 490 years, in the covenant renewal effected by the Messiah and the spirit. That is the foundation, in particular, for Romans 8 and Romans 10, though you would never know it from the de-Judaized and decovenantalized readings of Paul in the Western tradition.

All this, at last, enables us to read 3.1–8 with some prospect of understanding, and, with it, to find a clear path through into 3.21—4.25 as a whole.[23] Keep in mind that Paul is working with the single-plan-through-Israel-for-the-world, with all the problems that plan has now run into. The key is then 3.2: Israel was *entrusted* with 'the oracles of God'. This does not mean that Israel was *given* God's oracles for its own possession; the strange word 'oracles' may well reflect what Paul has already said at more length in 2.17–20, that the Torah was designed to enable Israel to be the light of the world. 'Entrusted' means 'given something in trust, to be used or passed on for someone else's benefit'. If I 'entrust' a letter to you, the letter is not for you, but for the person to whom I am asking you to deliver it. The 'advantage' of Israel, and the 'use' of circumcision (3.1: it is natural that, after 2.21–29, Paul would raise that as a question) was that Israel was in the privileged position of being called by the creator God to the crucial, and never-to-be-rescinded, task of bringing his healing message to the world. And Israel had been 'unfaithful'. Once again, if we fail to read what Paul actually says in 2.17–20, we will fail to understand this as well.[24] 'Unfaithful' here does not mean 'unbelieving' in the sense simply of 'refusing to have faith in God'. It means 'unfaithful to God's commission'. It summarizes 2.21–24. Israel has been charged with shining God's light into the world, and has instead provided a good deal of darkness. Those are the prophets' words, not something Paul has made up in scurrilous rejection of his former self and his fellow Jews! Would any first-century Jews have been prepared to claim the contrary, that Israel was a shining example to the world, obeying Torah in such a way that the nations, looking on, were saying to themselves, 'What a people! What a god!'?

The question of 3.3b, then, is: Will God now revoke the single-plan-through-Israel-for-the-world? Does the fact that the 'through Israel' part of the plan has collapsed mean that God can no longer be faithful to his ancient promises? *This is of course the question of the 'righteousness of God'*, as the next verses show explicitly, and with this the whole attempt to deny the meaning of 'covenant faithfulness' for *dikaiosynē theou* crashes to the ground like a felled oak.

Of course, as the literature shows abundantly, summaries of the 'doctrine of justification' down the years have regularly answered the question with 'yes'. God will revoke his plan! Torah will be set aside as a failed first attempt to rescue humans! The 'through Israel' part of the plan can now safely be ignored, and we are back with the simple narrative of 'humans sin; God sends Jesus; all is well', or perhaps 'God is righteous; humans sin; God justifies them'.[25] Yes, and you can forget Romans 9—11 as well, and condemn yourself to being unable to understand Galatians along with it!

But Paul, unlike many of his interpreters, answers his own question with a resounding *mē genoito*, 'certainly not' (3.4). God will be vindicated, as Psalm 51 declares in the face of massive human sin (specifically, David's sin, to which Paul will return in 4.7f.). Somehow – Paul does not yet say *how*, he only, but strongly, affirms *that* – God will be true to his single plan. Israel's 'unrighteousness' (her covenant failure, no less: her failure to be the middle term in the single-plan-through-Israel-for-the-world) will only make God's righteousness (his covenant faithfulness, no less: his determination to put that selfsame plan into effect) shine out all the more brightly. This, and not a shrunken or diminished version of it, is the platform for the complex but utterly coherent theology of 3.21—4.25.

The claim that God is going ahead with the plan despite the failure of Israel then raises a string of questions which, as I have often noted in other places, anticipates exactly the string of questions in Romans 9. Has God's word failed? Is God then unjust? Why does he still condemn? and, this time anticipating Romans 6.1, Why not continue in sin that grace may abound? Why not do evil that good may come? If God can take human failure and use it as a moment for his grace to shine out all the more brightly, why worry? He will do it anyway. Paul has no time at this point in his argument for such foolishness. Well, he says (3.8b), condemnation is clearly just for people who say *that* kind of thing!

This paragraph, for all it is regularly ignored, is all about God: God's oracles, God's faithfulness,[26] God's truth, God's vindication, God's victory, God's righteousness, God's justice, God's judgment, God's truth (again), and ultimately (verse 7) God's glory. It is surprising that theologians, to say nothing of preachers, would so readily skip over such a sequence of thought.

But how then *is* God going to be faithful to the single-plan-through-Israel-for-the-world? This problem only becomes more acute, it seems, when the basic indictment of 1.16—2.16 is repeated in 3.9–20. Yes, the Israel-plan was divinely intended and is not abrogated; but no, this doesn't mean that Israel has an inside track, can avoid the condemnation which comes on all people. (Recognizing the actual subject-matter of 3.1–8 means we can laugh off the remarkably arrogant suggestion of C. H. Dodd, that Paul, having given his question 'what's the point of being a Jew' the answer 'a great deal' in 3.1 and found it led nowhere, returns to it in 3.9 and tries the opposite tack, 'not a lot, actually'.) No: Jews join Gentiles in the dock. Here the lawcourt language comes strongly to the fore: 'I have already laid a charge against them' (3.9); 'every mouth is to be stopped, and the whole world is liable to God's judgment' (3.19). In between those two, of course, is the lengthy catena of Old Testament passages, designed to show without any more doubt that Israel's scriptures themselves declare Israel to be guilty. 'Whatever the law says' (including these quotations, mostly from Psalms and Proverbs, under the heading of 'law'), 'it speaks to those who are under the law': in other words, to Israel. Israel cannot claim that Torah sets it apart from the rest of the nations, enables it to avoid the judgment which hangs over the whole world, and establishes it as the people of God for the world. The law itself says: you are guilty too. 'By the works of the law shall no flesh be justified before God, since through the law comes the knowledge of sin.'

This is the point – before we even get to 3.21—4.25 – where we begin to realize at last how the emphases of the old and new perspectives belong so intimately together.

(a) The overarching problem has always been human sin and its effects – idolatry, pride, human corruption and ultimately death.

(b) God launched a rescue operation, the single plan, through Israel, to save the world.

(c) But Israel, too, is part of the original problem, which has a double effect:
  (i) Israel itself needs the same rescue-from-sin-and-death that everyone else needs;
  (ii) Israel, as it stands, cannot be the means of the rescue operation that God's plan intended.

(d) therefore the problem with which God is faced, if he is to be faithful to his own character and plan in both creation and covenant, is
  (i) he must nevertheless put his single plan into operation, somehow accomplishing what Israel was called to do but, through faithlessness to his commission, failed to do;

(ii)   he must thereby rescue the human race and the whole world from sin, idolatry, pride, corruption and death;

(iii) he must do this in a way which makes it clear that Israel, though still of course the object of his saving love, is now on all fours with the rest of the world.

In other words, God must find a way of enabling 'Israel' to be faithful after all, as the middle term of the single plan; God must thereby deal with sin; and God must do so in such as way as to leave no room for boasting. We are ready, at last, to read Romans 3.21—4.25.

IV

'But now, God's righteousness is made manifest apart from the law.' Not 'apart from the single plan', apart from God's Israel-shaped purposes, but 'apart from the Torah'. 'God's righteousness', in the light of 2.17—3.8, must mean, and can only mean, God's faithfulness to his single plan, the plan through which he will deal with the problem of human sin and put the whole world right at last. That is not only what the Old Testament usage would demand;[27] it is not only what is indicated by the post-biblical second-Temple literature of which John Piper is so cautious. It is massively indicated by the argument of Romans itself to this point, provided we actually read what Paul says, particularly in 2.17—3.8, rather than merely assuming that we can read 1.18 and 3.19f. and conclude that everything in between is merely a way of saying 'so all are sinful and need saving'. And it is powerfully supported by the actual argument of 3.21—4.25.

In particular, it is supported by the emphatic conclusion of 3.25f., which can only mean that God is revealing *his own* 'righteousness'. Paul says it three times: 'to display his righteousness' (3.25), 'to display his righteousness' again (3.26), 'so that he might himself be *dikaios*, in the right (3.26). It is not only surprising, it is actually quite shocking, that people who claim 'the authority of scripture', and often mean by that simply 'the authority of Paul', 'the authority of Romans', and even 'the authority of Romans 3.21–26', have so often simply failed to read what this all-important section says. Translations such as the NIV, which I mentioned earlier on this point, have simply gone along for the ride, fudging the evidence by translating *dikaiosynē* in verses 25 and 26 as 'justice', not noticing what a mess they are thereby making of the inner coherence of the paragraph.[28] The confusion generated at this point runs right on through the literature, as witness Simon Gathercole's frequent but strange comments about 'righteousness' which indicate that he, like so many critics of the 'new perspective', have not in fact reckoned with the fully biblical and Jewish context of what they are discussing.[29]

The wider section, also, demonstrates that here Paul is talking about God's faithfulness to the single-plan-through-Israel-for-the-world. The whole point of Abraham in Romans 4, as I have said before in relation to Galatians 3, is not that he is an 'illustration' or an 'example', as though the saving plan consisted of the simplistic narrative, 'humans sin; God rescues; all is well (and, by the way, God has done this here and there in the past as well)'. No: the single plan *began with the promises God made to Abraham*, and if Paul is to show what, in 3.4f., he promised that he would show – that, despite the failure of Israel, God was going to be true to his single plan – then the place above all places to which he must go is Abraham. And particularly Genesis 15. That, as we saw, is where God made the covenant according to which Abraham's family would be rescued from slavery and given their inheritance – both vital within Romans 5—8. That is where, in particular, 'Abraham believed God, and it was reckoned to him as righteousness'. This is the covenant to which God has been faithful in Jesus the Messiah. That is why *dikaiosynē theou* in Romans 3.21, and by backward extension 1.17, and by long forward extension 10.2f., must mean 'God's faithfulness to the covenant, to the single plan through Israel for the whole world'.

How then is the plan put into operation? How can God not only do what the plan proposed, rescuing humankind as a whole from sin and death, but also – as he must if he is to be faithful, as 3.4f. says he will be – do so by the *means* which he has promised to employ, that is, through Israel? What was lacking, as we saw in 2.21–24 and particularly, and sharply, in 3.3, was *faithfulness* on the part of Israel, not some kind of meritorious behaviour through which Israel would rescue itself, but a faithfulness to God and his covenant purposes that would enable Israel to live up to its calling as the light to the dark world, and so on (2.17–20). And what Paul now proposes, with as much a flourish of trumpets as 'the righteousness of God' itself, is that God has accomplished this Israel-shaped world-redeeming plan *through the faithfulness of the Messiah.* That is the meaning of 3.22.

This is not to say that I hereby endorse *every* suggestion that has been put forward for reading *pistis Iēsou Christou* here in terms of a subjective genitive (as opposed to the objective genitive, 'faith *in* Jesus Christ'). I do not think Paul is referring to Jesus' own 'faith', as though (in some sense or other) he too had to live 'by faith, not by works'.[30] That makes no sense, certainly at least no Pauline sense. Nor, of course, is the idea of faith *in* Jesus Christ hereby rendered unnecessary: that is the very next thing Paul says in 3.22, exactly as in Galatians 2.16. God's righteousness is unveiled *through the faithfulness of Jesus the Messiah* on the one hand, and *for the benefit of all who believe* on the other. Actually, as some have pointed out, unless you read the verse this way the second phrase is in danger of being redundant.

But what is 'the faithfulness of Jesus Christ'? Clearly, since Paul immediately goes on to expound it, it is his faithfulness unto death, the redeeming death, the dealing-with-sin death, the death that then makes it possible for sinners to be justified, to be declared 'in the right', not because of any moral worth in themselves but only because Jesus has done what Israel was called to do but, because of its own sin, could not do. (Hence, by the way, the importance of the theme of Jesus' sinlessness, as in 2 Corinthians 5.21. It was not so much that 'God needed a sinless victim', though in sacrificial terms that is no doubt true as well, as that 'God needed a faithful Israelite', to take upon himself the burden of rescuing the world from its sin and death.)

The dense details of atonement theology in 3.24–26 fall into place. God's grace accomplishes the new exodus, the *apolytrōsis*, the 'redemption', in and through the representative Messiah, whom God 'put forward' (the language is sacrificial) to be the place and means of propitiation (*hilastērion*), through his faithfulness (this phrase could mean 'through human faith', but Paul is still talking about what God has done, not how humans appropriate that for themselves) and by his sacrificial blood. The result is that, though in his forbearance God had previously 'passed over' sins, not dealing with them as they deserved, the cosmic moral deficit has now been put right, displaying God's faithfulness and justice to the world. And all this – returning to and emphasizing the 'but now' of 3.21 with 'in the present time' in 3.26 – means that he is indeed unveiled as righteous, 'just', faithful to the covenant with Israel and through Israel to all creation. And, within this very same faithful justice, he 'justifies' *ton ek pisteōs Iēsou*, literally 'the one out of the faith of Jesus', 'the Jesus-faith person', which looks as though it is a telescoping together of both halves of 3.22, 'through the faithfulness of Jesus for the benefit of all who have faith'.

How then does 'justification' actually work? The main point to notice is that this 'justification' occurs *now* (3.21), 'in the present time' (3.26). Think eschatology as well as covenant, lawcourt and Christology. This is the *present* verdict which *anticipates* the verdict that will be issued on the last day, the verdict Paul has described in solemn terms in 2.1–16. We are not yet told, though we are given a few hints, how the present verdict and the future verdict will correspond to one another. How can God possibly declare someone 'in the right', promising thereby that this verdict will be echoed on the last day, when all they have done is to believe in Jesus the Messiah? Paul, once again, keeps us waiting, insisting *that* it is so without yet telling us *how* it is so. By the end of chapter 8, and then particularly when we follow through to chapter 10, it will be more obvious. But at the moment his particular argument is going elsewhere.

If eschatology, so also covenant. When we look back a generation or two in scholarship, it is fascinating to see how Ernst Käsemann and some of his followers tried to make sense of all this. Käsemann was desperately anxious to prevent Paul having anything to do with the 'covenant', lest his theology collapse back into Jewish particularism. He nevertheless conceded that 3.25f. certainly looked like a Christian version of Jewish covenantal theology. He therefore had to postulate something which we might have thought hugely unlikely, namely that here, at one of the most sensitive and vital moments in his letter, Paul had simply incorporated, without proper assimilation and reworking, a fragment of an earlier Jewish-Christian covenantal confession into his otherwise non-covenantal discourse.[31] All this was, no doubt, partly because Käsemann and his followers were Lutheran rather than Reformed. I remember with fondness an angry Lutheran review of *The Climax of the Covenant*, in which the reviewer was fairly cross with me for daring to suggest that Paul held a covenantal theology, but far more cross with Fortress Press, a Lutheran publishing house, for daring to put out such a thing. Surely that's Reformed theology! We Lutherans shouldn't be supporting it! But also, more to the point, it will have been because Käsemann thought that 'covenant' would import a measure of bland, flattened-out 'salvation history', a straightforward affirmation of Israel which left no room for the cross, a smooth continuity rather than a dramatic inbreaking of God's fresh saving power, into Paul's apocalyptic train of thought.[32] I hope it is clear that when we understand Paul's reading of the single divine plan such fears are shown to be groundless. God's action in Jesus the Messiah, resulting in his affirmation of all those who belong to him, is the fulfilment of the covenantal promises made in Genesis 15.

And, of course, there is the lawcourt, which Paul has so carefully set up in 3.10 and 3.19f. God is the judge; all human beings alike are in the dock, guilty as charged, with nothing to say in their defence. But, six verses later, the judge is declaring them 'righteous'! How can this be?

We need to remind ourselves severely (because the point is so easily forgotten or allowed to slide sideways out of consciousness, making room for other competing notions) that 'righteous' here does not mean 'morally virtuous'. It means, quite simply, that the court has found in your favour. That is why the declarative verb *dikaioō*, 'to justify', can be said to indicate the *creation* of something, the *making* of something. But, as we noted earlier, the thing that is made is not a moral character, not an infused virtue, but a *status*. God really does, by virtue of his declaration, create this status for all those who belong to the Messiah. 'They are justified freely, by his grace, through the redemption which is in the Messiah, Jesus' (3.24). 'God is both righteous, and the justifier (the "rightwiser", to make the verbal link) of "the Jesus-faith person"' (3.26).

Notice what has *not* happened, within this lawcourt scene. The judge has not clothed the defendant with his own 'righteousness'. That doesn't come into it. Nor has he given the defendant something called 'the righteousness of the Messiah' – or, if he has, Paul has not even hinted at it. What the judge has done is to pass judicial sentence on sin, in the faithful death of the Messiah, so that those who belong to the Messiah, though in themselves 'ungodly' and without virtue or merit, now find themselves hearing the lawcourt verdict, 'in the right'. And the point, putting covenant and lawcourt together, is that *this is what the single-plan-through-Israel-for-the-world was designed to do!* The covenant purpose is accomplished, being turned into the single-plan-*through-Israel's-faithful-representative*-for-the-world. And 'the world', therefore, must now include the rest of Israel as well as the Gentiles.

Underneath all this, then, is Christology. Here again is the truth to which, at its best, the doctrine of 'imputed righteousness' can function as a kind of signpost. God has 'put forth' Jesus so that, through his faithful death, all those who belong to him can be regarded as having died. God raised him up so that, through his vindication, all those who belong to him can be regarded as being themselves vindicated. Since that is more or less exactly what Paul says in 4.25, and spells out at length in chapter 6, the point ought to be fairly clear. 'The faithfulness of the Messiah' is a shorthand way of saying that in Jesus, as Israel's representative (and hence the new, personal, middle term in the single-plan-through-Israel-for-the-world), God has accomplished what he always said he would. 'The faithfulness of the Messiah' is, actually, a way of stressing – as one might have thought any good Reformed theologian would welcome! – the sovereignty of God and the unshakeable, rock-bottom reality, within the events of justification and salvation, not of the faith of those being justified, but of the representative and therefore substitutionary death of Israel's Messiah, Jesus. Does this mean, then (as has been asserted), that I am saying that we should 'put our trust in anyone or anything other than the crucified and resurrected Saviour?' Don't be ridiculous. This way of reading Romans *emphasizes* the crucified and resurrected Saviour in a way that nothing else (in my humble but accurate opinion) can do.

Why then does human faith play the part it does within this scheme of thought? We are so used to the fact that it *does* play this part that we do not normally enquire as to the reason. Three possible options initially present themselves. The first is decidedly sub-standard (though it points, ultimately, in the right direction), and the second and third, though much better, still do not get to the root of the matter.

1 It will not really do to say, baldly, that faith is the proper, appropriate response, as though we were to measure various possible

181

'religious attitudes' against some invisible yardstick, some measuring scheme for rival spiritualities, and to conclude that faith was the best of them. That caricature is sometimes carried over into the present passage, so that, for instance, Genesis 15.6, quoted in 4.3, is glossed with the idea that God has been looking for a genuinely 'righteous' person, and discovering that when he makes Abraham a promise Abraham believes him, declares 'Yes! That's the sort of "righteousness" I was looking for! "Faith" is the real thing, the genuine article, far more important than all that moralistic self-help stuff.' That is not what 4.3, or for that matter Genesis 15.6, is about, as we shall see. There is a grain of truth here, but to tease it out we shall have to wait a moment.

2 It is true, but not the whole truth, that 'it must be by faith because it cannot be by the law' in the sense (the new perspective) that, if it were through the law, only Jews would benefit, so it must be by some other means in order that Gentiles can come in too.

3 Likewise, it is true, but not the whole truth, that 'it must be by faith because it cannot be by the law' in the sense (the old perspective) that, if it were through the law, nobody would qualify since all have sinned, so that it must be by some other means in order that sinners can still be saved. This, in fact, makes if anything less sense than the previous one, since 'faith' itself, in the full Christian sense, is not, as Paul well knew, something that anyone can just summon up out of a supposedly 'neutral' mindset. As today's atheists and their anxious onlookers will testify, 'faith' in almost any religious sense seems hard to the point of impossibility for many, and this is probably not such a new phenomenon as post-Enlightenment persons sometimes suppose.

Three better answers are available.

1 First, Paul has anchored his view of faith to the two biblical texts already mentioned, Habakkuk 2.4 and Genesis 15.6. These are not, as we have seen, merely decontextualized prooftexts. Habakkuk speaks of a time when the cosmos seems to be shaking, and God's people are called to be faithful while they await the revelation of God's covenant justice and faithfulness. God promised Abraham certain things which encompassed the entire single-plan-through-Israel-for-the-world, and the proper response to a promise – particularly a promise from God! – is

to believe it. Sanders was right that Paul privileged these two texts in both Romans and Galatians, but he never saw that they create a context of expectation within which he might be said to have made the crucial connection: if God justifies people in the present, ahead of the final judgment, faith must be the characteristic of those thus justified.

2 A second answer, further away in some senses and nearer at hand in others, may be found in the gospels. Throughout all four gospels Jesus calls for faith, for belief, and declares repeatedly that when God acts in and through him he does so in the context of people's faith. 'Go home; your faith has saved you.' 'Your faith has made you well.' 'Let it be for you in accordance with your faith.' Faith is a major theme in John: 'as many as received him, as believed in his name, to them he gave the right to become God's children'. We cannot prove that Paul knew any of this tradition, or that it formed part of the climate in early Christianity because of which 'faith' came to play the role it did in his theology. But the link is striking, and all the more so for not being made as often as perhaps it should be.

3 The third answer, which goes to the roots of it all, is found eventually (if only, we sometimes think, Paul had followed our rhetorical needs rather than the needs of his own argument!) towards the end of chapter 4. *Faith of Abraham's kind is the sign of a genuine humanity, responding out of total human weakness and helplessness to the grace and power of God, and thus giving God the glory.* That is the point of 4.19–21, where Paul demonstrates how in the case of Abraham we may witness the reversal of the catastrophic sequence of idolatry, the denial of God's power and glory, and the consequent dehumanization that he had catalogued in 1.18–25. This is the point at which the grain of truth in the first view I mentioned a moment ago at last emerges. But that view, as often expressed, makes it sound extremely arbitrary, or as though God is really an existentialist who simply wants an 'authentic' response rather than an 'external' one. Putting it this way brings out the full flavour: the faith of Abraham, which Paul sees as the exact model for the faith of the Christian (4.23–25), is the faith which indicates the presence of genuine, humble, trusting, and indeed we might say image-bearing humanity (compare Colossians 3.10). And, within that,

'faithfulness' has all along (so it seems) been the thing that God requires from his people, the 'Israel' who are the middle term in his single plan. If the plan has been fulfilled by the Messiah's faithfulness (*pistis*), the badge of the covenant people from then on will be the same: *pistis*, faith, confessing that Jesus is Lord and believing that God raised him from the dead (10.9). Faith of this sort is the true-Israel, true-human sign, the badge of God's redeemed people.

How then does this faith arise? Have we not backed ourselves into a corner where 'faith' of this sort has become a 'work', a really good, indeed striking and remarkable, 'religious' attitude which then commends itself to God? Not at all. Paul does not explain the full answer at the present point of Romans, but he has hinted at it. 'The gospel is God's power for salvation': the preaching of the gospel, in the power of the spirit, is the means by which, as an act of sheer grace, God evokes this faith in people from Abraham to the present day and beyond. It is a mystery, but it is held within the larger mystery of that same overarching divine grace. 'Nobody can say "Jesus is Lord"' (the basic Christian confession of faith) 'except by the Holy Spirit.'[33] When the word of the gospel is proclaimed, the spirit goes to work in ways that the preacher cannot predict or control and which often take the hearers, and the responders, by surprise as well.[34] 'Faith comes by hearing, and hearing by the word of the Messiah' – in other words, the announcement of the gospel of God concerning his son.[35] This is what Paul means in Galatians 3.2 and 5 when he talks of the *akoē pisteōs*, often translated the 'hearing of faith' or 'hearing with faith'. The word *akoē* can mean 'the act of hearing', or indeed either the faculty of hearing or its appropriate organ, i.e. the ear. But most commentators have concluded, rightly in my view, that the meaning here, an equally likely one in terms of the word's use elsewhere, is that of 'report', a message: 'the message which elicited faith'.[36] Paul can say the same thing in several different ways, but the underlying reality is the same. What he refers to as God's 'call' (Romans 8.29 and frequently) is the moment when, out of sheer grace, the word of the gospel, blown on by the powerful wind of the spirit, transforms hearts and minds so that, although it is known to be ridiculous and even shameful, people come to believe that Jesus is Lord and that God raised him from the dead. Faith is itself the sign of grace. Paul has not spelled that out at this point in his argument, but the other passages at which we have glanced tell that uniform story.

V

'Where then is boasting? It is excluded' (3.27).

By now it should be not only boasting that is ruled out, but also any lingering doubt about Paul's meaning. The 'boast' in question is the 'boast' of 2.17–20: the 'boast' that Israel could take its place within the single-plan-through-Israel-for-the-world, the boast not merely of superiority (and perhaps salvation) because of Torah-possession (and the attempt at Torah-keeping) but of a superior *calling* within God's purposes. Paul will have none of it. Drawing on 2.25–29, he insists: Torah, which you are using to prop up this boast (despite all the things that Torah then tells you about your own failures), this Torah itself declares that your boasted position in God's purposes has been taken away and given to others. 'If the uncircumcision keeps the commandments of Torah, will not its uncircumcision be reckoned as circumcision?' (2.26). 'Boasting excluded – by what Torah? A Torah of works? No – but by the Torah of faith' (3.27). Who are God's people? They are those who keep the Torah – but *whose Torah-keeping consists of faith.*

They are, in other words, those Paul has already spoken of from one angle in 2.7, 10, 13–16 and 25–29. Working back through those remarkable advance statements, they are 'the circumcised-in-heart', 'the Jew-in-secret people', 'the ones who keep Torah and thus have circumcision reckoned to them'; 'the ones who do the Torah and so will be justified on the last day, even though they are Gentiles and don't have the Torah as their ancestral possession', 'the ones who through patience in well-doing seek for glory and honour and immortality'. Now at last we can see not only who these strange people are but what Paul has meant all along by his cryptic and polemical statement of their defining characteristics. True, it will take him until chapter 10 fully to explain what he means, in turn, by this revelation, but nothing is gained by allowing the dead hand of a deliberately obtuse would-be exegesis to flatten 'law' here into 'principle' ('boasting is excluded: on what principle? Works? No, on the principle of faith'). Clearly *nomos* means 'Torah' throughout, as verses 29–31, not to mention 19f. and 4.13–16, indicate. God's people are *those who keep Torah not by works but by faith*, as Paul more or less repeats in 9.31f.

The meaning of the all-important verse 3.28 is held firmly in place by the verses on either side. Verse 27 indicates that 'the Torah of faith' excludes the 'boasting' of 2.17–20. 'The Jew' who claims that possession of Torah is sufficient to establish him or her as part of God's people, those through whom God is bringing light to the world, is confronted with an apparently different 'Torah' which says, 'No, not so fast: this faith-fulfilment is what I had in mind all along, and it eliminates your boasting as surely as if it was drowned in the depths of the sea.' And 3.29 says, 'God was all along the God of Gentiles as well as Jews.' The tiny word *ē* at the start of that verse says, loud and clear for those who are committed to letting every word of the text count instead of eliminating those that are inconvenient for their theories, 'if it were otherwise – if justification were by the works of Torah rather than by faith – then it would mean that God was indeed the God of the Jews only.'

How then must we read 3.28? As the decisive statement which explains (as the *gar*, 'for', indicates) the dramatic claim of 3.27, and as the statement whose immediate implication is that God has one family, not two, and that this family consists of faithful Gentiles as well as faithful Jews (3.30, anticipating 4.11f. and 4.16f.). In other words, 3.28 is saying: God declares a person to be 'righteous' on the basis of faith, apart from those 'works of Torah' which (a) would have established a status for Jews and Jews only and (b) were in any case impossible because Torah would then only have proved that Jews too were sinful. In other words, let's go beyond the new perspective/old perspective divide: both are necessary parts of what Paul is actually saying.[37]

How then does 3.28 play out in terms of the four aspects of justification we have already set out? First, the lawcourt setting, so strong in 3.19f., picking up the 'last Assize' theme of 2.1–16 and the attendant imagery of e.g. 3.5f. This is not 'one metaphor among others', but the *appropriate* metaphor, given that Paul's Jewish theology insists on God as the righteous judge who will put the whole world right at the last. The claim of 3.28, exactly in line with the dense advance statement in 3.22f. and 3.26, is that God, the judge, will give his verdict and will thus, as a declaratory, performative act, *make* certain people 'righteous', *always remembering that 'make righteous' here does not mean 'make them morally upright or virtuous' but rather 'make them "people-in-whose-favour-the-verdict-has-been-given"'*. The idea that what sinners need is for someone else's 'righteousness' to be credited to their account simply muddles up the categories, importing with huge irony into the equation the idea that the same tradition worked so hard to eliminate, namely the suggestion that, after all, 'righteousness' here means 'moral virtue', 'the merit acquired from lawkeeping', or something like that. We don't have any of that, said the Reformers, so we have to have someone else's credited to us, and 'justification' can't mean 'being made righteous', as though God first pumps a little bit of moral virtue into us and then generously regards the part as standing for the whole. No, replies Paul, you've missed the point; you haven't gone far enough in eliminating the last traces of mediaeval misunderstanding. 'Righteousness' remains the status that you possess as a result of the judge's verdict. For the defendant in the lawcourt (3.19f.) it simply means 'acquitted', 'forgiven', 'cleared', 'in good standing in the community as a result of the judge's pronouncement'. 'Imputed righteousness' is a Reformation answer to a mediaeval question, in the mediaeval terms which were themselves part of the problem.[38]

In good standing in the community: where does that take us? The second element in justification is of course (in terms of our previous analysis) that of the *covenant*. The question is, exactly as in Galatians 2.11–21, Who are the members of God's single family, and how can you tell? This is the theme which began to emerge in 2.25–29 and which will come through strongly in chapter 4. This is not to elevate some strange, extraneous notion of 'covenantal theology' over and above all the other things that are going on in the passage (not least in Paul's exposition of Genesis 15 in chapter 4). It is to recognize that this is part of the root meaning of the words Paul is using, that Torah itself was the covenant charter which left Israel with the puzzling question, how it could be fulfilled and thus do its job of designating God's people and keeping them on track. 'The works of Torah' could not do it, partly because Israel failed lamentably to perform them (2.21–24) and partly because, to the extent that those 'works' focused on the things which kept Jews separate from Gentiles, they would have prevented the establishment of the single family God always had in mind – just as we saw in Galatians 3. But this 'covenantal', and hence 'ecclesiological', meaning of 'justification' – once again, am I wrong to detect in some 'old perspective' supporters a deep fear of 'ecclesiology', as though to give an inch at this point will mean that they have to take the church more seriously than they have previously done? – is not to be played off against the whole theme of the acquittal of sinners through the faithful death of Jesus the Messiah. That faithful death remains the foundation; that acquittal and all that flows from it remains the joyful result. But those who believe the gospel – who 'believe in the God who raised Jesus from the dead' (4.25), who 'believe in their hearts that God raised him from the dead' (10.9) – are thereby constituted, not as a bunch of saved individuals, but as *the single family which God promised to Abraham*. The reasons why this matters are clear from Galatians, and are also clear in Romans chapters 14 and 15.

Along with lawcourt and covenant goes *eschatology*. Paul has set up a further question which will take him until chapter 8 to address fully. The new note he strikes in 3.21–31 (justified in the present on the basis of nothing but faith!) sounds initially all wrong in terms of the tune he was playing in 2.1–16 (justified in the future on the basis of the entire life!). He has set himself the challenge of filling in the intervening harmony and showing how, in fact, it is exactly what was required. 'But now' (3.21) is not simply a logical statement, 'but as it is' or something like that. It is the indication that the verdict of the last day, the verdict which Paul spent so much time setting up in 2.1–16, has already been announced, in advance of the whole life of the persons concerned. The judge has declared the verdict before the evidence has been produced! He has told us the result of the trial just as the lawyers were getting ready to deliver their carefully prepared speeches for and against the defendants – and when the defendants were already hanging their heads in shame, knowing that they were guilty (3.19f.)! What on earth is going on? How can such a judge be 'righteous' in the good Old Testament terms of being true to the law, hearing the case fairly, punishing the wicked and upholding the virtuous? And yet Paul has declared that this judge is indeed 'in the right'. What sense does this make?

All the sense in the world; because it is based on the fourth element in justification, namely *Christology*. The bringing-of-the-future-verdict-forward-into-the-present is rooted, grounded, rock-bottom established, on the bringing-of-the-Messiah-forward-into-the-present; more specifically, on the extraordinary, unprecedented and unimagined fact of the *resurrection itself* coming forward into the present. The Messiah is not simply a figure who will emerge at the very end. Resurrection is no longer simply a last-day event in which God will raise all his people. Messiah and resurrection are middle-of-history events in which God has come to inaugurate his kingdom, his sovereign, saving rule of all creation. In and through the Messiah, God has dealt with the whole problematic fact of idolatry, sin and death and so has begun, in the Messiah's resurrection, the new creation which is the great new Fact standing in the middle of time, space and human culture.

This Christology, this message about Jesus which is at the very heart of Paul's gospel, is the basis for the lawcourt verdict, the covenant announcement, the bringing of the future verdict forwards into the present. When God raised Jesus from the dead, he said in the deafening language of actual historic event what he had said in the strange descent of the dove at Jesus' baptism: 'This is my beloved son, in whom I am well pleased.' In other words: this is the faithful Messiah, in whom my purpose for, and my call to, Israel is fulfilled. And what God said about Jesus in that moment, he said and says about all those who belong to Jesus the Messiah. His unique and decisive death is the reason why the verdict 'in the right' can be announced in advance of the final day. His unique and decisive resurrection is the defeat, already in the present, of death itself, and of sin which was its cause. That is why the verdict can rightly be announced. That is why we can tell, in the present time, who belongs to the covenant family. Christology and eschatology together undergird the lawcourt scenario and the covenant definition.

This brings us back once more to the question: But why is faith the badge? Paul has not yet explained that; he has merely asserted *that* it is so. The crucial answers to the question are given in 4.18–25 and 9.30—10.13, and we shall get to them in due course. For the moment we merely note his dramatic, but now thoroughly comprehensible, conclusion to the present argument. Justification by faith on the basis of Jesus' faithful death and triumphant resurrection, revealing the 'righteousness' of the creator God, his faithfulness to the covenant-through-Israel-for-the-world – this justification means that God now declares circumcised and uncircumcised alike 'in the right', 'members of the covenant family', the former 'on the basis of faith' and the latter 'through faith' – a small but perhaps important distinction.[39] And, just in case anyone should imagine that all this was a way of sweeping the Torah aside as irrelevant, the Torah is, to the contrary, hereby established. Torah always intended *both* that God would fulfil his purpose for and through Israel *and* that ethnic Israel could not be God's people alone. That mystery lies at the heart of Romans 7, which is outside the reach of the present book, though ultimately part of the same continuous argument. But we have said enough to turn the page and launch into one of Paul's greatest expositions of God's covenant and how it is fulfilled.

VI

We cannot say it too often. Abraham is not simply an 'example' of someone who is justified by faith. Romans 4 is not just an 'illustration', or even a 'biblical proof', of the theological point Paul has just made. You might as well say that the American Constitution was just a good 'example' of political theory – when in fact it continues to provide the framework for what that whole great country is and does. Nor is Paul simply indulging a piece of clever rhetoric, guessing that his implicit or actual opponents will say, 'What about Abraham?' and trying to outdo them in advance.

None of those proposals, all of which have been prominent in exegesis and preaching, comes near to doing justice to what Paul has in mind here as well as in Galatians 3. He sees God's promise to Abraham as the foundation of the single-plan-through-Israel-for-the-world, in short, the covenant. Yes, there are other covenants: Noah, Moses, Phinehas even, David, and so on. These are not unimportant, and for Paul (as for some of his contemporaries) the spelling-out of the covenant in Deuteronomy 27—30 in terms of a historical sequence of events was particularly significant. But Abraham is where it all starts. Abraham is where things get shaped.

And it is God's faithfulness to his promises to Abraham that, as in many passages of the Old Testament, is the key central meaning of 'God's righteousness'. The section which began at 3.21 did not finish at 3.31; it merely sets up the fuller exposition of the same point, the *dikaiosynē theou*. The tragedy of much Reformation reading of Paul is that, by using up the language of 'God's righteousness' on the unnecessary project of 'finding someone's righteousness to impute to the believer' as though 'righteousness' was that sort of thing in the first place, and as though the theological point were not already taken care of 'in Christ', this entire point was not just sidelined but binned. And with that the entire single narrative, the entire *Jewish* narrative, was lost from view. (Which was the chicken, and which the egg? Did the church, and exegesis, first reject the Jewish narrative and then ignore 'God's righteousness', or did it first misunderstand that key phrase and then reject the Jewish narrative?) No wonder chapters 9—11 were stranded at the same time, like an ocean-going vessel high and dry in the harbour after the tide has gone out. Pull out Abraham, and you won't just pull out a single loose thread from the sweater. You will unravel the whole thing.

The point of Romans 4 is, in any case, not simply about 'how people get justified'. The flow of thought from verse 9 onwards indicates that the question towards which Paul is working in the opening verses is rather the question – much as in Galatians 3! – of 'Who are the family of Abraham?' Who are his 'seed' (4.16)? Is this a family of Jews only, so that Gentiles have to come in either as second-class citizens or as actual proselytes? Or, once we have established that Abraham himself was uncircumcised when God 'reckoned it to him as righteousness' in Genesis 15, might it actually be a family of *un*circumcised people, i.e. Gentiles, into whom Jews might struggle for admittance (4.12)? Verses 16 and 17, so often misunderstood and mistranslated when the purpose of the chapter was forgotten or ignored, are the answer to all this, the central statement of what is going on: the promise is valid for 'all the seed', that is, for the entire family, for Jews and Gentiles alike, because Abraham is the father of us all, in accordance with what Genesis had said, and, behind that, in accordance with the very character of God himself. In a fairly literal translation, these key verses read:

> Therefore it is by faith, so that it might be in accordance with grace, so that the promise might be confirmed for all the seed, not only that which is from the law but also that which is from the faith

of Abraham, who is the father of us all, as it is written, 'father of many nations have I appointed you,' before the God in whom he believed, who gives life to the dead and calls non-existent things into existence.

That is the subject of the chapter: the one true family, Abraham as its father, and the God who, by being the lifegiver and creator, has been true to his promise.

And that is why far and away the best translation of the normally puzzling first verse is a question, not about something that Abraham (who happens to be our father) had 'found', but about *in what sense we have found Abraham to be our father.* This proposal, made originally by Richard Hays (though with some distant antecedents) and modified (with Hays's approval) by myself, has been rejected by most subsequent writers but without, I think, being understood.[40]

'What then shall we say? Have we found Abraham to be our forefather according to the flesh?' Grammatically this works very well indeed, a great deal better than the normal translations which have to insert extra words. Literally, more or less word by word, the sentence reads, 'What then shall we say to have found Abraham our forefather according to the flesh?' The usual translation keeps it as a single sentence, and supposes that Paul is going to talk about 'how Abraham got justified', and so makes 'Abraham' the subject of 'to have found': 'What shall we say that Abraham found [in this matter]' – which is an odd way of saying even what the normal theory wants Paul to have said. The alternative proposal starts from the observation that Paul often begins a new argument with 'What then shall we say?', followed by a suggestion of what we *might* expect to say which Paul will then refute. (Remember that the earliest manuscripts of the New Testament have no punctuation, and indeed no breaks between words, so that suggestions like this are very much in order.) And from what we have already seen about the emphasis of the chapter, particularly from verse 9 onwards, it makes excellent sense to suppose that Paul's putting forward of a view which he is then going to reject would concern the limiting of Abraham's family to Judaism according to the flesh. The main theme of the chapter is the single family, Abraham as its father, and God as the one before whom Abraham stood and in whose promises and, ultimately, character he trusted. The following translation, which works extremely well with the Greek, brings this out:

> What then shall we say? Have we found Abraham to be our forefather according to the flesh? For if Abraham was justified by works, he has a boast – but not in the presence of God.

This sets up exactly that question to which verses 16–17 are the answer, towards which the rest of the chapter is building and from which the conclusion flows. We are back once more with the question of 'boasting', not simply of 'Has this person got some moral achievements to be proud of?' but 'Can this person, in and of himself, be the one through whom God is going to accomplish his purposes?' The question, just as in 2.17–20, is not so much about Abraham's own accomplishment, justification and so on, but about that justification as part of the larger question of the whole chapter. Was there something about Abraham which made him specially appealing to God? There were, after all, many theories among ancient Jews as to why God chose Abraham. Was he a man of special virtue? Is that why he became the father of this family-through-whom-God-would-save-the-world?

Paul's answer is an emphatic No. Scripture says that God made a promise to Abraham, that Abraham believed it, and that God 'reckoned it to him as righteousness'. What follows in 4.4–8 makes it crystal clear that 'reckoned it as righteousness' means that although Abraham was 'ungodly', a 'sinner', God did not count this against him. The covenant of Genesis 15, in other words, was a matter of sheer grace from its very first moments (as stressed in 4.16: 'by faith, so that it might be by grace').

Reading the passage this way means that 4.3–8 does not constitute, as Simon Gathercole and others have argued, a 'smoking gun' indicating that Paul is after all working with an 'old perspective' framework rather than a 'new perspective' one.[41] Yes, of course, he is arguing that Abraham was 'ungodly' when God called him, and that it was his faith in 'the one who justifies the ungodly' (4.5) – corresponding to his faith in 'the God who raises the dead and calls the non-existent things into existence' (4.17) – that simply clung on to the promises despite that ungodliness. And the 'promise', after all, which Abraham believed – and remember that here, as usual, Paul is far more aware of the biblical context of the passages he is quoting than most of us are – was not, as the 'old perspective' might have imagined, 'the promise that his sins would be forgiven and that he would go to heaven when he died'. It was, rather, *that he would have a family* as numerous as the stars in the heavens (Genesis 15.5). Paul has not, in other words, suddenly stopped talking about Abraham's family and started talking about 'how you can have your sins forgiven', still less 'how you can go to heaven when you die'. The point he is making is that, in calling Abraham and promising him his innumerable descendants, God was thereby acting in sheer grace, irrespective of the fact that Abraham had no merit to commend him. The brief discussion in verses 4 and 5 about people 'earning a reward' (or not as the case may be) does not mean that Paul is after all talking about proto-Pelagianism, self-help moralism or whatever, except to this extent: that he is ruling out any suggestion that Abraham might have been 'just the sort of person God was looking for', so that there might be some merit prior to the promise, in other words, some kind of 'boast'. As Psalm 31 indicates, even the great king David, joined interestingly with Abraham here as in Matthew 1, counted his 'blessing' from God simply in terms of the non-reckoning of sin. He may have been 'the man after God's own heart', but this had nothing to do with antecedent merit which commended him.

Forgiveness – the non-reckoning of sin – is thus right at the heart of the larger picture which Paul is sketching, but we must not for that reason ignore that larger picture. *The point of God's covenant with Abraham, to give him a single great family, always was that this was how sins would be forgiven, and the initial establishment of that covenant embodied the same principle.* That is how 4.3–8 plays its proper part within the ongoing argument of 3.21—4.25.

The rest of the chapter now falls into place. 4.9–12 asks the same question as 4.1, from a different angle and a more specific point of view: to whom do the Abrahamic promises belong? Do they belong only to the circumcised, or to the uncircumcised as well? Paul has not forgotten 2.25–29 and 3.29f.; this is still central to his concern. 'Have we found Abraham to be our forefather according to the flesh?' – because, if we have, the blessing will *only* come on those who share Abraham's circumcision, and we will be back with the Galatian agitators.[42] No: in Genesis 15 Abraham was still uncircumcised, and when he was circumcised in Genesis 17 this was as a sign of the covenant already made in chapter 15. As we saw earlier, 4.11 expounds Genesis 17.11, so that where Genesis says 'covenant' Paul says *dikaiosynē*, 'righteousness', which is why we are right to understand the latter term, here at least but then by implication in many other places, as 'covenant status'. Abraham received circumcision as a sign and seal *of the covenant status he had by faith while in uncircumcision*, so that he might be the father of all believers, whatever their state. Thus 4.11–12 provide a clear answer to the question of 4.1 within the more specific terms of circumcision and the covenant, with a remarkable extra twist: 4.12 indicates not only that uncircumcised believers are welcome into Abraham's family but that the circumcised are welcome too *if they too believe*.[43]

If that is true for circumcision, the same is true if we ask the question in terms of Torah (4.13–17). Doing so brings the developing picture to a remarkable new stage. In Genesis 15 and elsewhere, God promised Abraham the holy land; but Paul, in line with some other second-Temple Jews, interpreted this in terms of God's design out beyond the land, to reclaim the entire creation, the whole world. Again, the point of this whole chapter is not about how Abraham got saved, or justified, but about *the single promise through Abraham for the world*. And once again the point about the Torah is twofold: (a) to cling to it would be to embrace the wrath which results from having broken it; (b) to highlight it would be to restrict the covenantal promises to Jews only. Both perspectives matter, and the two fit snugly together within Paul's overall view of God's call and promise to Abraham. 4.16b is the climactic answer to the question of 4.1: Abraham is the father of us *all*, the law-people and the non-law people, Jews and Gentiles alike, the dead who need to be brought back to life and the non-existent who need to come to life for the first time (4.17).

The whole chapter, then, is not about 'how Abraham got justified by faith' so much as 'God's faithfulness to his promises to Abraham, giving him a worldwide family whose badge is the same faith that Abraham himself had'. Abraham's own 'justification by faith' is thus part of the picture, but it is not the whole, or the main frame. Verses 18–22 explore Abraham's faith, and probe to see what exactly it was that he believed, in such a way as to highlight the fact that it all depended on God's promise and God's power. Abraham's faith consisted of looking away from his own situation and possibilities and continuing to trust God and give him the glory – the reverse of the idolatrous human race as described in 1.18–23. And the crunch-point of the chapter, the ultimate answer to the question of 4.1, the long-term result of the revelation of God's righteousness apart from Torah in 3.21, is stated in 4.23–25: all those who believe in 'the God who raised Jesus our Lord from the dead' are part of Abraham's single family, which means that they, too, have their sins forgiven. Genesis 15.6 is not a detached, long-range prediction or type, otherwise unrelated to the present status of Christians. It is the foundation charter of Abraham's family, and it has not changed from that day to this.

What has changed is that now, at last, we can see, so to speak, how it works. How can God act in such a way, declaring Abraham and all other believers 'in the right', 'acquitted', even though they are ungodly and sinful? Answer: Jesus. He 'was handed over because of our trespasses' (the echoes of Isaiah 53.5, 12 should be unmistakable), 'and raised because of our justification'. The old debate about the precise significance of *dia* here ('because of') should not be a problem in the light of all that we have said so far. 'Our trespasses' were the reason for his death. The successful dealing with those trespasses on the cross, the overcoming of sin and the accomplishment of 'our justification', was the reason for his resurrection. Or, to put it another way, echoing 1 Corinthians 15.17: if the Messiah is not raised, you are still in your sins, because if the cross had dealt with sin it would also have dealt with death. But in fact Jesus' resurrection, the primary object of foundational Christian faith, here and in 10.9, is the direct result, and hence the demonstration, of the fact that on the cross sins were indeed dealt with. God's purpose in establishing the covenant with Abraham – to create a worldwide family whose sins were forgiven – is thereby accomplished, with the one and only badge of faith: faith both in 'the God who raised Jesus' and, for the same reason, in 'the God who justifies the ungodly'. Paul has now shown that these amount more or less to the same thing. This faith is the direct response to the faithfulness of God, the glad acknowledgment of the power and glory of God. It is not itself a 'work', an 'achievement' even in the so-called 'religious' sphere, because – and here of course many 'old perspective' writers get it quite right – it consists simply of looking away from oneself to God the creator and lifegiver.

This exposition of chapter 4 demonstrates how exactly 3.21f. ('But now, God's righteousness has been manifested apart from Torah' etc.) sums up in advance the whole argument of 3.21—4.25, not simply 3.21–31 with chapter 4 as an explanatory appendix or 'proof from scripture'. Looking back to 3.21f., we can re-read it in exactly the terms of chapter 4 as we have expounded it: 'Now, God's covenant faithfulness has been manifested apart from Torah, though with Torah and prophets bearing witness to it: God's covenant faithfulness, his faithfulness to the promises he made to Abraham and through Abraham to the whole world, put into operation through the faithful death of the Messiah, Jesus, for the benefit of all who share Abraham's faith.' The whole passage is about the forgiveness of sins, because the whole passage is about something larger, namely God's covenant purpose to put the world right through his chosen people, Abraham's family. And from here there is a straight line to 8.19. The whole creation, already promised to Abraham in 4.13, is now longing for God's entire family of children to be raised from the dead, so that God's ultimate purpose, his promise-through-Abraham's-family-for-the-whole-creation, might at last come true. But to get there we must set 8.19 in the context of the justification-teaching of chapters 5—8 as a whole.

VII

Most readers who go looking for Paul's theology of justification give up exhausted at the end of Romans 4, and assume that he now passes on to some other topic, for instance 'sanctification' or 'salvation', or perhaps – with an eye to 8.29f. – 'glorification'. The last of those is the most accurate in terms of the text of the letter, and it is true that the opening summary of the argument so far in 5.1 ('Being therefore justified by faith') indicates that Paul believes he has now expounded that topic in such a way that he can build something else upon it. Fine. But there is still much to learn about justification itself from the continual backward glances that Paul throws, during the argument of chapters 5 and 6, towards chapters 3 and 4. And, most importantly, he still has not explained how it is that 3.21—4.25 fit together with 2.1–16: how, in other words, the verdict issued *in the present* on the basis of faith in God the creator and lifegiver who raised Jesus from the dead (3.21—4.25) will correspond to the verdict issued *in the last day* over those who 'by patience in well-doing seek for glory and honour and immortality' (2.7), those who 'do the law' (2.13, 26).

The opening paragraph of chapter 5 suggests that precisely these thoughts are not far from his mind. We boast, he says, in our hope of God's glory; and also in our sufferings, because suffering produces patience, patience produces character, and character produces hope, a hope that does not disappoint. It sounds as though he is picking up the theme of chapter 2, in order to say: the people who are already justified by faith are the people who will live the sort of life I described earlier on, those who will have the present verdict confirmed in the future. Chapters 5—8 is, in fact, a single great argument for *assurance*, the Christian doctrine that 'those whom God justified, them he also glorified' (8.30). In other words, that the verdict *already* announced is indeed a true anticipation of the verdict *yet to be* announced. The journey from 5.1–5 to 8.31–39 is also the journey from 3.21–31 back to 2.1–16.

Note, first, the strong and clear summary statements of what justification is and how it has been achieved. Chapter 5 expands the opening statement of verses 1 and 2, which means that there is repeated reference back to 'being justified'. But, interestingly, after verse 2 Paul never again in the chapter refers to 'faith'. Indeed, the *pistis* root, having played such a prominent role in chapters 3 and 4, is found nowhere at all after 5.2 until the end of chapter 9.[44] Instead, Paul concentrates on attributing justification, not to anything at all on the part of those who are justified, but to the work of the Messiah. The Messiah died, at the right time, for the ungodly (5.6 echoes 'God justifying the ungodly' in 4.5); he died for us while we were still sinners (5.7b, echoing the summary of 'the gospel' in 1 Corinthians 15.3), and this is the demonstration-in-action of God's love for us (5.7a, echoing 'God put him forth' in 3.25). This can all be summarized as 'being therefore now justified in his blood' (5.9a), the reference to 'blood' taking us back again to 3.25, and this in turn can be interpreted as 'when we were enemies, we were reconciled to God through the death of his son' (5.10a), which is clearly the point at which 'being justified' in 5.1 shades over into 'we have peace with God'. Justification, itself the product of God's self-giving love, effects reconciliation between God and humans.

But justification and reconciliation are not the same thing. Paul clearly distinguishes them in 5.1. 'Justification', as we have seen, is the act of God that brings about the new situation in terms of the lawcourt, the covenant and eschatology, on the basis of God's achievement in the Messiah. This act of 'justification' enables God to deal, as a consequence, with a different problem, which Paul has not mentioned up to now, namely the *actual relationship* between God and humans. (Many, seeing correctly that 'justification' is a 'relational' concept, make a mistake here, sliding between the law-court and actual inter-personal relationships without realizing that the two are different kinds of things.) Formerly they were at enmity; now they are reconciled. Once again, this is not simply 'another metaphor for the atonement'. It is, rather, a further and essentially different point from that of the lawcourt. In the lawcourt, the point is not that the defendant and the judge have fallen out and need to re-establish a friendship. Indeed, in some ways the lawcourt is more obviously fair and unbiased if the defendant and the judge have no acquaintance before and no friendship afterwards.

The question then presses as to why Paul has introduced this new topic. The answer he himself suggests is that the next stage of the letter's argument (chapters 5—8) is framed by the strong doctrine of God's *love*. With this we realize, of course, that we have not in fact left behind one key element of justification, namely the covenant. The covenant, as the notion developed in Israel, became seen as the marriage bond between YHWH and his people, so that the re-establishment of the covenant (Isaiah 54) following the work of the Servant (Isaiah 53) might bear fruit, the fruit of new creation (Isaiah 55). The idea of God's unbreakable bond with his people over-arches the entire discussion, with justification as one outworking and reconciliation as another, the latter consequent upon the former.

But it is the language of justification, not so much of reconciliation, that dominates the summary (in 5.12–21) of where the argument has got to so far. The force of the Adam–Christ contrast grows directly out of the long argument concerning Abraham, since God's purpose in calling Abraham, as we have seen, was to deal with the problem created through Adam. If God has now been true to the promises to Abraham, it must mean that the long entail of sin and death has been overcome, so that the way is clear to the rescue of human beings and, through them, the rescue of the whole of creation.

After the opening setting of the scene (5.12–14), Paul develops the point in two moves. First, he shows that there is in fact a gross imbalance between (a) sin and its effects and (b) grace and its effects (5.15–17). Then he shows that, granted this imbalance, one can at last view, as though from a great height, the victory of God over all the forces of evil through Jesus the Messiah (5.18–21), taking in at a single glance the map of all that territory which the Christian now inhabits and in which, through the spirit, God's people move from justification to glorification. In other words, 5.15–21 provide the foundation for that further exposition which will occupy Paul in chapters 6—8. Or, to put it another way, 5.15–21 offers an extended summary of 1.18—4.25 which then paves the way for the expansion of 5.1b–5 which will occur in 6—8.

Thus, throughout 5.15–21, Paul summarizes the achievement of God in Christ in terms of 'righteousness' and 'justification' (remembering still that these share the same Greek root):

> 5.16b: the gift following many trespasses led to 'the verdict "righteous"' (*dikaiōma*);
> 5.17b: how much more will those who receive the abundance of grace and of the gift of righteousness (*dikaiosynē*) reign in life through the one man Jesus Christ;
> 5.18b: even so, through a single 'righteous act' (*dikaiōma*), to all people, to 'justification of life' (*dikaiōsis zōēs*);
> 5.19b: even so, through the obedience of the one man the many will be established as 'righteous' (*dikaioi*);
> 5.21b: [so that] ... even so, grace might reign through righteousness (*dikaiosynē*) to 'the life of the age [to come]' through Jesus Christ our Lord.

What do we conclude from this? That Paul has in mind a consistent frame of thought in which (a) *a judicial event* takes place, consisting of (b) the *righteous act* of Jesus, also designated as his 'obedience', and referring to the same event as his 'faithfulness', in other words, his death (3.24–6; 5.6–10), as a result of which (c) *human beings are declared to be 'in the right'*, now enjoying the status of 'righteousness' as a result of the verdict which God has announced (*dikaiōma*) and as God's free gift, so that (d) they might inherit 'the age to come', and not only inherit it but also share

Christ's reign within it. All this simply confirms what we have seen up to this point. There are of course numerous interesting exegetical and theological details which we could in principle explore, but this is not necessary for our overall case. We note in particular that the 'obedience' of Christ is not designed to amass a treasury of merit which can then be 'reckoned' to the believer, as in some Reformed schemes of thought, but is rather a way of saying what Paul says more fully in Philippians 2.8, that the Messiah was 'obedient all the way to death, even the death on the cross'. Jesus Christ has been 'obedient' to the saving plan which was marked out for Israel. He has been the faithful Israelite through whom God's single-plan-through-Israel-for-the-world is now fulfilled.

That is why (in line with the 'for the world' bit) Paul twice hints at the larger picture, out beyond the justification and salvation of human beings. Not only are human beings to be saved; they are to be the agents of God's rule over the renewed creation (5.17). This will be the 'reign of grace' (5.21), the grace which brings about not only 'eternal life' for individuals in God's new world, but that whole new world itself, the 'age to come' for which Israel had longed. This points on to 8.18–26, where the point is that when humans are renewed, creation itself is to be renewed. All this is in line with the promise not just *to* Abraham but *through* Abraham. He was promised that he would 'inherit the world' (4.13), and the entire ancient Israelite understanding of God's covenant purposes for Israel in the land – the virtuous circle of promise, obedience and blessing – is now to come true in a global, and cosmic, sense.

As most exegetes are aware, 5.12–21 forms a kind of platform on which the argument of chapters 6—8 is then constructed; or, changing the metaphor, a quarry from which are cut the great rocks out of which Paul's developing argument is built. That is relatively uncontroversial, but the conclusion we draw from it is often missed: that the notion of 'being in Christ' which Paul develops in these chapters is rooted in, and fully dovetails with, the doctrine of justification. It is not the case, in other words, that one has to choose between 'justification by faith' and 'being in Christ' as the 'centre' of Paul's thought. As many Reformed theologians in particular have seen – though one would not know it from reading John Piper, Stephen Westerholm, and many others – the two must not be played off against one another, and indeed they can only be understood in relation to one another. We are, after all, 'justified in Christ' (Galatians 2.17), so that when Paul summarizes the great argument of Galatians 3 in verses 23–29 we find justification by faith and being in Christ (seen, as in Romans 6, in terms of baptism) held together. And the point is this: there, as here in Romans, they belong together not by being subsumed under one another, either way round (as has always been a danger in Pauline scholarship at least since Wrede and Schweitzer), but by playing their proper role within the larger Pauline whole, namely once again God's single plan through Israel for the world, now fulfilled in the Messiah. 'If you are Christ's, you are Abraham's seed' is the conclusion to Galatians 3. The rhetoric of Romans does it differently: Abraham's family (chapter 4) is founded on God's justifying action in Christ (chapter 5), which is then explained in terms of membership in the Messianic family (chapter 6).

We should not be surprised, then, to find the language of 'righteousness' continuing to crop up in chapter 6 – though not, we note again, any mention of 'faith'.[45] Having established in 6.1–11 that what is true of the Messiah (dying to sin, rising to new life) is now to be 'reckoned' as true of all those who are baptized into him, Paul can use the language of 'unrighteousness' and 'righteousness' to denote the contrasting quality of actions performed in sin on the one hand and in obedience on the other (6.13). When he develops this further in 6.15–20 there are no fewer than four occurrences of *dikaiosynē* in five verses:

> 6.16: Do you not know that you are slaves of the one to whom you yield yourselves in obedience, whether of sin which leads to death or of obedience which leads to *dikaiosynē*?
> 6.18: Having been set free from sin you were enslaved to *dikaiosynē*.
> 6.19b: . . . So now yield your members as slaves of *dikaiosynē* unto sanctification.
> 6.20: For when you were slaves of sin, you were free in regard to *dikaiosynē*.

Here *dikaiosynē* is being used as a way of *denoting* the state into which one comes through baptism and faith, while *connoting* the fact that this state is (a) the result of God's righteousness at work in the gospel, (b) properly described in itself as the state of having-been-declared-in-the-right (the lawcourt perspective) and members-of-God's-people (the covenant perspective), and (c) not just a state, but a state which carries obligations, so that one can be said, after a manner, to be 'enslaved' to it. A moment's reflection on Romans 6 (I have developed this much more fully in my commentaries) suggests the framework within all this makes sense, so that one need not say, as some have done, that Paul is using his technical terms loosely here, or that 'righteousness' has simply collapsed into being a term of 'ethics' as opposed to doctrine. Romans 6 is all about the slaves who come through the water and so are set free; it is, in other words, exodus theology. Baptism recapitulates the story of Israel's escape from Egypt and, as in Romans 8, of the journey to the promised land – in this case, the entire new creation. This opens all sorts of fascinating perspectives on the letter and on Paul in general, but the sharp-edged point for our purpose is this. God's action to free Israel from Egypt was the archetypal *covenantal* action, in fulfilment of the promises to Abraham, resulting in Israel's being bound to God in the covenant made on Sinai. That covenant began with grace ('I am YHWH your God who brought you out of the land of Egypt'), continued with obligation (the commandments) and ended with the promise of blessing on obedience and the warning of curse on disobedience (Deuteronomy). Now, granted the range of meaning available for the word *dikaiosynē*, it carries centrally, as we have seen, the notion of *covenant faithfulness* as well as *covenant membership*, and indeed intertwines those two in exactly the same way as we see in these verses. I therefore conclude that the overarching category which enables Paul to hold together 'justification' and 'being in Christ' is precisely the covenant: the covenant God made with Abraham and fulfilled in Jesus the Messiah. This, as I say, has all sorts of implications for how we read the rest of Romans, not least chapter 7 where Paul necessarily has to deal with the question of the Sinai covenant. But it shows, as Piper and others like him never seem to grasp, the deep and rich integration of Paul's theology and hence the multiple dimensions and connections of 'justification' itself.

There follows from this an exceedingly important point within the present debate. John Piper is rightly concerned to safeguard the great Christian truth that when someone is 'in Christ' God sees them, from that moment on, in the light of what is true of Christ. But, in line with some (though by no means all) of the Protestant Reformers and their successors, he insists on arriving at this conclusion by the route of supposing that the perfect obedience of Jesus Christ – his 'active obedience' as opposed to the 'passive obedience' of his death on the cross – is the ground of this security. Jesus has 'fulfilled the law', and thus amassed a treasury of law-based 'righteousness', which we sinners, having no 'righteousness' of our own, no store of legal merit, no treasury of good works, can shelter within. I want to say, as clearly as I can, to Piper and those who have followed him: this is, theologically and exegetically, a blind alley – but you can get the result you want by a genuinely Pauline route if you pay attention to what is happening here in Romans 6. Three points are vital here.

First, there is no suggestion that when Paul speaks of the 'obedience' of Jesus Christ he refers to his moral uprightness, still less, more specifically, his obedience to the Law of Moses. As we saw in Romans 5, the 'obedience' of Jesus (5.19, with cross-reference to Philippians 2.8) refers back, in line with the 'obedience' of the Isaianic servant, to the achievement of his death. The law arrives as an extra on the stage (5.20), adding a new spin to the whole process but not providing the foundation for a theology of Jesus' supposed righteousness-earning 'active obedience'.

Second, Paul's entire understanding of the Mosaic law is that it never was intended as a ladder of good works up which one might climb to earn the status of 'righteousness'. It was given, yes, as the way of life (7.10), but it was the way of life *for a people already redeemed*. Let's sharpen this up: God did not say to Israel in Egypt, 'Here is my Torah; if you keep it perfectly for a year or two, then I will liberate you from your slavery', but 'I am liberating you now because I promised Abraham I would do so; when, and only when, I have done so, I will give you the way of life that you will need for when you come into your promised land.' This narrative sequence is of enormous importance when we come, as we shortly will, to the outworking of justification in Romans 8. Yes, Israel several times wanted to go back to Egypt, because it was easier to live in slavery than to walk through the wilderness with God and his law. Yes, Israel's rebellion and idolatry in the wilderness did threaten to forfeit the promised inheritance – but God's grace (and Moses' prayers) overcame that as well. Yes, the Mosaic law continued (within the narrative of scripture as it stands) to warn successive generations that they must make real for themselves that freedom from slavery and idolatry that was God's gift by grace in fulfilment of promise. And of course, later on, the worst that God could threaten was that Israel would lose the promised land, would be sent either back to Egypt or off to Babylon. But the fact remains that the Torah, the Mosaic law, was never given or intended as a means whereby either an individual or the nation as a whole might, through obedience, earn liberation from slavery, redemption, rescue, salvation, 'righteousness' or whatever else. The gift always preceded the obligation. That is how Israel's covenant theology worked. *It is therefore a straightforward category mistake, however venerable within some Reformed traditions including part of my own, to suppose that Jesus 'obeyed the law' and so obtained 'righteousness' which could be reckoned to those who believe in him.* To think that way is to concede, after all, that 'legalism' was true after all – with Jesus as the ultimate legalist. At this point, Reformed theology lost its nerve. It should have continued the critique all the way through: 'legalism' itself was never the point, not for us, not for Israel, not for Jesus.

Third, have we thus abandoned the wonderful good news of the gospel? By no means. Paul has a different way, a far more biblical way, of arriving at the desired conclusion. It is not the 'righteousness' of Jesus Christ which is 'reckoned' to the believer. It is his death and resurrection.[46] That is what Romans 6 is all about. Paul does not say, 'I am in Christ; Christ has obeyed the Torah; therefore God regards me as though I had obeyed the Torah.' He says: 'I am in Christ; Christ has died and been raised; therefore God regards me – and I must learn to regard myself – as someone who has died to sin and been raised to newness of life.'

The answer he gives to the opening question of chapter 6 is an answer about *status*. Jesus' death and resurrection is the great Passover (1 Corinthians 5.7), the moment when, and the means by which, we are set free from the slavery of sin once and for all. The challenge to the believer – indeed, one might almost say the challenge of learning to believe at all – is to 'reckon' that this is true, that one has indeed left behind the state of slavery, that one really has come now to stand on resurrection ground (6.6–11). All that the supposed doctrine of the 'imputed righteousness of Christ' has to offer is offered instead by Paul under this rubric, on these terms, and within this covenantal framework.

I cannot stress too strongly the point of principle. We must read scripture in its own way and through its own lenses, instead of imposing on it a framework of doctrine, however pastorally helpful it may appear, which is derived from somewhere else. There are many things which are pastorally helpful in the short or medium term which are not in fact grounded on the deepest possible reading of scripture. That is simply a testimony to the grace of God: we don't have to get everything right before anything can work! But if the church is to be built up and nurtured in scripture it must be *semper reformanda*, submitting all its traditions to the word of God. And when we bring the doctrine of 'imputed righteousness' to Paul, we find that he achieves what that doctrine wants to achieve, but by a radically different route. In fact, he achieves more. To know that one has died and been raised is far, far more pastorally significant than to know that one has, vicariously, fulfilled the Torah.

From Romans 6 we leap straight into Romans 8. For a lifelong exegete to skip over Romans 7 is like a thirsty Irishman ignoring a pint of Guinness. But that is what we must do, because our theme sends us straight to the great chapter where so much of Paul's theology is summed up and celebrated. And in that chapter, despite the tradition of some exegetes that Paul has stopped talking about 'justification' and has now moved to other topics, Paul himself is still cheerfully working out the full implications of what he said in chapters 3, 4 and 5.

'There is therefore now no condemnation for those who are in Christ Jesus' (Romans 8.1). This is, if you like, justification by incorporation. Paul does not mention faith at any point in Romans 8, but the truth of justification is what the whole chapter is about, as Paul returns to the themes briefly sketched in 5.1–5 and develops them in detail, while drawing the narrative of the Christian exodus to its triumphant conclusion with the whole creation sharing the freedom of God's children (8.18–26). How can he say all this about justification, in 8.1–11 and 8.31–39, without mentioning faith? Answer: *because he is talking once more about final justification*, not present justification, and exploring the present status and task of Christians in the light of that. He is returning, in other words, to that much-neglected chapter Romans 2, and showing at last how it is that those who are in Christ, who have died and been raised with him and have received his spirit, are in fact those who 'do the law' in the extended sense he hinted at in 2.25–29, those who 'have the work of the law written on their hearts' as in 2.15, those who 'by patience in well-doing seek for glory and honour and immortality' in 2.7–11. And it is within this context, and only within this context, that we finally discover how Paul puts together the (to us) tricky jigsaw of Christian moral obedience within the celebration of the assurance of final salvation.

We note, first, what 'salvation' actually means. As I have argued at length in *Surprised by Hope*, we are not saved *from* the world of creation, but saved *for* the world of creation (8.18–26). Humans were made to take care of God's wonderful world, and it is not too strong to say that the reason God saves humans is not simply that he loves them for themselves but that he loves them for what they truly are – his pro-creators, his stewards, his vice-gerents over creation. To make this utterly Pauline move is not merely to adjust some nuts and bolts at the edge of his doctrine of salvation, but to shift the weight of the whole thing away from where it has been in the Western church since long before the Reformation and – without losing the necessary Western emphases on the cross – back towards the cosmic focus which Eastern Christians never lost. (Eastern Orthodoxy may have other problems, but at this point we Westerners need to learn from them. One of the greatest tragedies of the Schism of AD 1054 was that the West was able to develop a view of 'salvation' and the East a view of 'transformation', each of which needed the other for a balanced completeness. But that is another story.) 'Salvation' is from death itself, and all that leads to it and shares its destructive character (tribulation, hardship, persecution, famine, nakedness, danger, weaponry) and all the powers that use these things to oppress humans and deface God's world. 'Salvation' does not mean 'dying and going to heaven', as so many Western Christians have supposed for so long. If your body dies and your soul goes into a disembodied immortality, you have not been *rescued from* death; you have, quite simply, died. That is why resurrection means what it means: it is not a bizarre miracle, but the very centre of God's plan and purpose. God will renew the whole creation, and raise his people to new bodily life to share his rule over his world. That is 'what the whole world's waiting for' (Romans 8.19).

And Paul's doctrine of final justification is based solidly on the fact that this great rescue operation, this great renewal of all things, *has already been launched in Jesus Christ, and is already being put into operation through the spirit.* This is Paul's framework for what we have come to think of as 'Christian ethics'. Let me put it like this: if we begin simply with 'justification by faith', as traditionally conceived within much Protestantism, we will have the obvious problem that 'what we now do' appears to get in the way of the 'faith from first to last' by which alone we are justified. But if we follow Paul and see justification by faith (as in 3.21—4.25) *within the larger framework of his biblical theology of God's covenant with and through Abraham for the world, now fulfilled in Christ,* we will discover that from within that larger, and utterly Pauline, framework there is a straight and easy path to understanding (what is sometimes referred to as) the place of 'works' in the Christian life, without in any way, shape or form compromising the solidity of 'justification by faith' itself.

Here's how it works. The opening sentence of the chapter, 'there is therefore now no condemnation for those who are in Christ Jesus' (8.1), forms a circle with the closing one, 'nothing shall be able to separate us from God's love in Christ Jesus our Lord' (8.39). This is the great Pauline truth which preachers in the Reformation tradition have always rightly celebrated, though not always understanding the framework of Pauline thought within which it all fitted together. What has been lacking in much of the tradition has been the interlocking Pauline features of (a) the renewal of creation and (b) the indwelling of the spirit. The point is stated decisively in 8.4: 'the righteous intention/decree/verdict/judgment of the law (*to dikaiōma tou nomou*) is fulfilled in us who walk not according to the flesh but according to the Spirit'. The 'righteous judgment' of the Torah is, as Paul indicates in 7.10 and 8.9–11, to give life – the life which overcomes death, the new life of resurrection itself. By itself the Torah could not accomplish this, because of the 'flesh' – i.e. the sinful, rebellious human nature – of those to whom it was given. That is the paradox of the Mosaic law, which Paul has explored (though we have not in the present book) in chapter 7. But now the paradox is explained, because the reality to which the law pointed forwards has arrived in the person and the saving death of Jesus the Messiah, and the consequent gift of the spirit. As Paul had hinted in 2.28–29, echoing the new covenant promises of Jeremiah and Ezekiel, the spirit is the one through whose agency God's people are renewed and reconstituted *as* God's people. And it is by the energy of the spirit, working in those who belong to the Messiah, that the new paradox comes about in which the Christian really does exercise free moral will and effort but at the same time ascribes this free activity to the spirit. And the point is this: what is going on when this happens is the anticipation, in present Christian living, of the final rescue from sin and death. Thus, 'though the body is dead because of sin, the spirit is life because of righteousness' (8.10). Paul has not stopped talking about 'righteousness', even if most of his interpreters have by this point. As in chapter 6, the appearance of this word indicates that he is still thinking within the map sketched out in 5.12–21. 'Righteousness' here serves as a catch-all term for the entire sequence of covenantal and lawcourt thinking developed in the earlier parts of the letter.

With this paradox (the spirit works within us, we freely work) comes a careful balance. Paul never says that the present moral life of the Christian 'earns' final salvation. It looks towards it, it 'seeks for' it (2.7). It partakes of it in advance. Nor does he say that one must attain moral perfection before any of this can be meaningful; one can never collude with half-hearted moral effort, but one can never imagine that repentance and forgiveness are not possible for the Christian who still sins. At the same time he insists that the signs of the spirit's life must be present: if anyone doesn't have the spirit of Christ, that person doesn't belong to him (8.9), and 'if you live according to the flesh you will die' (8.13). There can be no passengers in God's family. All are called to make, through the spirit, the hard moral choices which cut against what the world wants to do, what the physical body wants to do, what the proud and arrogant human spirit wants to do. Where there is no sign of these choices being made and acted upon, Paul would warn that there is no sign of life, and would challenge that person to the faith he describes in Romans 6: if you are in Christ, reckon yourself to be dead to sin and alive to God.

You cannot, in short, have a Pauline doctrine of assurance (and the glory of the Reformation doctrine of justification is precisely assurance) without the Pauline doctrine of the spirit. Try to do it, and you will put too much weight on human faith, which will then generate all kinds of further questions about types of faith, about faith and feelings, about what happens when faith wobbles. This, in turn, will generate worried reactions, as people look on and see a supposed Protestantism which appears to regard strong emotional certainty of being saved as the criterion for being saved in fact. And from that muddle there spring other things, too, not least the anti-moralism which has bedevilled a certain kind of liberal theology, which, whenever it hears a moral command, protests that it believes in grace, not law. All this could be avoided if we would only stick with Paul himself.

For Paul himself the final glorious statement of assurance (8.31–39) contains no mention of faith whatsoever. It *expresses* faith, of course, but for that very reason it does not *refer to* faith, just as when I talk about God I am using my tongue but am not speaking about my tongue. Faith is the breath which enables us to praise God, not to praise breath. And this great, decisive, climactic, sober but exalted statement of faith is faith not in faith itself – the classic Protestant dilemma, if it isn't careful – but faith in the God who has acted out his all-powerful love in the death and resurrection of Jesus Christ his son. This closing paean of praise, like 5.1–11 in its way and 5.12–21 in its, rests all its weight, not on anything in ourselves, but only on God's achievement in Christ. The hidden presupposition of the passage is of course the identity of the 'we' who are speaking: the 'we' who cannot be separated from the love of God in Christ are 'those who are in Christ' as in 8.1, those 'who believe in the one who raised Jesus from the dead' (4.23–25). The 'we' are those in whom the spirit is working his life-giving, free-Christian-holiness-producing revolution (8.5–8; 12.1–2). Another paradox: the more the spirit is at work in someone's life, the less they will be even thinking about their hard moral effort, their work for God's kingdom, as 'earning' anything or 'qualifying them for' anything, because the more they will be looking away from themselves and celebrating the unique triumph of the creator's love in the death and resurrection of the Messiah. If you try to understand justification by faith within a smaller framework than this, don't be surprised if the jigsaw pieces don't quite fit. And if, when you have the larger Pauline framework pointed out to you, your inclination is to say, 'But the sun still does go round the earth – look, there it goes!', then remember, and Romans 8 is the best place to help you remember this, that salvation is not simply God's gift *to* his people but God's gift *through* his people.

Why then does Paul not discuss faith between 5.2 and 8.39, even though the whole passage is 'about' justification in the sense of the final verdict which remains founded on God's love in the death and resurrection of Jesus? It's hard to prove a negative. But it could just be for two reasons. First, at no point throughout this long argument is he needing to stress that the people of God consist equally of Jews and Gentiles. He has already made that point in 3.21—4.25, and will return to it shortly in 9.30—10.13. And this is closely cognate with the second point: throughout this passage he has his eye on the future day when God will put the whole world right and raise his people to new life. 'Justification by faith' is about the *present*, about how you can already tell who the people are who will be vindicated on the last day. He celebrates that in chapter 8, not by providing a further discussion of it as though to supplement 3.21—4.25, but by looking on from it to the *final* moment of resurrection, ultimate vindication, and new creation.

The linguistic point about Romans 5—8 (the absence of *pistis*) thus points to an underlying theological point, of enormous significance for our whole topic. Loose talk about 'salvation by faith' (a phrase Paul never uses; the closest he gets, as we have seen, is Ephesians 2.8, 'by grace you have been saved through faith') can seriously mislead people into supposing that you can construct an entire Pauline soteriology out of the sole elements of 'faith' and 'works', with 'works' of any sort always being ruled out as damaging or compromising the purity of faith. For Paul, a stress on 'justification by faith' is always a stress on the *present status of all God's people in anticipation of the final judgment*. But when he puts this into its larger, covenantal context, alongside and integrated with 'being in Christ' and all the other elements of his complex thought, it is always filled out with talk of the spirit. The implicit charge that the Pauline theology I have articulated might lead people to put their trust in 'anyone or anything other than the crucified and resurrected Savior' (Carson, in the blurb on Piper's book) is seriously misleading. Paul invites his hearers to trust *both* in Jesus Christ *and* in the father whose love triumphed in the death of his son – *and in the holy spirit who makes that victory operative in our moral lives and who enables us to love God in return* (5.5; 8.28). The trouble with some would-be Reformation theology is that it is not only insufficiently biblical. It is also insufficiently Trinitarian. These two go together, of course, and join up with two other insufficiencies. First, much Western Protestant thought is insufficiently creational (some, of course, slides all the way into radical dualism). Second, much Western Protestant thought is insufficiently Israel-focused (some, of course, slides all the way into radical anti-Judaism). It is this second danger which highlights the importance of our final exegetical section.

VIII

If they do not believe Moses and the prophets, declared Abraham in Jesus' parable, neither will they believe even if someone should rise from the dead.[47] In the same way we might declare: if you fail rightly to understand God's-single-plan-through-Israel-for-the-world, neither will you understand the place of Romans 9—11 within the letter and within Paul's thought as a whole. There is no space here, of course, for a treatment of the whole section, and I refer again to my other writings.[48] We must concentrate on the section which is as central to the theology as it is to the literary structure: 9.30—10.13.

The subject of this passage is God's righteousness, the righteousness of God's people, their salvation and how it might be attained, and above all the covenant. These, of course, fit together. It is because God is 'in the right', both as the world's rightful judge and more specifically as Israel's covenant God, that there is now a status of 'righteousness' for his people, the result of which is 'salvation', that is, rescue from death and all that causes it. At this point Paul has moved from one end of the Pentateuch to the other, but still within the same framework of thought. Having rooted his exposition of justification in Abraham, in chapter 4, and developed it with echoes of the exodus story in chapters 6—8, he concludes it with Deuteronomy.

Deuteronomy 30 is so obviously a 'covenant' chapter that it is surprising, given its clear centrality in Romans 10, that people have not tumbled to the centrality of covenantal thinking here and elsewhere in Paul. The problem, I think, is that the relevant passage (10.5–11) has appeared so dark and difficult that exegetes have tiptoed their way through it without daring to look to right or left lest monsters emerge from the bushes to devour them, and theologians have ignored it altogether and carved out a doctrinal bypass route which avoids the problem. But when we look, even briefly, at the place of Deuteronomy 30 in its own setting and in its use by other Jews of Paul's period, all sorts of things become clear. As often happens, the passage which was initially puzzling turns out to contain the clues to everything else as well.

We must understand, as the framework, the line of thought which began in 9.6 and is still continuing at this point. Paul has been telling the story precisely of Israel and the covenant, beginning with Abraham, Isaac and Jacob (9.6–13) and continuing to Moses and Pharaoh and the episode of the Golden Calf (9.14–18). He then carries on to the period of the prophets, the period (that is) when God warned his people that failure to live by the covenant would mean the judgment of exile with the prospect only of a remnant (9.19–29). As we know from other contemporary retellings of Israel's story, that brought matters more or less 'up to date', with many Jews still regarding themselves as in the 'exilic' period and awaiting the 'new exodus' that would produce covenant renewal and all the long-promised and long-awaited blessings. For many, as we know from other texts, this meant examining ancient scriptures that spoke of God restoring the fortunes of his people. Among such texts Deuteronomy 30 had an important place, as we know from Baruch and the Scroll known as 4QMMT.[49]

It may help to consider briefly the inner logic of Deuteronomy 27—30. Chapters 27—29 outline the covenantal obligations God is placing on Israel and the assured results of both obedience and disobedience. The sequence concludes with a terrifying picture of the exile which will result from disobedience, and with the promise of restoration the other side of that exile.

The inner logic of all this ought to be clear. Israel is carrying God's purposes for the world; Israel's stewardship of the land of Israel, and God's blessing upon that stewardship, is the advance sign of that eventual purpose (which Paul has expounded in 8.18–26). Exile is therefore not an arbitrary punishment for disobedience. It is the inevitable consequence of Israel's idolatry and rebellion. Creation is designed to flourish under wise human stewardship reflecting the love of God the creator. When the humans rebel, creation suffers too. The humans must therefore be put out of the garden. Israel recapitulates the primal sin of Adam and Eve. As Genesis opened with the vision of created blessing and vocation, turning into disaster and tragedy, so Deuteronomy, drawing towards its close, envisages Israel going through the same exile-from-the-garden – only now with the promise of redemption, of covenant renewal. Abraham's people will inherit the land, but be exiled. If they are still to carry the long promises of God (Romans 3.1–8), it will be necessary for that exile to be undone, for the story to reach the point Moses had predicted in chapter 30, the point to which prophets like Jeremiah and Ezekiel had looked back in order to gain fresh hope.

Paul's message in Romans 10 is that this point has been reached with the Messiah. To understand the significance of the Messiah's work, he says, look at it in terms of Deuteronomy's picture of covenant renewal. This passage is not, as is often implied, an oblique and difficult way of saying 'to get to heaven, you don't have to perform good moral deeds, you only have to believe'. That is a severely distorted caricature of part of what Paul is saying. The truth to which that caricature points is the truth contained, once more, within Paul's much larger scheme of thought. In order to address the question of God's faithfulness to Israel – the question, that is, of the 'righteousness of God' – he must continue to tell the story of that faithfulness, not simply from Abraham to the present but through the decisive revelation of that covenant faithfulness (3.21) in Jesus the Messiah and on, outwards, to the new work which is going ahead, in and through which that faithfulness is being put into powerful salvific operation 'for all people, the Jew first and also the Greek' (1.16). Paul has set up the question of Israel's salvation in 10.1, giving fresh urgency and a sense of direction at this point to the ongoing narrative of God and Israel which continues from 9.6 right through to 10.21. The question is to be answered, and can only be answered, in terms of God's renewal of the covenant in Christ and by the spirit, and in terms of the covenant membership (chief among whose blessings is salvation itself) already hinted at in 2.25–29.

Within this context I have no hesitation in saying that *dikaiosynē* in 9.30 and 9.31 must be understood in terms of *membership within the covenant*. Gentiles were not looking for such membership, but have found it; Israel, hunting for it, did not attain it. Or rather – since as usual Paul does not say quite what we expect him to say – Israel, 'pursuing a law of covenant membership, did not attain to that law'. The force of this must not be blunted, as it often has been in Protestant exegesis, as though one should try to prevent Paul saying anything positive about the law. The problem is not the law itself; Paul has already established that in 7.7—8.11. The problem is the Adamic nature of Israel (as Paul puts it, 'the law was weak through the flesh', 8.3). So, when Israel tried to attain the privileges of covenant membership by keeping the law, the attempt was a failure, again as in chapter 7: the commandment which had promised life proved to bring death. We are now back, not only in chapter 7, but in 3.19–20: the law brings knowledge of sin. Embrace the God-given law, Paul says to his fellow Jews (to his own former self!) and you are embracing that which must declare you to be a transgressor, a law-breaker, on all fours with the 'sinners' who are outside God's covenant.[50]

The problem, then, is not that Israel is attempting 'works-righteousness' in the old Reformational sense, that is, trying to earn favour in God's sight through the performance of good moral deeds. Israel, we recall yet once more, is the people whom God rescued at the exodus, whose law was the way of life for a people already redeemed. No: Israel's mistake, here as elsewhere, was to imagine that the purpose of God was not the single-purpose-through-Israel-for-the-world but a single-purpose-for-Israel-apart-from-the-world. Israel was taking God's wider purpose and focusing it back on itself. Martin Luther saw the essence of sin in being 'turned in on oneself'; Israel was acting out that primal sin through the attempt to carve out and cling on to a covenant membership which would be for Jews and Jews only, a national identity marked out by the 'works of Torah' which proclaimed Jewish distinctiveness. That is what Paul means when he says that 'they did not pursue the law by faith, but as though it was based on works' (9.32). But the whole point of Romans 9—11 is this: *even this failure was not outside the strange purposes of God*, as indicated by Isaiah when he spoke about a stone of stumbling that God himself had placed in Zion (9.32–33). Israel's failure, ironically, was the same as that of many exegetes: to ignore the single-plan-through-Israel-for-the-world, in other words, the covenant plan and God's faithfulness to it.

That is exactly what Paul then says in starting to answer his own implied question about Israel's salvation (10.1). Referring once more not only to his contemporaries but to his own former self, he declares that they have 'a zeal for God' which is sadly 'not in accordance with knowledge'. The zeal is misdirected, because they have not understood God's single plan and how it was supposed to work not just *for* them but *through* them. 'They are ignorant of God's *dikaiosynē*, and they are seeking to establish their own *dikaiosynē*, and so they did not submit to God's *dikaiosynē*.' In other words, they have not recognized the nature, shape and purpose of their own controlling narrative, the story Paul has been telling since 9.6, and have supposed that it was a story about themselves rather than about the creator and the cosmos, with themselves playing the crucial, linchpin role. But God's single plan has won out nevertheless (Paul is here very close to the earlier transition from 3.1–8 into 3.21–31) because the plan always was the single plan *through Israel in the person of the Messiah, alone*, for the world. 'The Messiah is the culmination of the Torah, so that there may be *dikaiosynē*, covenant membership, for all who believe.' Thus 10.4, one of the most controversial verses in Paul (because *telos* can mean 'end' and 'goal', and because Paul seems to mean some combination of the two with the weight on the latter), gives off its full resonances not within the Lutheran scheme whereby the law is a bad thing abolished in Christ, nor within the Calvinist scheme whereby the law is a good thing which Christ obeyed and thus procured 'righteousness' (works-righteousness, we note) to be then 'imputed' to those who believe, but within Paul's own Jewish framework of thought, the narrative of God and his faithfulness to Israel which has reached its destination in the Messiah.

The result is that the long-awaited covenant renewal spoken of in Deuteronomy has at last come about. Yes, Moses does indeed say that the one who 'does these things' shall live in them (Romans 10.5, quoting Leviticus 18.5). But what does 'doing these things' now mean? Paul is not thinking in terms of a detached profit-and-loss account system of soteriology in which one either 'does' good works to earn God's favour or decides to trust God's forgiveness instead. He is thinking in terms of the promised covenant renewal which, when it arrives, will enable a 'doing of the law' of quite a different sort to anything previously imagined – exactly as he had hinted in

2.25–29 and such other apparently odd passages as 1 Corinthians 7.19 ('neither circumcision nor uncircumcision matters; what matters is keeping God's commandments!'). He is thinking, in fact, of a covenant renewal which will be recognizably that of which Deuteronomy 30 was speaking when it spoke of a 'doing of the law' which was not difficult, requiring someone to bring it down from heaven or out of the depths of the sea. This 'doing of the law', Paul declares, is announced by 'the righteousness of faith', that is, by the message of the faith-based covenant renewal. We recall how Paul analysed Abraham's faith – the faith that God would give life to his and Sarah's dead bodies – so that it turned out to be the same faith that Christians have when they believe 'in the God who raised Jesus from the dead' (4.23–25). Now he does the same with the covenant renewal spoken of in Deuteronomy 30. There he read of a new condition, one in which God's word would be 'near you, on your lips and in your heart', as though God had sent it down from heaven and brought it up from the abyss. Yes, he says: this is the condition you find in Christian faith, in confessing that Jesus is Lord (in other words, that he is the very embodiment of YHWH himself) and believing in your heart that God has raised him from the dead. *When people believe the gospel of Jesus and his resurrection, and confess him as Lord, they are in fact doing what Torah wanted all along, and are therefore displaying the necessary marks of covenant renewal.*

The 'people' in question are of course anybody and everybody, Jews and Gentiles alike.[51] The single plan has at last come to fruition, through Israel's Messiah, for the world. Justification by faith is intimately correlated with the inclusion of the Gentiles, not because Paul has stopped being interested in soteriology and substituted something less exciting, namely ecclesiology, instead, but because soteriology itself is rooted in the single-plan-through-Israel-*for-the-world*. The worldwide availability of this faith, and hence of this salvation, is the sure sign, not so much of the truth of one particular abstract scheme of salvation over some other, but of the fact that the new day has dawned, the covenant has been renewed at last, and 'salvation' is to be found, by anyone and everyone, not in fiercer adherence to the covenant the way it was – which merely intensifies the problem of Romans 7 – but in God's decisive achievement in Jesus the Messiah, the Lord. Those who will 'not be ashamed' (10.11, quoting Isaiah 28.16 and thereby echoing 9.33) are not those who cling to the badges of national privilege, but those who see that their national purpose has been fulfilled in their Messiah. I hope it is clear that this means a rich and strong affirmation of the goodness and God-givenness of the people of Israel and their law, simultaneous with the affirmation that Israel's destiny is to be understood as leading to Jesus as Messiah.

Nor is the spirit absent from this exposition, even though unmentioned. 'All who call upon the name of the Lord will be saved' (10.13): Paul is quoting another passage about covenant renewal, this time from the prophets.[52] This passage is important because Paul is continuing to answer the implied question of verse 1: How will Jews be saved? But echoes arise from the whole section of the prophet in question, the very passage quoted by Peter in Acts 2 on the day of Pentecost. 'I will pour out my Spirit on all flesh . . . and then all who call upon the name of the Lord will be saved.'[53] This, Paul declares, is how Israel's God is fulfilling his ancient promises. This is the renewal of the covenant. That is why there now needs to be a Gentile mission. And that is why we must at once face the question (chapter 11) of where ethnic Israel belongs within this new world, this new covenant.

These are questions for other times and places. But my contention here has been that this covenantal reading of 9.30—10.13 makes far better and more detailed sense of this whole passage than the usual Reformational readings, whether those in the Lutheran tradition, with a negative view of the law, or those, in the Calvinist tradition, with a positive view. (If we had to choose between those two, I would of course choose the Calvinist, but I believe the view I have sketched transcends both.) Justification by faith – God's declaration in the present time that all those who believe that God raised Jesus from the dead, all those who confess him as Lord, are true members in the renewed covenant, and are assured thereby of final salvation – belongs inextricably, for the reasons now abundantly given, within the framework of Paul's vision of God's single plan of salvation, through Israel and hence through Israel's Messiah, for the sake of all the nations and ultimately of the whole cosmos. To shrink this larger picture is to squash all the doctrines within it out of shape. To stand back and gaze at the full picture is to be overawed once more by the depth of the riches and mercy and purposes of

God (11.33–36). The attempts in some quarters to imply that the so-called 'new perspective on Paul' involves a diminution, a scaling down, a replacement of the majesty of a great soteriology with the banal statements of a pragmatic ecclesiology, simply miss the point. Once again, if we had begun with Ephesians how different everything would have appeared. At least we can now see the full majesty of Paul's full picture. Nothing that the Reformation traditions at their best were anxious to stress has been lost. But they are held in place, and I suggest even enhanced, by a cosmic vision, a high ecclesiology generated by Paul's high Christology and resulting in a high missiology of the renewal of all things, and all framed by the highest doctrine of all, Paul's vision of the God who made promises and has been faithful to them, the God whose purposes are unsearchable but yet revealed in Jesus Christ and operative through the holy spirit, the God of power and glory but above all of love.

There remains one final note. Paul does of course highlight the saving death of Jesus when he is giving his thumbnail sketch of the gospel in 1 Corinthians 15.3–8. But it is interesting that in the two crucial passages where he speaks of the faith of the Christian as embodying the faith spoken of in the Old Testament – 4.23–25 and 10.6–11 – it is the resurrection that takes centre stage. This is not, of course, an either/or. The resurrection remains the resurrection of the crucified one, and its significance is not least that it signals that the cross was a victory, not a defeat (1 Corinthians 15.17). And in 4.23–25 Paul quickly adds that Jesus 'was put to death for our trespasses'. But the second half of that stanza is that he was 'raised for our justification'. There seems to be something about the joining together of resurrection and justification which some of our Western traditions have failed to grasp. Justification is more than simply the remitting and forgiving of sins, vital and wonderful though that is. It is the declaration that those who believe in Jesus are part of the resurrection-based single family of the one creator God. Any preaching of justification which focuses solely or even mainly on Jesus' death and its results is only doing half the job. Justification is not just about 'how I get my sins forgiven'. It is about how God creates, in the Messiah Jesus and in the power of his spirit, a single family, celebrating their once-for-all forgiveness and their assured 'no condemnation' in Christ, through whom his purposes can now be extended into the wider world. All this, of course, might have been clear from a reading of the gospels, but, alas, the same Western tradition that has highlighted the cross at the expense of Paul's full theology of resurrection has also highlighted a supposed Pauline soteriology at the expense of the gospels' theology of the kingdom of God. That, too, is naturally another story.

8

Conclusion

What shall we say to these things? If Paul is for us, who can be against us? The text is the text. As Ernst Käsemann said a generation ago, we must assume that the text has an inner logic to it, even if it is initially not entirely comprehensible to us.[1] That is my starting and finishing point: which account of particular themes, subjects, even 'doctrines', makes most sense of the text itself? I give considerable weight to the noble traditions that have sustained the church throughout the years. They do not, of course, always agree, and among the Reformers themselves, and their various strands of successors, there have been major disagreements which indicate that further work is necessary, perhaps even involving various paradigm shifts.[2] This, too, is in line with Reformation beliefs: God has always more light and truth to break forth from his holy word. So spoke the Puritan John Robinson as he bade farewell to the pilgrims on the *Mayflower* in 1620. Had the teachers of old, he said, been now living, 'they would be as ready and willing to embrace further light as that they had received'. This is of course a dangerous doctrine; many groups teaching many extraordinary things have claimed this 'more light' as the justification for their strange proposals. But if the light comes, and can be shown to come, from the word, from scripture itself, there is no tradition so strong, venerable or previously fruitful that it should not be prepared to learn from it.[3] That is the foundation of all that I have tried to do. Let me now sum up where I think we have got to.

What comes out of the text, above all, is the fact, and the achievement, of Jesus Christ himself. In ways that the Western tradition, Catholic and Protestant, Lutheran and Calvinist – yes, and Anglican too! – has often failed to recognize, scripture forms a massive and powerful story whose climax is the coming into the world of the unique son of the one true creator God, and, above all, his death

221

dily resurrection from the dead. All Christian
raying and living takes place in that light. But
Jesus Christ is the focal point is the story of
i, focused then on Abraham and his family and
ange promise-bearing people; and it is also the
ied, of what Jesus Christ continues to do and
is holy spirit, in advance of the day when what
God did for Jesus at Easter he will do not only for all his people
but for the whole creation. Any attempt to give an account of a doctrine which screens out the call of Israel, the gift of the spirit, and/or
the redemption of all creation is doomed to be less than fully
biblical. And where that happens, you can expect distortions. And
squabbles between the distorters – and between them and anyone
who tries to open their eyes to larger worlds. This is not, of course,
a claim that I have got it all right and my critics have got it all
wrong. It is an attempt to suggest that our disagreements need to
be mapped on a larger canvas than we have usually done.

In particular, as we get the picture of God, Jesus and the spirit
in better focus, we discover what I have, perhaps loosely but I still
believe helpfully, referred to as *covenant* theology, the belief that the
creator God called Abraham's family into covenant with him so that
through his family all the world might escape from the curse of sin
and death and enjoy the blessing and life of new creation. To regard
this, as John Piper and others have done, as somehow a side-issue,
an avoidance of the message of free forgiveness and assurance of
life in God's new world, is to me inexplicable. I can only conclude
that I must still have failed to make myself clear – a situation which
I hope the present work has gone some way towards remedying.

Within this covenant theology, the God-given means for putting
the whole world right, we discover the running metaphor of the
lawcourt. This is not arbitrary, as though it was simply one metaphor
among others for how God forgives people their sins, brings them
into a relationship with himself, and assures them of their future
hope. It is the utterly appropriate metaphor through which Paul can
express and develop the biblical understanding that God, the creator, must 'judge' the world in the sense of putting it right at the
last – and that God has brought this judgment into the middle of
history, precisely in the covenant-fulfilling work of Jesus Christ,
dealing with sin through his death, launching the new world in his

resurrection, and sending his spirit to enable human beings, through repentance and faith, to become little walking and breathing advance parts of that eventual new creation. According to this judgment, this 'verdict' which is accomplished and publicly announced through the death and resurrection of Jesus, all those who are 'in him' are 'reckoned' to have died and been raised with him, so that from God's point of view their sins are no longer accounted against them and they stand on resurrection ground, free at last to live as genuine human beings. And the sign of this spirit-given membership of the family of God's renewed covenant is neither more nor less than faith – specifically, the faith that Jesus is Lord and that God raised him from the dead. This faith, by being equally open to all, Jew and Gentile alike, indicates in its reach as well as its content that here we are witnessing the beginning of that cosmic renewal, that coming together of heaven and earth, which declares to the principalities and powers that God's rich wisdom has come to birth in Jesus Christ the Lord.[4]

Finally, as is already clear from the above, this lawcourt verdict, implementing God's covenant plan, and all based on Jesus Christ himself, is announced both in the *present*, with the verdict issued on the basis of faith and faith alone, and also in the *future*, on the day when God raises from the dead all those who are already indwelt by the spirit.[5] The present verdict gives the *assurance that* the future verdict will match it; the spirit gives the *power through which* that future verdict, when given, will be seen to be in accordance with the life that the believer has then lived. 'There is no condemnation for those who are in Christ Jesus, *because* the law of the Spirit of life in Christ Jesus has set you free from the law of sin and death.' This opens the way both for a clear and utterly Pauline account of the final judgment and for an equally clear, and equally Pauline, account of and motivation for the present vocation, mission, holiness and unity of the church as a whole, and within that the vocation, holiness and membership within the one body of Christ of every believer.

Where then is the boasting in human traditions (including those of the Reformation)? It is excluded. By what theology? Some kind of revisionist nonsense? No: by the theology of Paul himself. For we reckon that a doctrine is established by the whole scripture, in relation to the whole Trinity, and not by partial readings of scripture or imbalanced reliance on the work of one member of the Godhead alone. God is one, and will set forth his glory as creator, as incarnate son, and as powerful spirit, thereby embracing both the truths the Reformers were eager to set forth and also the truths which, in their eagerness, they sidelined. Do we then overthrow the Reformation tradition by this theology? On the contrary, we establish it. Everything Luther and Calvin wanted to achieve is within this glorious Pauline framework of thought. The difference is that, whereas for some of their followers it really did look as though the sun was going round the earth, we have now glimpsed the reality. The risen son is the fixed point in whose orbit we move, the one who holds his people by his power and sustains them by his love, the one to whom, with father and spirit, be all love and all glory in this age and in the age to come.

Notes

1 What's all this about, and why does it matter?

1. John Piper, *The Future of Justification: A Response to N. T. Wright.* Wheaton, IL: Crossway Books, 2007. For the variety of views among the Reformers and their successors, see McGrath 1986 and several essays in Husbands and Treier 2004; McCormack 2006.
2. Barbara Brown Taylor, 'Failing Christianity', *The Christian Century,* 17 June 2008, 35.
3. Earlier volumes: *The New Testament and the People of God* (1992) (*NTPG*); *Jesus and the Victory of God* (1996) (*JVG*); *The Resurrection of the Son of God* (2003). All published by SPCK (London) and Fortress (Minneapolis).
4. See e.g. Piper, 60f. A good example of this current trend is the work of Guy Waters, e.g. 2004.
5. 1 Cor. 4.3–5.
6. R. Olson, *Reformed and Always Reforming: The Postconservative Approach to Evangelical Theology.* Acadia Studies in Bible and Theology. Grand Rapids: Baker Academic, 2007.
7. Dunn 2008, 7 n. 24; Wright, 'The Paul of History and the Apostle of Faith', 1978.
8. As e.g. Piper, 27.
9. e.g. Hays 1989; 2002; 2005; Campbell 2005 (and a larger, forthcoming work, entitled *The Deliverance of God*); Donaldson 1997; Longenecker 1998.
10. Watson 2007.
11. <www.thepaulpage.com/Bibliography.html>; see Bird 2007, 194–211.
12. Packer 1962.
13. Dunn 2008, ch. 20.
14. Westerholm 2004.
15. Especially Hays 1989.
16. Ps. 115.1 in the LXX.
17. Refs. in Wright 'The Paul of History and the Apostle of Faith', 1978: see esp. Käsemann 1971, 60–78; Stendahl 1976, 78–96.

2 Rules of engagement

1. Clowney, in Carson 1992, 44.
2. At this point (60) he suggests that I am also jettisoning 'Orthodox', i.e. Eastern Orthodox, readings, which is peculiar since Orthodoxy has no special theology of justification, the relevant debates having taken

place entirely in the West, following Augustine. See Bray, in Packer et al. 1986; and McGrath 1986, 3f.
3. Thiselton 2007.
4. Bird 2007, 70, 87; Packer 1962, 685.
5. Piper, 37.
6. Piper, 34f.
7. Whiston n.d.; Edersheim 1883. Both works went through many editions; these are the ones I have to hand.
8. Carson et al. 2001 and 2004.
9. Piper, 36 n. 5.
10. Piper, 24.
11. Piper, 37.
12. Piper, 25 n. 31, quoting Scott Manetsch.

3 First-century Judaism: covenant, law and lawcourt

1. Mishnah *Sanhedrin* 10.1.
2. See e.g. *NTPG* Part III.
3. For the calculations, see e.g. Beckwith 1981; and *NTPG* 173, 312f.
4. Jer. 25.11; cf. 29.10.
5. 2 Chron. 36.21; Ezra 1.1; Zech. 1.12; 7.5.
6. Dan. 9.24.
7. Dan. 9.25–27.
8. *Jewish War* 6.312; cf. 3.399–408.
9. Neh. 9.36; Ezra 9.7–9.
10. See *NTPG* 269f., with refs., and *JVG* xviif.
11. The attempt by Carson 2001, 546f., to ward off this conclusion, drawing on the thesis of S. M. Bryan, has in no way dampened my enthusiasm for this viewpoint.
12. See Exod. 2.23–25 and variously thereafter.
13. Piper is wrong to suggest that I collapse lawcourt language into covenant language (54f.). It is proper to see the connections and implications; but the lawcourt still matters, even though you only understand its full Pauline meaning when you see it within the covenantal framework.
14. Piper, 62 n. 13.
15. Packer 1962, 683 – though unfortunately Packer then turns away from the point when applying it to Paul.
16. Wright, *Romans*, 2002, 452–5, 464–507.
17. Piper, 68 n. 17.
18. Piper, 70 n. 18.
19. Piper, 71.
20. Gen. 38.26.
21. 1 Sam. 24.17.

22. I am still puzzled, in the same vein, that Mark Seifrid (2000, 59) should suppose I am arguing from a *modern* lawcourt situation. The passage he cites (*What St Paul Really Said*, 96–99) explains quite clearly that we are dealing with the ancient Hebrew lawcourt.
23. Piper, 71.
24. See pp. 201–6, on Rom. 6.
25. Clowney, in Carson 1992, 25.
26. Full list in Bird 2007, 195.
27. Deut. 4.7f.; Ps. 147.20.
28. Sanders 1977, 409–18.
29. Carson et al. 2001.
30. Piper, 133–61.
31. Wright, '4QMMT', 2006.
32. Mishnah *Sanhedrin* 10.1.
33. Piper has simply not understood this (149): he thinks that what the sectarians will have performed is 'simple obedience to what the law requires'.

4 Justification: definitions and puzzles

1. McGrath 1986.
2. McGrath 1986, 1.2 (emphasis original).
3. McGrath 1986, 1.2f. (emphasis original).
4. Torrance 2000.
5. Hays 1992, 1133. Even Hays, however, in his otherwise excellent article, suggests that Paul sees the story of Abraham as an 'illustration' (1131).
6. McGrath 1986, 1.2f.
7. McGrath 1986, 1.2f.
8. Wrede 1904.
9. Westerholm 2004, 257f.
10. Westerholm 2004, 285 n. 57.
11. Westerholm 2004, 440–5.
12. Schweitzer 1931, 225.
13. McGrath 1986, 2.36f.
14. See *NTPG* 42–6, 98–109.
15. Sanders 1977 and esp. 1983.
16. Piper's warnings about 'the kind of gospel preaching that will flow from Wright's spring' (101; cf. too e.g. 165) should be read in the context of my many books of published sermons, e.g. *The Crown and the Fire* (London and Grand Rapids: SPCK and Eerdmans, 1992), or the 'Reflections' sections in my large commentary on Romans (2002).
17. e.g. Piper, 164.
18. Seifrid 2000a, 124.

19. Thus he manages to write a substantial piece on 'righteousness' language, in relation to Jewish claims about 'covenant', without ever making a connection with the key writings like 4 Ezra where the question of God's righteousness is all-important: Carson et al. 2001, ch. 14.
20. Westerholm 2004, 286f.
21. See Dunn 2008, ch. 20.
22. See, much more fully, *Climax* ch. 8.
23. Interestingly, Piper does not include Gal. 3.15–18, or any part of it, in his index, an omission matched by Seifrid 1992; and the refs. in Seifrid 2000 do not address the question. Westerholm does note the point, but hastily neutralizes it by saying that Paul has only chosen the word *diathēkē* because it can also refer to a 'will' (2004, 287 n. 60). It is remarkably easy to sustain a point if you simply do not deal with the evidence that runs the other way.
24. A full discussion can be found at *JVG* 202–9.
25. On all this see *Climax* chs 2–3.
26. See not least Gal. 3.13, on which see p. 103.
27. Rom. 8.1–3.
28. One still occasionally meets the strange idea that in Rom. 1.3f. Paul is saying that Jesus only *became* 'son of God' at his resurrection. That this cannot be correct is clear from e.g. 5.10 and 8.32, in each of which Jesus is 'son of God' at the point of his death, and 8.3, where he is 'son of God' already at the point of his becoming human.
29. For an early statement, see my (1983) edition of John Frith, 29–32; and e.g. Torrance 2000.
30. Carson, quoted on the cover of Piper's book.
31. Dunn 2008, ch. 18, and other chapters in the book. Dunn seems to me significantly to underplay the messianic theme in Paul.
32. See my *Paul: Fresh Perspectives*, 2005, ch. 7.
33. Phil. 2.10.
34. Rom. 2.16.
35. 2 Cor. 5.10, resonating with Rom. 14.10, 'we must all stand before the judgment seat of God'.

5 Galatians

1. I note that the Eastern Orthodox once used the same passage to damn the Anglican church for ordaining women, saying that this was 'another gospel'. They now tend to say that, since there has never been a general Council on the subject, they do not know, officially at least, where their church stands. See *The Church of the Triune God: The Cyprus Agreed Statement of the International Commission for Anglican–Orthodox Theological Dialogue 2006*. London: Anglican Communion Office, 2006.

2. Gal. 1.3–5.
3. Acts 10.28; 11.9.
4. See John 4.9; 18.28; Acts 10.28; 11.3.
5. On the recent debate between Hays and Dunn, see Hays 2002, 249–97, where the principal statements of both writers are printed.
6. See too Rom. 5.12–14.
7. I am aware that John Piper puts a great deal of store by technical meanings, within Reformed debates, of the word 'basis' (e.g. 117f.). I have to say that, since Paul does not use a phrase which corresponds to this, I am not convinced that this is the way to clarity.
8. Cf. Rom. 4.16, 'therefore by grace, so that by faith'. This passage is closely linked to our present one.
9. This is the underlying point of the 'vindication of Torah' in Rom. 7.7–8.11.
10. See too *Climax*, ch. 7.
11. See Bird 2007, 109.
12. Though Michael Bird's work is helpful in other respects, he sometimes simply reinforces this false antithesis.
13. See, classically, Sanday and Headlam 1902 [1895], 278: 'while the old method was hard and difficult the new is easy and within the reach of all'; 283: the Jews 'had not submitted to the method (as will be shown a much easier one) which God himself had revealed'; cf. too 287, 'faith is not a difficult matter since Christ has come'.
14. Exod. 4.22.
15. At a late stage in revising this book for publication, my colleague Ben Blackwell pointed out to me that I should really have added two further paragraphs, on the place of the spirit and of life, in this argument. Paul, after all, closely aligns 'receiving the spirit by faith' (3.1–5) and 'being justified by faith' (3.6–9), and the end result of Christ receiving the curse on 'our' behalf (3.10–14) is 'that we might receive the spirit by faith'. And, as in Romans, the spirit is the one who gives life (3.11f., 21). To develop these points further would, I believe, strengthen my overall argument.

6 Interlude: Philippians, Corinthians, Ephesians

1. This remark is directed particularly at Harink 2003: neither of these passages, nor indeed Galatians 2.19f., appear in his index, or apparently in his mind.
2. See e.g. O'Brien, in Carson 1992, 88, quoting also Gundry.
3. See details in Wright, '4QMMT', 2006.
4. That, we note, is a summary of how Saul of Tarsus saw it at the time. As Westerholm rightly points out (in Barclay and Gathercole 2007, 76

n. 16), Paul the Christian would hardly have said 'blameless' over a life that included persecuting the church.

5. Contrast Piper's attempt (171f.) to say that the 'natural implication' of this verse is that Christ's righteousness is imputed to us. If Paul did mean that, and if it was as important for him as it is for Piper, why does he not say it straight out? Saying that 'the implication seems to be that our union with Christ is what connects us with divine righteousness' (172) only serves to show how imprecise Piper's language and thought is at this point.

6. Compare Rom. 3.22, on which see below.

7. It is remarkable how those who try to prevent Paul saying anything about the covenant either ignore this passage or pretend it's only there because he is replying to opponents who were going on about Moses, or try to belittle the idea of 'covenant' itself – so e.g. Seifrid 2000, 110, saying that it is 'somewhat misleading'.

8. The little phrase 'in him' is vital to my understanding here (against Piper, 177).

9. See Dunn 2008, chs 8, 17, 19 and frequently elsewhere.

7 Romans

1. See, early on in the present round of debate, Williams 1980, and many since.

2. This is the suggestion of Ed Sanders, the first great 'new perspective' exponent.

3. I cannot follow Simon Gathercole (2002, 197–200) in saying that 'the Jew' is the *primary* or even the only addressee of this passage, still less in what he builds on that assumption.

4. This is another place, by the way, where Mr New Perspective himself, Ed Sanders, confessed himself baffled, and concluded that Paul just dropped in an old synagogue-style sermon at this point even though it didn't really fit with his argument (Sanders 1983, 123–32).

5. By what right does Piper say (110), against my exegesis of this verse, that 'the verse was not written to carry that much freight'? The question is, does Paul mean what he says or not? Who are we to say, of a clear statement, that Paul didn't really mean it?

6. Acts 17.31.

7. Refs. and discussion in Dunn 2008, ch. 18.

8. Other ancient authorities read 'of Christ', but this looks like an assimilation to 2 Cor. 5.10.

9. Quoting Isa. 49.18 and other passages.

10. See Wright, *Paul: Fresh Perspectives*, 2005, ch. 7.

11. Thus when Piper says (22) that 'Wright makes startling statements to the effect that our future justification will be on the basis of works', I want to protest: it isn't Wright who says this, but Paul.

12. See e.g. Piper, 166f.
13. We might note that Paul still appears to be working, as he was in chapter 4, with Psalm 116 in mind: Psalm 116.9 uses the same word, 'pleasing the Lord in the land of the living'.
14. Don Carson, quoted on the back of Piper's book.
15. This is why the thesis of Barry Smith (2007) is so radically mistaken both in theology, exegesis and pastoral relevance. He argues that Paul's doctrine of final judgment according to works is not 'synergistic' – the great bugbear of those schooled in the mediaevally shaped Reformation theology – because the spirit destroys the Christian's free will, so that the works which carry forward to judgment are *purely* the work of the spirit, and not at all of Christians themselves. That, in fact, functions as a kind of *reductio ad absurdum* of an entire way of thinking.
16. Mark 7.21–23; John 8.34.
17. See Wright, 'Romans 2', 1996.
18. Matt. 25.21, 23.
19. The Hebrew *Judah* means 'praise': see Gen. 29.35.
20. Ps. 44.8; cf. Ps. 34.2; Jer. 9.24.
21. Isa. 52.5; Ezek. 36.20, 23.
22. Ezek. 36.24–36.
23. Piper, 69f. simply fails to grasp what the whole paragraph is about, contenting himself with raiding it for a few 'nuggets' that seem, super-ficially, to support his reading of 'God's righteousness'.
24. See, e.g. Seifrid in Carson 2004, 135–7, who manufactures out of thin air the idea that the 'oracles' are the words that should have told Israel about sin and salvation, which Israel refused to 'believe'.
25. McGrath 1986, 1.5. For a large-scale statement of this, spelling out a supposedly biblical framework in considerable detail and omitting the Israel-dimension altogether, see Jeffrey et al. 2007, ch. 3. For the authors then to suggest that G. Aulén comes close to Marcionism invites Jesus' remark about the speck and the plank. Why am I not surprised to find that the Foreword to this book was written by . . . John Piper?
26. *Pistis*, we note: the word can mean 'faith' or 'faithfulness', and there is good reason for thinking that someone like Paul would not have recognized such a hard-and-fast distinction between those two as we normally suppose.
27. And, in particular, what Psalm 143, referred to in the previous verse, would strongly suggest, as Richard Hays pointed out long ago in a piece now reprinted in Hays 2005, 50–60.
28. Today's New International Version (TNIV) has superficially improved this, translating 3.21 'but now apart from the law the righteousness of God has been made known . . .', but without allowing this to have any effect on the rest of the paragraph. Piper, 67f., tries to exegete

3.25 with no regard whatever for the flow of thought of the larger paragraph.
29. Gathercole 2002.
30. I first met this in Hanson 1974, 39–45. Hanson discusses earlier writers taking similar views.
31. Käsemann 1960, 96–100; Käsemann 1980, 98f.
32. See his debate with Stendahl, on which see my 1978 article and the brief mention earlier.
33. 1 Cor. 12.3.
34. 1 Thess. 1.5; 2.13.
35. Rom. 1.3f.; 10.17.
36. See Danker 2000, 36; for the other reading, Williams 1998.
37. It is bizarre for Piper to say (43) that 3.28 is most naturally interpreted in terms of 4.6. Yes, there is a parallel in the thought; but 3.28 is most naturally interpreted as part of the flow of thought of 3.27–31.
38. See e.g. Piper, 128: 'We have no perfect obedience to offer . . .'.
39. See my 2002 commentary, 483.
40. The original piece is now in Hays 2005, 61–84. See my 2002 commentary, 489f.
41. Gathercole 2002, 250. Piper, 168f. discusses 4.3–8 without giving the slightest hint that they mean what they mean within the context of the whole chapter, and hence without beginning to engage with what the chapter as a whole is about and how these verses nest within it.
42. It is ironic that Gathercole (234) accuses me of over-harmonizing Romans with Galatians. If anything, that is what a traditional Lutheran reading has always tended to do – granted, of course, that it is the Lutheran Romans assimilated to the Lutheran Galatians.
43. Thus developing 2.25–29 and anticipating 10.1–13 and 11.23.
44. Except for 6.8: 'we believe (*pisteuomen*) that we shall also live with him', which is not about justification.
45. Apart from 6.8, as mentioned in the previous note.
46. Piper, tellingly, speaks (184) not of 'death and resurrection' at this point but of 'death and righteousness'.
47. Luke 16.31.
48. Especially *Climax*, ch. 13, and my 2002 Romans commentary.
49. See again Wright, '4QMMT', 2006.
50. Gal. 2.17.
51. Piper, predictably but frustratingly, manages (90f.) to screen out this central element of Paul's exposition.
52. Joel 2.32 (LXX 3.5).
53. Joel 2.28, 32.

8 Conclusion

1. Käsemann 1980, viii.
2. On the substantial disagreements within the 'family' of Protestant interpretations, see the various essays in Husbands and Treier 2004, particularly those by McCormack, Seifrid, Kolb, Collins and above all Lane.
3. Piper explicitly rules this out (25).
4. See Eph. 1.10; 2.11–21; 3.10. The theme of judgment is also prominent, of course, in John's gospel, in ways which dovetail fascinatingly with what we find in Paul.
5. See esp. Rom. 8.9–11.

Bibliography

1. Relevant works by N. T. Wright (sometimes as 'Tom Wright')

Books

2007 *Surprised by Hope*. London: SPCK; San Francisco: HarperOne (US edn 2008, with subtitle *Rethinking Heaven, Resurrection and the Mission of the Church*)

2005 *Paul: Fresh Perspectives*. London: SPCK; Minneapolis: Fortress (US title: *Paul in Fresh Perspective*)

2004 *Paul for Everyone: Romans*. 2 vols. London: SPCK; Louisville: Westminster John Knox

2003 *Paul for Everyone: 1 Corinthians*. London: SPCK; Louisville: Westminster John Knox

2003 *Paul for Everyone: 2 Corinthians*. London: SPCK; Louisville: Westminster John Knox

2003 *Paul for Everyone: The Pastoral Letters*. London: SPCK; Louisville: Westminster John Knox

2003 *The Resurrection of the Son of God*. Volume III of Christian Origins and the Question of God. London: SPCK; Minneapolis: Fortress

2002 *Paul for Everyone: Galatians and Thessalonians*. London: SPCK; Louisville: Westminster John Knox

2002 *Paul for Everyone: The Prison Letters*. London: SPCK; Louisville: Westminster John Knox

2002 *Romans* in the *New Interpreter's Bible*. Vol. X, 393–770. Nashville: Abingdon

1999 *Romans and the People of God: Essays in Honor of Gordon D. Fee on the Occasion of his 65th Birthday* (co-ed., with Sven K. Soderlund). Grand Rapids: Eerdmans

1997 *What St Paul Really Said*. Lion, Oxford; Grand Rapids: Eerdmans

1996 *Jesus and the Victory of God*. Volume II of Christian Origins and the Question of God. London: SPCK; Minneapolis: Fortress

1992 *The New Testament and the People of God*. Volume I of Christian Origins and the Question of God. London: SPCK; Minneapolis: Fortress

1991 *The Climax of the Covenant: Christ and the Law in Pauline Theology*. Edinburgh: T&T Clark (October 1991); Minneapolis: Fortress (February 1992)

Bibliography

1988 *The Interpretation of the New Testament, 1861–1986* (with Stephen Neill). Oxford: Oxford University Press

1987 *The Epistles of Paul to the Colossians and to Philemon.* Leicester: Tyndale; Grand Rapids: Eerdmans

1983 *The Work of John Frith.* Courtenay Library of Reformation Classics, no. 7. Appleford: Sutton Courtenay Press

Major articles

2008 'Faith, Virtue, Justification and the Journey to Freedom', in *The Word Leaps the Gap: Essays on Scripture and Theology Sparked in Honor of Richard B. Hays*, ed. J. R. Wagner, C. K. Rowe and A. K. Grieb. Grand Rapids: Eerdmans

2007 'Paul as Preacher: The Gospel Then and Now', *Irish Theological Quarterly* 72, 131–46

2006 '4QMMT and Paul: Justification, "Works," and Eschatology', in *History and Exegesis: New Testament Essays in Honor of Dr E. Earle Ellis for His 80th Birthday*, ed. Sang-Won (Aaron) Son. New York and London: T&T Clark, 104–32

2006 'New Perspectives on Paul', in *Justification in Perspective: Historical Developments and Contemporary Challenges*, ed. Bruce L. McCormack. Grand Rapids: Baker Academic, 243–64

2004 'Redemption from the New Perspective', in *Redemption*, ed. S. T. Davis, D. Kendall and G. O'Collins. Oxford: Oxford University Press, 69–100

2002 'Coming Home to St Paul? Reading Romans a Hundred Years after Charles Gore', *Scottish Journal of Theology* 55, 392–407

2001 'A Fresh Perspective on Paul?', *Bulletin of the John Rylands Library* 83.1, 21–39

2000 'Paul's Gospel and Caesar's Empire', in *Paul and Politics: Ekklesia, Israel, Imperium, Interpretation. Essays in Honor of Krister Stendahl*, ed. Richard A. Horsley. Harrisburg, PA: Trinity Press International, 160–83. (Slightly edited update of 1999 article with same title.)

2000 'The Letter to the Galatians: Exegesis and Theology', in *Between Two Horizons: Spanning New Testament Studies and Systematic Theology*, ed. Joel B. Green and Max Turner. Grand Rapids: Eerdmans, 205–36

1999 'New Exodus, New Inheritance: The Narrative Substructure of Romans 3—8', in *Romans and the People of God: Essays in Honor of Gordon D. Fee on the Occasion of his 65th Birthday*, ed. S. K. Soderlund and N. T. Wright. Grand Rapids: Eerdmans, 26–35

1996 'Paul, Arabia and Elijah (Galatians 1:17)', *Journal of Biblical Literature* 115, 683–92

1996 'The Law in Romans 2', in *Paul and the Mosaic Law*, ed. J. D. G. Dunn. Tübingen: J. C. B. Mohr (Paul Siebeck), 131–50

Bibliography

1995 'Romans and the Theology of Paul', in *Pauline Theology*, vol. III, ed. David M. Hay and E. Elizabeth Johnson. Minneapolis: Fortress, 30–67. (Republished, with minor alterations, from *SBL 1992 Seminar Papers*, ed. E. H. Lovering, 184–213.)

1995 'Two Radical Jews: A Review Article of Daniel Boyarin, *A Radical Jew: Paul and the Politics of Identity* (University of California Press 1994)', *Reviews in Religion and Theology* 1995/3 (August), 15–23

1994 'Gospel and Theology in Galatians', in *Gospel in Paul: Studies on Corinthians, Galatians and Romans for Richard N. Longenecker*, ed. L. Ann Jervis and Peter Richardson, Journal for the Study of the New Testament, Supplement Series 108. Sheffield: Sheffield Academic Press, 222–39

1993 'On Becoming the Righteousness of God: 2 Corinthians 5:21', in *Pauline Theology*, vol. II, ed. D. M. Hay. Minneapolis: Augsburg Fortress, 200–8

1992 'Romans and Pauline Theology', *SBL 1992 Seminar Papers* (see 1995 above)

1991 'One God, One Lord, One People: Incarnational Christology for a Church in a Pagan Environment', *Ex Auditu* 7, 45–58

1991 'Putting Paul Together Again', in *Pauline Theology*, vol. I: *Thessalonians, Philippians, Galatians, Philemon*, ed. J. Bassler. Minneapolis: Augsburg Fortress, 183–211. Adapted and reprinted in *The Climax of the Covenant*, ch. 1

1990 'Poetry and Theology in Colossians 1:15–20', *New Testament Studies* 30, 444–68. Reprinted in *The Climax of the Covenant*, ch. 5

1987 'Reflected Glory? 2 Corinthians iii.18', in *The Glory of Christ in the New Testament: Studies in Christology in Memory of George Bradford Caird*. Oxford: Oxford University Press, 139–50. Considerably emended, and reprinted, in *The Climax of the Covenant*, ch. 9

1986 'ἁρπαγμός and the Meaning of Philippians 2.5–11', *Journal of Theological Studies*, 37.2, October, 321–52. Considerably expanded for *The Climax of the Covenant*, ch. 4

1983 'Adam in Pauline Christology', *SBL 1983 Seminar Papers*, ed. K. H. Richards. Chico, CA: Scholars Press, 359–89. Adapted and reprinted in *The Climax of the Covenant*, ch. 2

1982 'A New Tübingen School? Ernst Käsemann and His Significance', *Themelios* 7, 6–16

1980 'The Meaning of περὶ ἁμαρτίας in Romans 8:3', in *Studia Biblica 1978*, vol. III, ed. E. A. Livingstone. Sheffield: JSOT Press, 453–9. Reprinted (updated) in *The Climax of the Covenant*, ch. 11

1978 'The Paul of History and the Apostle of Faith', *Tyndale Bulletin* 29, 61–88

Website

Various other materials are available, including some otherwise unpublished lectures, at <www.ntwrightpage.com>.

2. Other works referred to in the text (fuller bibliographies in most of these, not least that by Michael Bird)

Barclay and Gathercole 2007: John M. G. Barclay and Simon J. Gathercole, eds, *Divine and Human Agency in Paul and his Cultural Environment*. London: T & T Clark

Beckwith 1981: Roger T. Beckwith, 'Daniel 9 and the Date of Messiah's Coming in Essene, Hellenistic, Pharisaic, Zealot and Early Christian Computation', *Revue de Qumran* 40, 521–42

Bird 2007: Michael F. Bird, *The Saving Righteousness of God: Studies on Paul, Justification and the New Perspective*. Milton Keynes: Paternoster

Campbell 2005: Douglas A. Campbell, *The Quest for Paul's Gospel: A Suggested Strategy*. London and New York: Continuum

Carson 1992: D. A. Carson, ed., *Right With God: Justification in the Bible and the World*. Carlisle: Paternoster; Grand Rapids: Baker

Carson et al. 2001 and 2004: D. A. Carson, P. T. O'Brien and M. A. Seifrid, eds, *Justification and Variegated Nomism*, vol. I: *The Complexities of Second Temple Judaism*; vol. II: *The Paradoxes of Paul*. Tübingen: Mohr Siebeck; Grand Rapids: Baker

Danker 2000: F. W. Danker (rev. and ed.), *A Greek–English Lexicon of the New Testament and Other Early Christian Literature*, 3rd edn. Chicago: University of Chicago Press

Donaldson 1997: Terence L. Donaldson, *Paul and the Gentiles: Remapping the Apostle's Convictional World*. Minneapolis: Fortress Press

Dunn 2008 [2005]: J. D. G. Dunn, *The New Perspective on Paul*, rev. edn. Grand Rapids and Cambridge: Eerdmans

Edersheim 1883: Alfred Edersheim, *The Life and Times of Jesus the Messiah*, 2 vols. London: Longmans, Green & Co.

Gathercole 2002: Simon J. Gathercole, *Where Is Boasting? Early Jewish Soteriology and Paul's Response in Romans 1—5*. Grand Rapids and Cambridge: Eerdmans

Hanson 1974: Anthony T. Hanson, *Studies in Paul's Technique and Theology*. London: SPCK

Harink 2003: Douglas Harink, *Paul among the Postliberals: Pauline Theology Beyond Christendom and Modernity*. Grand Rapids: Brazos Press

Hays 1989: Richard B. Hays, *Echoes of Scripture in the Letters of Paul*. New Haven and London: Yale University Press

Hays 1992: Richard B. Hays, 'Justification', in D. N. Freedman, ed., *Anchor Bible Dictionary*. New York: Doubleday, 3.1129–33

Bibliography

Hays 2002 [1983]: Richard B. Hays, *The Faith of Jesus Christ: The Narrative Substructure of Galatians 3:1–4:11*, rev. edn. Grand Rapids: Eerdmans

Hays 2005: Richard B. Hays, *The Conversion of the Imagination: Paul as Interpreter of Israel's Scripture*. Grand Rapids: Eerdmans

Husbands and Treier 2004: Mark Husbands and Daniel J. Treier, *Justification: What's at Stake in the Current Debates*. Downers Grove, IL: IVP; Leicester: Apollos

Jeffrey et al. 2007: Steve Jeffrey, Mike Ovey and Andrew Sach, *Pierced for Our Transgressions: Rediscovering the Glory of Penal Substitution*. Nottingham: IVP

Käsemann 1960: E. Käsemann, 'Zum Verständnis von Römer 3.24–26', in *Exegetische Versuche und Besinnungen*, vol. I, Göttingen: Vandenhoeck & Ruprecht, 96–100

Käsemann 1971: E. Käsemann, *Perspectives on Paul*. London: SCM Press

Käsemann 1980: E. Käsemann, *Commentary on Romans*. London: SCM Press

Longenecker 1998: Bruce W. Longenecker, *The Triumph of Abraham's God: The Transformation of Identity in Galatians*. Edinburgh: T & T Clark

McCormack 2006: Bruce L. McCormack, ed., *Justification in Perspective: Historical Developments and Contemporary Challenges*. Grand Rapids: Baker; Edinburgh: Rutherford House

McGrath 1986: Alister E. McGrath, *Iustitia Dei: A History of the Christian Doctrine of Justification from 1500 to the present day*. Cambridge: Cambridge University Press

Olson 2007: Roger Olson, *Reformed and Always Reforming: The Postconservative Approach to Evangelical Theology*, Acadia Studies in Bible and Theology. Grand Rapids: Baker

Packer 1962: J. I. Packer, 'Justification', in *New Bible Dictionary*, ed. J. D. Douglas. London: IVP, 683–6

Packer 1986: J. I. Packer and others, *Here We Stand: Justification by Faith Today*. London: Hodder

Piper 2007: John Piper, *The Future of Justification: A Response to N. T. Wright*. Wheaton, IL: Crossway Books

Sanday and Headlam 1902 [1895]: W. Sanday and A. C. Headlam, *The Epistle to the Romans*, 5th edn. Edinburgh: T & T Clark

Sanders 1977: Ed P. Sanders, *Paul and Palestinian Judaism: A Comparison of Patterns of Religion*. London: SCM Press

Sanders 1983: Ed P. Sanders, *Paul, the Law and the Jewish People*. Philadelphia: Fortress Press

Schweitzer 1931: Albert Schweitzer, *The Mysticism of Paul the Apostle*. London: A & C Black

Seifrid 1992: Mark A. Seifrid, *Justification by Faith: The Origin and Development of a Central Pauline Theme*. Leiden: Brill

Bibliography

Seifrid 2000: Mark A. Seifrid, *Christ our Righteousness: Paul's Theology of Justification*. Leicester: Apollos; Downers Grove, IL: IVP

Seifrid 2000a: Mark A. Seifrid, 'In What Sense is "Justification" a Declaration?' *Churchman* 114, 123–36

Smith 2007: Barry D. Smith, *What Must I Do To Be Saved? Paul Parts Company with his Jewish Heritage*. Sheffield: Sheffield Phoenix Press

Stendahl 1976: Krister Stendahl, *Paul Among Jews and Gentiles and Other Essays*. Philadelphia: Fortress Press

Thiselton 2007: Anthony C. Thiselton, *The Hermeneutics of Doctrine*. Grand Rapids and Cambridge: Eerdmans

Torrance 2000: Alan Torrance, 'Justification', in A. Hastings et al., eds, *The Oxford Companion to Christian Thought*. Oxford: Oxford University Press, 362–4

Waters 2004: Guy Waters, *Justification and the New Perspectives on Paul: A Review and Response*. Phillipsburg, NJ: P & R

Watson 2007: Francis B. Watson, *Paul, Judaism and the Gentiles: Beyond the New Perspective*. Grand Rapids and Cambridge: Eerdmans. (A completely rewritten version of the book with the same title, though a different subtitle (*A Sociological Approach*), published by Cambridge University Press in 1986.)

Westerholm 2004: Stephen Westerholm, *Perspectives Old and New on Paul: The 'Lutheran Paul' and his Critics*. Grand Rapids and Cambridge: Eerdmans

Whiston n.d.: William Whiston, *The Whole Genuine Works of Flavius Josephus*, 4 vols. Glasgow: Blackie & Sons

Williams 1980: S. K. Williams, 'The "Righteousness of God" in Romans', *Journal of Biblical Literature* 99, 241–90

Williams 1998: S. K. Williams, 'The Hearing of Faith: *AKOE PISTEOS* in Galatians 3', *New Testament Studies* 35, 82–93

Wrede 1904: William Wrede, *Paul*. Boston: American Unitarian Association

Index of biblical references

Index of names

Index of topics

Index of topics

Israel: in Adam 171; call of 18–19; disobedience 83, 177; in Egypt 204; in God's plan 49, 74, 216, 218

Jesus 81, 82; God's wisdom 134; as judge 86, 159; obedience 204–5; redemption 134–5; righteousness 134, 135; sanctification 134; sinlessness 178; *see also* Christ
Jews, ethnic identity 95
Judaism 37–58; second-Temple period 75; *see also* Israel; Torah
judgment, last 158–62, 165
justification: by faith 115, 211, 217–18; by works 123–4

kingdom of God 149–50
knowing God 126

last judgment 158–62, 165, 167
Law *see* Torah
lawcourt terminology 49–51, 69–70, 78–9, 96, 112–13, 180–1, 186–7, 199, 223
Lord, Jesus as 82
love 117, 163

male and female 110
merit 163
Messiah 81–7, 108–14; and Abraham's seed 102, 104; and Christ 61–2; a curse 103; death of 113–14, 114; faithfulness 181, 204–5; as Israel's representative 19; knowing him 126; resurrection 84–5, 100, 125–6, 189
mistakes 4
Moses 53, 76–7, 204–5

new age 80
New International Version of the Bible 35–6, 176–7
Noah 77

obedience 83, 201
oracles of God 173
Orthodoxy, Eastern 207

Pentecost 218
Peter 94–5, 100
Pharisees 124–5
pleasing God 162–4, 167
purpose, God's, in history 18–19

Qumran 124–5

redemption 133, 134–5
Reformation tradition 6, 218–19, 221, 223

representation 84
resurrection 207–8; of Christ 84–5, 100, 125–6, 189, 196, 219; in first-century Judaism 38, 57
righteousness 47–51; of believers 133–4, 217; of Christ 133–5; of God 44–52, 131, 140–1, 153–4, 173, 176, 212; imputed *see* imputed righteousness; and justification 67–8; meaning 50, 67–71, 100–1, 113, 209; status 127–8, 180–1; within the Torah 121–4
Romans (Paul's letter to the) 24
Romantic movement 20

sacrificial system 57
salvation 52, 60, 146, 207, 212; purpose 7–8; through the Jew 169
sanctification 133, 134
Sarah and Hagar 116
scripture 6–7; and tradition 28
sin 78, 84, 97–9, 99, 111–12, 215; *see also* forgiveness
son of God 82
soteriology 105–6, 217
spirit *see* holy spirit
substitution 84, 181
supercessionism 120
synergism 164, 167

table-fellowship 94–6
Tamar 49
Temple 148
Titus 92
Torah 53–8, 76–7, 95; and covenant renewal 216–17; curse of 114; embodiment of truth 169; and faith 185–6; and freedom 93, 223; and the Messiah 115–16; pointer to sin 101, 215; and the promise to Abraham 102–3; purpose 106–8, 114; righteousness within 121–4, 208; as tutelary deity 115; works of the law 96–7, 125, 148, 187–8
tradition 6–7, 28
transformation 207
transgression 99
Trinity 115, 164

'unfaithful', meaning of 173

virtue 50, 164, 168

wisdom 132–5
women *see* male and female
works of the law 96–7, 125, 148, 187–8